D1577080

THE 10
FOOTBALL MATCHES
THAT CHANGED
THE WORLD

THE 10

FOOTBALL MATCHES

THAT CHANGED
THE WORLD

... AND THE ONE THAT DIDN'T

JIM MURPHY

\B^b\

First published in Great Britain in 2014 by
Biteback Publishing Ltd
Westminster Tower
3 Albert Embankment
London SE1 7SP

ISBN 978-1-84954-698-0

10 9 8 7 6 5 4 3 2 1

A CIP catalogue record for this book is available from the British Library.

Set in Sabon by Soapbox
Printed and bound in Great Britain by
CPI Group (UK) Ltd, Croydon CR0 4YY

MIX
Paper from
responsible sources
FSC® C020471

THIS BOOK IS dedicated to the memory of the remarkable men whose love of football played a part in them volunteering for the British Army in the First World War.

Contents

Introduction

SPORT'S IMPACT ON the world is as great as any government's, and no sport ever played has been more influential than Association Football. From the moment it was codified and taken out of Britain's public schools, it has been a constant companion of change across the globe.

The industrial revolution coincided with a transformation in football's appeal. As the twentieth century dawned, wherever you found Britons you found football. It became the nation's most successful export. Football quickly became more than just a pastime: it has bolstered and deposed tyrants; started and stopped wars; been an incubator of racism at home while helping bring down a racist regime abroad. It has assisted in building nations, influencing elections, shaping cities and inspiring resistance. Its impact is as dynamic, contradictory and compelling as the game itself.

Each chapter's story includes first-hand accounts from those closest to the events across the decades, including international footballers, Prime Ministers, political prisoners, Cabinet ministers and journalists. There are fresh insights and revealing answers to questions, some of which have never before been asked.

The difficult part of this book was not finding ten crucial games; the problem was cutting the list down to just ten. Many of the people I discussed it with tended to think for a few seconds, before asking: 'Are you going to include that game between...?' More often than not, though, their candidate for inclusion was a match involving their team. Instead, I've opted for a mix of British and international games, such as Sir Alex Ferguson's first European final, which set Tony Blair on the road to Downing Street. There are chapters about the role of football in saving Rupert Murdoch's satellite empire, helping post-war Germany believe again, and standing up to racism. Also covered are games that cemented some of the sport's fiercest rivalries, from Celtic and Rangers to Barcelona and Madrid, as well as a chapter on Hillsborough and how the UK government belatedly made the right decision to deliver justice for the ninety-six.

The title of this book changed while I was researching it for one very simple reason: the truth. When I first put pen to paper, I had assumed the most famous football story of them all, the 1914 First World War Christmas truce, would be among the ten that changed the world. Instead, it deserves a chapter of its own as 'The One That Didn't'. When those few hours of peace ended, a war that was meant to be over by Christmas had simply paused for a single Christmas Day. Eight million more were still to lose their lives.

The stories of all those footballing warriors, from every corner of this and other lands, deserve to be told, respected and remembered.

Jim Murphy
2014

THE 10
FOOTBALL MATCHES
THAT CHANGED
THE WORLD

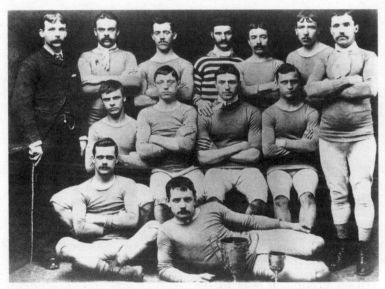

The first working-class champions. The relaxed Blackburn Olympic squad of 1883 that triumphed over the Old Etonians.
© *Press Association*

Chapter One

The Rebirth of Football:
Old Etonians v Blackburn, 1883

FOOTBALL ALMOST DIED. But a single match helped rescue the sport, and, with one unexpected victory, it finally broke free from its ghettos in the nation's public schools and British Army officers' messes.

The ailing game was violent, with very few agreed rules. It was run by and for the elite and, in a nation with very few sports fields, had been banned from public streets. In England, the FA Cup was colonised by university, public school and regimental teams.

In the 1883 FA Cup final, the former pupils of Eton College lined up against Blackburn Olympic at the Oval cricket ground. It was to be the very first time a northern working-class team prevailed. Until that March afternoon, the trophy had normally been won by teams made up of former public school boys, Oxford University or the British military. In a single 3-2 defeat, Eton's blue-blooded boys, destined to run Britain's empire, surrendered control of the sport they had been keeping alive.

That second half of extra time proved that the game had changed, and changed forever. It ensured that, as Britain ruled the waves, Queen Victoria's subjects were taking with them a sport that was freshly energised, codified and newly open to all. As Britain exported Britons, they travelled with a game inspired by the appeal of the 1883 final. The first global working-class sport was now made in the image of the working-class men of England's north and Scotland's west. From this point forward, football would be the most democratic sport in the world. Even those without shoes on their feet or a shilling in their pocket, in possession of nothing more than a freedom of spirit, could play and win.

1883 was the moment football announced to the world it was heading their way. Before this point, as Britain had forged its empire, football had failed to take root, but henceforth, as Britons emigrated to work in the heavy industries, they took with them an old sport bearing a new identity. The traditional exporters of football had been the factory and mill owners, the men who had previously been the football-playing boys of Eton and other fee-paying schools. British expat mill owners in Russia, aristocrats in Austria and professional classes in places like Genoa were among British football's initial ambassadors. But a new breed of football innovator was also born. They were more Blackburn Olympic than Old Etonian. In South America, British railway workers helped introduce the sport to Colombia, Uruguay and Argentina. A school-teaching Scot, Alexander Watson Hutton, set up the Argentine FA. In Chile, British sailors and, in Venezuela, British miners were among the first to play. In Spain, Brazil and Italy, Brits planted their proletarian footballing roots. AC Milan was created by a Nottinghamshire lace worker, Herbert Kilpin. Athletic Bilbao was formed from a joint effort by British miners, shipyard workers and local students.

Today, Eton continues to churn out Prime Ministers. And a team by the name of Blackburn Olympic lives on. They play in the Blackburn Combination Neales Waste Management Second Division.

I decided to drive south to the north-west of England in search of Olympic. The original team folded years ago but

\B\ \Rp\

Biteback Publishing and **The Robson Press**
Westminster Tower, 10th floor, 3 Albert Embankment, London SE1 7SP
+44 (0) 20 7091 1260 | info@bitebackpublishing.com
www.bitebackpublishing.com **www.therobsonpress.com**

With Compliments

another group of football fanatics now bears their name. Blackburn Olympic have their base next to the Cherry Tree train station on Blackburn's Old Preston Road. It was there, in the station pub, that I had arranged to meet up with them in their pre-kick-off pub HQ.

The first thing I noticed was that the barman treats the players as though they belong to the pub. The second is that no one in the team is drinking anything stronger than a can of Red Bull. The half-hour get-together is the only time they see one another between games. Olympic sit second in the league and have high hopes of promotion. But today's game is a break from league duty for the glamour of a cup quarter-final. Blackburn Olympic is a team that never trains. Their home ground is just a two-minute drive from their Cherry Tree spiritual home. It's impossible to miss; all you have to do is follow the signs for the Pleasington Playing Fields Cemetery.

The place where the teams get ready is a maze of Soviet-style cold echoing corridors, each leading to a changing room designed for a five-a-side team. Each room is lit by a single strobe light unprotected by any lampshade. It's impossible to imagine that there might be hot water in the showers. The team is a real mix of characters, including the dynamo-mouthed captain, Christopher Tomlinson, and the sullen Lee Grundy, who I'm told had real promise before a terrible injury. He arrives later than the others. And when he does, he turns up clutching a pack of ten Embassy Regal cigarettes in the way that players a few miles down the road at Blackburn Rovers might hold onto an energy drink.

The changing room echoes with news of who did what the night before and with whom. It's not clear which of the guys has the cloudiest hangover. No one is admitting to an early night as part of their quarter-final preparation. A friendly dispute seems to break out about who should be in possession of the JCM Steel Fabrication-sponsored number seven shirt.

The verbals are so rapid and the room so small, it's impossible to see or hear who says what. One of the midfielders says, 'If you're so keen to wear number seven, wear the number five and the number two. It's cold anyway, that'll keep you warm.' Right-back Bill Scott and centre-back Robert Plummer don't seem pleased about the idea of losing their shirts, but the dispute is somehow settled.

The coach, Dave Lloyd, is one of those unnoticed footballing heroes, the type that keeps the game alive. He gets no pay and lots of pain for his troubles; and he takes the kit home to wash every week. But he whispers to me just before his team talk, 'The thing for me is that, while they enjoy it, I enjoy it.' It's clear that he does. There's never an easy way to tell serious social footballers, like the Olympic lads, that they are on the bench. Dave has an unusual way of breaking the news to the substitutes. He starts to collect the players' match fees: £10 from those who are starting and a fiver from the subs – used or unused. That's the point when they first know if they're on the bench. No one seems pleased when he turns to them and asks them to pay half-price.

The room is full of a team talking. Centre-forward Joe Walmsley explains to me why he insists on wearing children's shin-guards. The entire midfield discusses how their horse-racing accumulator got on at the previous day's Cheltenham Festival. It's not just quick-witted banter that fills the pre-match changing room. It's also cluttered with mud and the sound of studs on concrete as the players bang their boots on the frozen floor to remove the dirt from last week's defeat.

The Olympic team is made up of painters, a pub manager, a policeman, an ex-trainee soldier; the goalie is a student in Middlesbrough. The patronising middle-class thing to do when going along on a visit like this is to sneeringly parody working-class life. I've seen it happen so many times but I've never done it because, as expected, these guys are confident,

clever, articulate and the opposite of the prejudice-based cari-
catures associated with working-class culture. They have the
dignity of working-class pride in the power of knowledge, a
sharp sense of humour and a readily deployed wit, often pack-
aged up in industrial language. Their swearing has the purpose
of instant anger, aimed at themselves for a misplaced pass or
a mistimed tackle. They have the ability to use the same swear
word as an adjective, verb or noun, which, as anyone who has
tried this knows, isn't easily done.

As assistant manager for the day, it's my job to carry the
water bottles and put the nets up. I leave the motivational
team talk stuff to Dave:

> You know how important this game is lads: quarter-final of
> the cup, Greenfields. We've played them three times already
> this season. We've beaten them twice, they beat us once. They
> are a good team. We need to keep on top of Chris Harrison,
> you know that. He scored the winner against us in that 3-2
> defeat. We know what we can do; we didn't do it last week.
> We were awful. We didn't turn up last week, most of us. We
> know what we can do; we've got a full squad this week,
> everybody's here today. Let's do it!

Captain Tomlinson adds, 'When we play football, we're the
best team in this league without a doubt. So let's go back to
playing footie. Let's not panic, yeah. If you can't go forward,
go back. Let's play football on the deck.'

Both teams are from Darwen and, surprisingly, despite
being local rivals there isn't any real animosity. One of the
strangest things about the game is that it's a match between
two all-white squads. On the pitch next to us is a game
between another all-white line-up against a totally Asian team.
Blackburn is a city of real diversity in so many ways but not, it
would seem, this morning on the Pleasington football pitches.

7

I know that people who don't play football sometimes wonder what a referee says to the players just before kick-off. So here's an insight into what our ref told the players as they went through their final stretches:

Jewellery, let's take it off, please, alright. Wedding rings off, yeah. If I see anyone with jewellery on, you go off for two minutes so be warned. On swearing, lads, let's keep it down, alright. Frustration ones you know I don't mind, but let's keep it long-distance ones, lads, alright. I'm supposed to send you off but I don't want to do that, you know what I mean. So let's keep it down, alright. You know me, lads, play to the whistle, alright. I'll try to play the advantage, alright, I'll wait a few seconds and if you have no advantage I'll bring it back and you'll get the free kick, alright. Just enjoy it, boys.

I'm not certain what he meant by 'long-distance ones'. Perhaps he didn't want them aggressively swearing up close and personal in one another's faces. But he was right to say, 'You know me, lads.' He had been an Olympic player for ten years.

As the players lined up to kick-off, I wondered if they could play as fluently and quickly as they talked. I had to wait longer than expected to find out. Some fool had put the goal nets on upside-down. The ref insisted on delaying kick-off until they were fixed. Embarrassingly, I pretended not to notice and got on with checking whether I had filled up the water bottles.

When the game eventually did get going, the tone was set in the first minute, when Joe Walmsley was fouled with a full-on swipe against his kids-size shin-guards. The crowd number ebbed and flowed from anywhere between two and ten. In a truism of football the world over, the main striker's girlfriend came to watch.

Richard Sholicar is a footballing cop from Burnley who misses one game in four due to his shifts. In truth, he misses more than that because of suspension. He is the most sent-off player in the Olympic team. In the fifth minute, he scored to put Olympic into a deserved lead. But three minutes later, Lee Steele, the most unusually shaped footballer, equalised. He defied his appearance as a slightly out-of-shape front-row rugby-forward to slot home after a subtle touch.

You don't realise how physical amateur football is until you watch it from the sidelines. In the twenty-fourth minute, Olympic went behind when Mitchell Pickup scored from a direct free kick. It seemed to go through a hole in our keeper's hands.

When I signed up to be the manager's assistant for the day, little did I know that my boss would then sign up to be the referee's assistant. I was left standing by myself among the subs, but, from the first minute, it was clear Dave hadn't really got the sense of his new role. He was more like a supporter with a linesman's flag. As he ran along the side of the pitch, he screamed, 'Let's put some crunching tackles in like they are!' He raised his flag for some pretty imaginative offsides against Greenfields. The former Olympic player-turned-ref ignored them all. Instead of accepting being over-ruled, Dave took to shouting ever louder across the breadth of the pitch: 'Ref, what's the point of me being here if you ignore every decision I give?!' After half an hour, the opposition's goalkeeping captain had clearly had enough of Dave. He shouted from his goal line at the ref standing on the halfway line, 'Take that flag off him and stick it up his arse!' One of our subs smiled. 'No one can run the line quite like Dave.' In the thirty-seventh minute, the linesman's team drew level at 2-2 with a stunning Sholicar strike from the right-hand corner of the box.

With hopes of holding on until half-time, and with the team talk being finalised in the linesman's head, Mitchell Pickup scored again for Greenfields. This time the ball managed to find a gap between the goalie's legs. It reminded me a lot of Kenny Dalglish's 1976 Hampden strike through Ray Clemence's wide-open legs.

Goals change attitudes, and it would appear they also alter team talks. Dave put his flag down and got stuck into the players:

> Do we want this or what? Do we want this or what? 'Cause it doesn't look like it on the pitch. Every tackle we are coming out second best. They want it more than we do. You can tell the way they are fighting for it. We're second best every time. We seem to think we can just pass it around. We can't.

Dave's anger incites a mini-rebellion in the team. 'You're wrong, Dave!' shouts one. Another says: 'It's just the basics. When you were at school you fucking learned to shout to each other, "Man on!", "Fucking time!" It's just the basic things that we're not doing.' A third rebel launches into his own mini team talk: 'Put a name on your passes. You're knocking it and expecting someone to find it.' In perhaps the least self-aware half-time declaration in amateur football history, the goalie announces, 'They ain't earned the goals!' The whole team looks at him as if to say, 'Piss off back to Middlesbrough.' More from the second half at Blackburn later...

***

Two hundred years ago, football was a minority sport. It also appears to have been a cross between two sports that I don't understand: modern-day cage fighting and Australian Rules football. It was played across vast areas, with the goals sometimes a mile apart, and was often violent and unforgiving. Confusingly, sometimes the aim was to score in your own goal. By the early 1800s, the highlight of the football calendar was the Shrove Tuesday challenge. The contests were officially football, but not as we now know it. In an era without public sports fields, it took place in built-up towns, with no agreed rules, and limitless time and players.

Then the Highways Act banned urban street football. Outlawed in the streets, football was also losing ground to the newly opened Industrial Revolution factory floors. Industrialisation brought longer working hours; workers' self-interest caused mass abstention from football's sporting violence. There were some isolated pockets of footballing resistance in places like the Orkneys, Workington, Shetland, Cornwall and Jedburgh, but there was no way of avoiding the truth: football was on its way out. Joseph Strutt wrote in his 1801 book *Sports and Pastimes of the People of England* that 'the game was formerly much in vogue among the common people, though of late years it seems to have fallen into disrepute and is but little practised'.

But there was one institution where the game lived on: the nation's public schools. For anyone from overseas reading this book, I should explain that peculiarly, in the UK, 'public schools' really means 'private schools'. While some were originally set up to educate the poor, they morphed into the classrooms of the cream of the British Empire.

The schools' affections for football coincided with an era of academic under-achievement and over-exuberance in many of these institutions. The pupils seemed to be in charge, rather than the staff. In 1797, the British Army were even summoned to quell a rebellion at Rugby School, and, in 1818, they fixed bayonets to put down trouble at Winchester College, their sixth visit in fifty years. The nation's public school elite were out of touch. In some places they appeared out of control, and in their commitment to football they showed just how culturally out of touch they were. The aristocratic kids, who dominated their middle-class teachers, insisted on playing this game.

Into the mêlée entered Thomas Arnold, the principal of Rugby School. He introduced a faith-based regime and a new focus on formal study for the mind and structured play for the body. His was a muscular Christianity about which it was declared: 'Through sport, boys acquire virtues which no book can give them: not merely daring and endurance, but better still, temper, self-restraint, fairness, honour, un-envious appropriation of another's success and all that "give and take" of life.' I'm not certain this is a description of the beautiful game that many of us would recognise today.

Each public school played its own variant of the sport. Distinct sets of rules and styles had evolved to fit into the physical layout of the individual schools. The playing fields of Eton had two games: the Eton Wall Game and the Eton Field Game. Harrow, with its water-sodden pitches, kicked a flat-bottomed ball, capable of travelling through the mud. Winchester had a kicking game to fill its long pitches. In contrast, Westminster played a short passing game within their confined cloistered spaces, while Rugby and Shrewsbury focused on picking the ball up.

Although they played by their own rules, sometimes, just sometimes, Eton were confronted by Association Rules. The first time this happened was in an 1880 game against workers from the local biscuit factory. One of the Eton players complained that, despite winning, they were unhappy because, firstly, they were unaccustomed to the workers' rules and, secondly, it was considered 'derogatory to the school to have entered for a competition which brought us into contact with such opponents'.

The game also travelled with the boys as they became young men at Oxford or Cambridge University. Later, they took their sport into the senior ranks of the Royal Navy or British Army, but there was, of course, no Royal Air Force in a pre-Wright brothers world. Football was played at Cambridge University as early as the seventeenth century. Oliver Cromwell played there in 1616 and was described as 'one of the chief match-makers and players at football, cudgels or any other boy strong sport'.

The two universities became the cultural melting pots of their day. Not in an American, Statue of Liberty, 'Give me your tired, your poor, your huddle masses...'-type way. Instead, theirs was a real collision of multiple footballing identities as groups of students within each university played the rules they had brought with them from their school. The only thing the games seemed to have in common was the name. To add to the confusion, there were distinct footballing rules in different parts of the country. Teams would often play forty-five minutes under one set of laws before switching to entirely different ones for the second half.

The first shot at creating universal regulations came in 1848, at Cambridge University. So frustrating had the mishmash of arrangements become that former public school boys from five different establishments with five different sets of rules got together to resolve things. Their main disagreements seemed to centre on whether handling of the ball should be allowed or not. A second-year pupil, Henry Malden, recorded that 'the Eton men howled at the Rugby men for handling the ball'. According to Hunter Davies in *Boots, Balls and Haircuts*, an illustrated history of football: 'The meeting lasted from four in the afternoon 'til midnight, with other students wandering in, thinking there must be an exam on, with all the bits of paper flying around, before they agreed what the rules should be.'

In 1862, it was left to a former Etonian, Charles Thring, to publish the first set of ten football regulations. Inevitably, many of the dos and don'ts in his 250-word guidance focused on violence, such as outlawing the hacking, kicking or back heeling of an opponent. He didn't find the space to explain how to enforce any of these rules, nor did he set out the punishment for their infringement, but perhaps the prevailing attitudes meant that enforcement might not be necessary. In his 1899 book *Association Football*, N. L. Jackson explained, in a way that now seems both quaint and naive:

> In the very early years of the game, when it was chiefly confined to old public school boys, the laws were strictly observed, any infringement being purely accidental. This was doubtless due to that honourable understanding which is cultivated among boys at the better class schools and which prevents them taking unfair advantage of an opponent.

It wasn't until a year after Thring set out his laws of the game that the first English FA rules were agreed. Initially, in those association rules, there was no place for an umpire or referee. Peculiar as it may sound to contemporary football, the two captains were expected to resolve any disagreements between themselves.

Hunter Davies also carries a good description of the dynamic of the 1860s game:

> Nine out of the eleven would have been chasing after the ball, leaving only two defenders. At the head of the charge was the best dribbler, followed by the 'backers-up', who would dribble till knocked off the ball, sometimes quite violently. Any sort of pass to someone ahead of you on your own side resulted in offside, so passing was virtually non-existent.

The ball had to be played by foot, but, until 1866, it could be caught by hand too. Indeed, this was a big year for the introduction of new rules as it was also when the offside rule first came into force. Thankfully, it was a simpler offside rule than today's, with a player remaining onside if three of the opposition were nearer their goal line than the attacking player. Sheffield was the first city to attempt to codify the sport. The South Yorkshire city's rules didn't catch on and it's not hard to work out why: they had decided that the goals should be only four yards wide. In 1863, at a meeting in the Freemason's Tavern in London, representatives of eleven old boys' teams met to draw up a single set of agreed rules. But yet again, disputes arose over whether players should be allowed to handle the ball and their right to 'hack'. Mr Campbell, the delegate from the Blackheath club, defended the right of his, and all, players to deliberately target their opponents' shins. He told the delegates that if they tamed football's aggression: 'You will do away with the courage and pluck of the game, and I will be bound to bring over a lot of Frenchmen who would beat you with a week's practice.' He lost the vote. In 1871, unresolved disputes about hacking and handling would eventually lead to the creation of the Rugby Football Union.

* * *

Eton believed itself to be educators of the blue-blooded societal thoroughbreds. The college taught their pupils the ethics and ideas that guided them on their predestined way to become the leaders of men, business and government. At the time of writing, no fewer than twenty British Prime Ministers have made the 23-mile journey from Eton to Downing Street. Is it any wonder that the college is described as 'the chief nurse of England's statesmen'?

A form of football has been played at the college for nigh-on five centuries. In 1519, William Horman wrote his *Vulgaria* about life at Eton. The Latin book offered a first insight into just how early a game resembling football may have been played at Eton. He wrote: '*Livsun erit nobis follies pugilari spiritu tumens*', which translated into the English of the time meant, 'We will play with a ball full of wynde'. Further evidence of Eton's attachment to football is contained in a 1766 list of games played by the pupils. This list includes the peculiar-sounding pastimes of battledores, shirking walls, headimy and cat gallows, but, more than any of these, it is football that is the crucial part of growing up there. A nineteenth-century school notice-board read: 'Any lower boy in this House who does not play football once a day and twice on a half-holiday will be fined half a crown and kicked.'

Unusually, the boys at Eton had a choice of two types of football: a game against 'The Wall' and one on the Eton Field. The Wall Game, introduced in 1717, was, and still is, played alongside a 120-yard wall, with teams of eleven chasing down the ball. A few yards in front of the goal is an area called a calx. From there, the team can have a shy, from where they can have a shot at goal. The goal at one end is a tree and at the other end is a door in a wall. That's my basic sense of the rules, so I hope it's all straightforward. If I haven't got the details about the goals exactly right, I'm not sure it really matters: it seems as hard to understand as it is to score. There have only been three goals in two hundred years of the big St Andrew's Day game. The last was scored in 1909.

***

The Old Etonians, the team made up of the school's ex-pupils, was one of the dominant footballing powers in the land. They had colonised a novel and newly introduced tournament by the name of the FA Cup. In the early years of the competition, they won it twice and were beaten finalists six times. Their power only dissipated after the professional game throttled amateurism. In the Eton College in-house newspaper, they offered an insight into Etonians' frustrations at how the FA Cup had become dominated by the pros:

It may be stated that in 1870 the competition was started for the promotion of the game, and was at first entered for almost exclusively by southern amateur clubs playing more or less in the neighbourhood of the metropolis; but before very long the interest in this particular form of the game spread so rapidly that clubs from all parts of England now enter for the competition, as may be instanced by the fact that this season no fewer than eighty clubs competed in the first round.

Nowadays, well over 700 teams try their luck by entering the tournament. I remember in the late 1990s being involved in a debate about whether the MPs' football team should enter the competition. We decided not to for one simple reason: under FA rules, the two female MPs in our team, Watford's Claire Ward and Sheffield's Meg Munn, wouldn't have been allowed to take up their places.

The inaugural year of the FA Cup had been a pivotal year for football. That November, the first sanctioned international took place in Glasgow. Following two unofficial Scotland v England encounters, it was an enormous hit. One of the reports of the time recorded 'the entire limit of the ground being lined by an enthusiastic array of supporters of both sides'. With no score by the break, England became more adventurous and their goalie joined the forwards in attack, allowing Scotland's seventeen-year-old Robert Crawford to score in the goalie-free goal. But as the Scots prepared to celebrate victory, Baker equalised in the final minute and the first honours were shared.

***

1881 was the pinnacle of public school football dominance. Old Carthusians defeated Old Etonians 3-0 in the FA Cup final. But that contest between the two teams of former public school pupils masked a truth: change was coming and it was coming in the shape of the Lancashire industrial towns, with an irreversible vengeance. That final between England's elites attracted just 4,000 of their ilk to the Oval. In the same year, more than double that number was at the Scottish Cup final watching Queen's Park defeat Dumbarton after a replay. So rapid was the growth of professional football's popularity among the working class that, by 1899, 73,000 would attend the FA Cup final at Crystal Palace to see Sheffield United take on Derby County. But back in 1881, more people watched the Lancashire and Yorkshire finals than the FA Cup final.

Power was almost wrested northwards in 1882 when Blackburn Rovers contested the FA Cup final against the Old Etonians. It was the first cup final in which one of the old public school teams took on one of the new, mill-powered forces of the north, and it was played across the centre of a cricket field, including the crease. This, and the novelty of a team from the north, boosted the crowd to 6,000. Rovers went into the final unbeaten that season and there was enormous interest and anticipation back home. The local newspaper, the *Blackburn Standard*, even brought out a special Saturday-night post-match edition, 'specially telegraphed from our reporter', although they had to unhappily print news of an Old Etonian victory. This delayed the demise of public school dominance for just one more year.

* * *

Having already been to Blackburn, I decided to head to one of the places where the peripheral sport of football had been sustained. As I arrived from Glasgow at Heathrow's Terminal Five, I was nervous about my journey into another world. Not a trip on one of Richard Branson's test flights into space, but instead a short walk over to stop D6 to catch a bus to Eton

College. I paid my £2.30 and travelled on the number 61 bus as it slowly wound its way through picturesque villages such as Wraysbury and Datchet. An hour or so later, I arrived at the home of Angus Graham Campbell, the Fulham- and St Johnstone-supporting Eton schoolmaster. The college appears to be the main purpose of the town of Windsor. Along its main street are an endless number of upmarket tailors' and drapers' shops trading exclusively in the school's paraphernalia. As you walk away from the college towards Windsor's small train station, you trip over estate agencies selling unaffordable homes and boutique cafés offering beautifully scented teas.

My arrival coincided with the last day of term and the culmination of school exams. Angus was good enough to use his break from officially overseeing exams to take me on a tour of Eton. As I sat in his upstairs living room, the sun shone through the window and curtains into a shadowy corner. Perched there, alone upon a small, elevated round table, was a hat. From my armchair across the room, the scarlet and bright blue quartered cap looked like the sort of thing an old jockey would have worn. Instead, Angus tells me, the little worse-for-wear cap belonged to a different Eton custom. The 'Captain of the Field' was, and still is, allowed by Eton tradition to have his own personal silk cap. I hadn't realised, but I was looking across at his father's captain cap from the 1930s.

Angus and I have at least two things in common: a love of football and the fact we both attended the same schools as our fathers. My family's school was Bellarmine in the Pollok housing scheme in Glasgow, and it's now the Silverburn shopping centre. Angus and his father were Etonians. He is steeped in the tradition of Eton's sport and holds a remarkable Eton sporting pedigree. When he was a boy at the school, he was captain of the Field Game team and a squad player on the football team. Since returning as a housemaster, he has served as the master of both the Field Game and the Wall Game.

Angus went out of his way to make me feel at home, but it wasn't really my world. In every single step through the college, I was gripped by a powerful caution. I felt like an outsider because, despite my host's warmth, that's what I was. It reminded me of how I was during my first three years as a new MP in the House of Commons. We went on a tour of the college and looked through a window into an original but empty classroom where boys had been taught since the day the college opened. We wandered onto the playing fields and looked at the Brew House. This is an important spot as it was where the pupils' beer had been brewed, since the water there was too dirty for them to drink originally.

Football lives on at Eton. There are twenty-four school teams and they maintain their original rivalries with the likes of Winchester, Westminster and Charterhouse public schools. In a school that prides itself on continuity, one thing has changed in an important way: it now plays against comprehensive schools in the Berkshire Schools League, although I'm not sure if they still play against the local biscuit factory. As we stood where I never thought I would, on the playing fields of Eton College, I remembered that this was the piece of grass that features in one of the world's most famous misquotes: the Duke of Wellington never did declare that 'the Battle of Waterloo was won on the playing fields of Eton'. I also thought to myself about how this place compared to my own school's gravel football pitches, the type where if you made a slide tackle it would tear the opponent's shorts, as well as the skin from your own arse. As we chatted about the history of the Field and Wall Games, there were boys playing football on a distant but standard pitch, shouting politely at one another.

The next stop on my tour was the archive room, which contains the school's official records. I was met by Penny, the Eton archivist, whose soft suggestion of 'Do come through' was the type of polite invitation that, in my head, felt much more like an instruction, and I knew it wasn't intended to be ignored. I signed the register, stated the purpose of my visit and displayed my photographic ID. I was then separated from my bag, which was stored away in another room. Penny whispered, 'If you'd like to take a seat...' – another quiet suggestion that I felt should have had an exclamation mark after it. Penny chaperoned me to where she had decided I would sit. I was delighted that she did, because there on the desk in front of me she had thoughtfully laid out the books and newspapers detailing some of the most important football matches in Eton's history.

I can't be the only one who has been somewhere so painfully quiet that you just sit and listen to the sound of nothing whatsoever, other than the noise of unbroken silence. I was agitated that the sound of my breathing would disturb the two other readers in the room. I only managed to relax once I had worked out that they definitely couldn't hear me; after all, I couldn't hear them and I was certain they must have been breathing. Above the din of the silence, the only interruption was the scraping of the razor-sharp Eton archive room-issued pencils scratching across notebooks (pens are banned in the archive room).

The *Eton Chronicle*, the in-house school newspaper, printed reports of the Old Etonians' progress towards the two FA Cup finals of 1882 and 1883. I anxiously turned the pages in the 130-year-old newspapers. Reading through the original leather-bound records, I found myself distracted by stories of school life from the eighteenth and nineteenth centuries: details of the school theatre; a boy's boating fatality on the Thames; Queen Victoria's decoration of a Lieutenant Edwards for his bravery at the Battle of Tel-el-Kebir. But the most regular coverage seemed to be about hunting. As I slowly turned the pages, I began to think that these must have been the luckiest hares on earth, or that they were simply pursued by the worst huntsmen in history.

Judging by the quantity of coverage, it's clear that the beagle runs must have been a focal point of school life. One copy after another of the *Chronicle* contained mind-numbingly detailed running commentaries of the ninety-minute pursuit of a lonely hare. I'm a vegetarian and voted in Parliament to ban fox-hunting, but so tediously prolonged were the beagle reports that even I silently cheered on the nineteenth-century hounds to catch their furry little prey, for no reason other than the hope that it might bring an earlier end to the article. Here's a flavour of the kind of sporting insights that passed for *Chronicle* news:

> We met at Aldin House ... We then crossed the canal, and found immediately in a few turnips; the hare ran nearly to Colnbrook village, but doubling back, took three or four very large rings and then went straight away to within a mile of West Drayton. She then doubled back...

And so it goes on, and on, and on, with pointless tours of, no doubt pretty, villages and dull dramas of hares outwitting the most expensively educated boys in the Empire by cunningly scampering through fields of Brussels sprouts. Oh, how the upper classes lived! Perhaps it's no surprise after all that Eton developed an interest in football.

Like those clever hares, I wanted to get away from the hounds, and so turned my attention to the reports of the 1883 football season. The Old Etonians' team began with the same eleven that had, the previous year, won the cup for their former school. They had remained largely unchanged throughout the 1883 run-up to what was to be their fourth final in five years. It's an easy case to make that the Etonians of the time were, in all likelihood, the best team in England. But the 1882 cup winners almost became the 1883 first-round cup casualties. Back then, only the Wanderers had gone through that embarrassment. The Old Etonians managed to scrape through against the Old Foresters in the opening round after drawing their initial game. In the subsequent rounds they disposed of Brentwood and then Rochester. From the fourth round onwards, they played every game at the cup final venue of Kennington cricket ground where the Old Etonians defeated, in turn, the Swifts 2-0 and Hendon 4-2. In the semi-final, they came from a goal down to beat Notts County 2-1 with strikes from Macauley and Goodhart. In Manchester, Blackburn Olympic easily overpowered Old Carthusians 4-0 in the other semi.

The final on the last day of March was a clash of class and sporting cultures. The result rocked the closeted world of the football establishment. The Old Etonians never trained or practised. They were committed amateurs who simply turned up to play and expected the same of their rivals. But they were shocked by their cup final opponents' preparations. Such was the consternation at Blackburn's pre-match behaviour that the school newspaper carried reports that, in plain speaking, were tantamount to the aristocrats accusing the Blackburn players of being paid cheats. 'So great was their ambition to wrest the cup from the holders that they introduced into football play a practice which has excited the greatest disapprobation in the south.' The reporters at the *Chronicle* went on to hint at a paid professionalism, which they were too polite to directly allege:

> To be brief, the Blackburn men were in splendid condition for the match and spared no pains to gain victory ... For three weeks before the final match they went into a strict course of training, spending, so report says, a considerable time at Blackpool, and some days at Bournemouth and Richmond. Though it may seem strange that a football eleven composed of mill-hands and working men should be able to sacrifice

three weeks to train for one match, and to find the means to do so too.

Despite Blackburn's Blackpool build-up, the former Eton pupils still went into the game as favourites. They were captained by the remarkable Arthur Kinnaird. He was a Scot who played in nine FA Cup finals, helped organise the first international and went on to serve as president of the English FA. The Eton school reporter hinted that a pre-match mindset contributed to an ungentlemanly complacency among Kinnaird's players:

> No one will deny that they were the better team of the two, but it was their very confidence in this fact which probably lost them the match. Had they only been non-favourites, the result would have been different, for their play during the first part of the game was too casual...

Acknowledging the superior physical condition of the Lancashire team, the report added 'and they should certainly have gained more than one goal while fresh'.

A record-breaking crowd of 8,000 turned up to watch, with many travelling from Lancashire. Both sides picked formations unimaginable today; none of your modern-day 4-4-2 or 'one in the hole behind a single striker' stuff. Instead, the teams set out with, what I would call, 'prime-number line-ups' of 1-2-3-5. Both played a goalie, two defenders, three half-backs and five forwards.

Eton took the lead after Kinnaird passed to Chevalier, who, after avoiding Ward's tackle, found Goodhart, who then scored. But, after half an hour, Eton were reduced to ten men, not by a red card (which didn't exist in those days) but by an injury (substitutes, like red cards, hadn't been introduced). As I read through the *Chronicle* of 1883 in that silent reading room, it reported that the competing footballing cultures continued even during the half-time break. The former public school boys stood together, chatted and relaxed. In contrast, Blackburn's assistant ran on with 'a large black bag containing grapes and other fruits, lemonades etc. for their refreshment'.

Perhaps unsurprisingly, the second half saw a turnaround in Olympic's fortunes after Eton went down to eight and two halves. Without any sense of grievance, the *Eton Chronicle* reported that:

> Dunn was severely injured and had to leave the field, and shortly afterwards Goodhart was seized with cramp in both legs, and Macaulay received a nasty kick on the knee. This completed the 'rot' which had by this time set in, and the Northerners were not long in making matters even.

Matthews equalised for Blackburn after sixty-five minutes. Against the pattern of the second half, the Eton captain Kinnaird scored a winner that wasn't. He put the ball in directly from a free kick at a time when all free kicks were indirect; the 'winning' goal didn't stand.

Despite their numerical advantage, their half-time refreshments and the Blackpool sea air, Olympic could only score that single second-half goal. The final ended all square.

It was Eton's conduct after the final whistle that was to be their undoing. The Etonians thought it unreasonable to ask Blackburn to go to the expense of coming back a week later for a replay. Exhausted and depleted in numbers, Eton honoured a sense of chivalry and Blackburn seized an opportunity. The former public school boys agreed to play extra time despite having only eight fully fit players. Olympic's strength in numbers and stamina from training helped defeat the tired, battered and reduced Etonians, and, when Crossley scored in the second period of extra time, the trophy was heading to a new home – the furthest from London it had ever travelled.

The *Chronicle* concluded its report in a way that, possibly, only it could. 'Considering that after half-time the Old Etonians played with ten men and that Goodhart and Macauley were practically "hors de combat" in the last half-hour, they did not do so badly.' That phrase, which translates as 'outside the fight', isn't the type of thing you normally read in a football summary. It's much more commonly ascribed to combatants in literature such as Alexandre Dumas's *The Three Musketeers*. The phrase might sound like it's laced with public school eccentricity (which it is), but it was also, in some ways, an accurate summing-up of the physical, rough and tumble, long-ball game from the north that triumphed that day.

Years later, long after he had hung up his boots, the Eton captain Arthur Kinnaird reminisced about Olympic's physical tactics, lamenting, 'I carry their marks to this day.' The defeat wasn't without recrimination; N. L. Jackson wrote in *Sporting Days and Sporting Ways* that:

> It was really Kinnaird who lost the Old Etonians the match, for although the extra half-hour was not then obligatory, his good nature prompted him to promise that concession because the visitors explained that a draw would mean their having to come up to London again, which they could ill afford.

In 1883, Olympic were the first northern and, in all likelihood – though no one admitted it – the first professional team to win the FA Cup. The game in parts of the north of England had become big money. When two teams from opposite ends of England met in a two-legged tie, the second legs in the south would sometimes attract just a tenth of the first game's attendance. The north of England's growing armies of paying supporters helped clubs entice the best players, particularly the best of the Scottish players. A process that had begun in 1879 with Darwen gathered an unstoppable momentum.

But so incensed were the men at the Football Association that they felt compelled to set up a commission of inquiry. When Preston North End were accused by Upton Park of paying players, including the two prominent Scots, Nick Ross and George Drummond, the commission summoned the club secretary. He stunned everyone by admitting to the payments. Preston was suspended from the FA Cup and the authorities acted to ban professionalism by insisting that all players non-native to the club's surrounding areas had to be registered. It might sound like a strange demand, but it was their way of trying to track down the subsidised out-of-town travelling professionals. What followed, however, was a massive rebellion emanating from Lancashire, as seventy clubs joined forces and threatened to set up the British Football Association. Finally, on 20 July 1885, in a meeting at the Anderston's Hotel in Fleet Street, the FA surrendered and legalised professionalism. When the professionals won the day, Scotland rebelled against the rebels, with the Scottish FA angrily compiling a list of sixty-eight 'outlaw' players who had been paid in England. It would be a further eight years before Scotland finally accepted professional football.

No one realised at the time, but the Old Etonians' victory of 1882 was to be the last time a group of amateur former public school boys would ever lift the trophy. No team from the south even reached the final again until Spurs in 1901.

After being reunited with Angus, I ask him about the 1883 final and the contrast between the two teams. While they may have had the same team formations, Angus explains that they were playing with totally different approaches.

> The field game is a kick-and-rush game; a dribbling game like
> little kids playing in the playground. You run with the ball

until you're tackled and all your mates run behind you and once you're tackled they get the ball. The Blackburn team would have been playing something that we would recognise as soccer, passing the ball, while the Old Etonians would be dribbling it until tackled. There were two completely different sets of tactics.

And Angus should know what he's talking about. He is the keeper of his very own Eton archive of football and has compiled a detailed hand-written record of Eton football going back to 1800. His tiny scribbled notes are a meticulously preserved goldmine of footballing history and in his A4 hardback book he has traced the story of sport at Eton back to the start of the nineteenth century. Each pre-printed line in the book contains a year in the life of results. He has lists of players from the cup final-winning runs, including details of the players, their ages and their subsequent careers.

As I stood next to him, determined not to spill my tea over his work, he announced, 'Here, take them away and read through them.' While I thought about taking his book into the next-door room, he told me, 'Take them away for a few days.' I wanted to say 'no', but how could I tell him I didn't trust myself (one of only three people I have known my entire life), when this man, whom I'd only met via email and in person for two hours, was willing to do so?

When we parted company, we made an arrangement to meet again at the next Fulham home game under a statue outside the stadium. Fulham fans will know there are two statues: one of legendary midfielder Johnny Haynes and the other of Michael Jackson. When I checked my bag into the flight back to Scotland later that week, I carried Angus's notebook on as hand luggage. I trusted British Airways luggage transit even less than I trusted myself. On the plane, and when I got home, I kept checking and re-checking that the notes hadn't been taken by an invisible thief; I've never known the old saying 'a watched kettle never boils' to have greater truth. It was a feeling I hadn't experienced before. I imagine it's a bit like one of those Saturday-night jackpot lottery winners who hide their winning ticket in an easy-to-remember, but impossible-to-be-stolen-from, place, waiting to claim their winnings on Monday morning.

For those few days these notes were among my most treasured possessions. They were the type of discovery that any researcher in any profession would wait years for. Angus's books weren't going to transform my life, but I was really unsettled by the fact that, if I lost or damaged these originals, it would surely affect his. Fast-forward and I was relieved to be walking towards Craven Cottage and finally reuniting Angus with his two centuries of Eton history. I wanted to ask him how he was going to keep them out of harm's way during the match, but I didn't. My mission had been accomplished: the package had been delivered and, under the watchful eye of the late Johnny Haynes, we said our goodbyes. I was relieved. A couple of hours later, I was certain Angus was even more pleased as Fulham overcame Bolton 2-0.

I wanted to conclude the story of football's revolution by going back to where I started: the report of the second half of my match at Olympic. Just as the second period got underway, I seized my big moment as the assistant manager. I spotted a tactical strength in Greenfields' line-up, which concerned their captain, Keith Robinson. He was better known as Cheggers, for no other obvious reason than the fact he shares a first name with the 1980s children's TV semi-celeb. It seemed to me that Cheggers had too much space all to himself in midfield. I told this to one of our subs, who passed the information to our right-back, Bill Scott. I knew that my instructions to try to close down in midfield were being communicated when I saw Bill lean over to ask the linesman to make the tactical switch.

I'm not sure how my advice got lost in the translation, but whatever change was made appeared to make the problem worse. Within a couple of minutes it was 4-2 as the opposition's centre-back, Mark Golding, scored with a screaming half-volley. The strike gave our goalie no chance to make a save, or a mistake.

In the sixty-fifth minute, Olympic had a great chance to get back in the game, but blasted over from ten yards. As they tired, it was only their mouths that didn't slow down. I've often wondered what frustrated subs say on the sidelines. Are they secretly hoping that the guy in their position messes up so they can get on the pitch? Not in this team. Left-back Ian Mason, who had been subbed earlier in the game, told me, 'I don't mind losing. It's just the manner in which you lose that annoys me. Today we didn't try hard enough.' The sub I spent most time with was Callum Stirling. At eighteen, he is the youngest player in the squad. He was training to be a soldier in the British Army until a knee injury led to his being medically discharged near the end of his basic training. 'If they get another, our heads will go down and it will get worse.'

As the game petered out towards a 4-2 defeat, I wandered over for a cup of tea at the van by the side of the pitch containing Kath's kitchen. I missed the fifth goal by Barry Devvitt, but, moments later, the ref blew for full-time and the cup dream was over for another year.

In the pub after the defeat, the pub owner treats Olympic like FA Cup winners, laying on free food for the team. As they dispute why they lost, one of their number, only half-jokingly, blames it on 'Dave's half-time team talk and our new assistant manager!' They debate what should have been and what can be put right the following week. Central midfielder Steve Round has an unusual explanation for why he was under-par: 'I was too sober today, that was my problem.' Chris, the goalie, explains the reason for the second of his gaffes: 'My knee got stuck in the mud.' His teammates seem surprisingly forgiving, although maybe that's because the previous keeper, as they then tell me, got the whole team barred from the entire town of Wigan with his antics during an end-of-season celebration.

As talk turns to the history of Blackburn Olympic and Eton, I ask them whether they would be interested in a rematch after all these years. Dave seems to speak for his entire team when he states: 'For more than a 120 years they've been bearing a grudge, so we'll play them.' Captain Chris Tomlinson quickly adds, 'But if they're going to give us cucumber sandwiches they can bugger off.'

Just as in 1883, a match between Old Etonians and Blackburn Olympic would promise to be a clash of football and culture. Bring it on.

The 1980 Old Firm cup final ended in an on-field riot between rival supporters. But Glasgow's football has happier origins, forgotten by most. *Picture: Courtesy of The Daily Record.*

Chapter Two

Glasgow's Football – Is it all Sir Isaac Newton's Fault?: *Rangers v Celtic, 1924*

NO OTHER BRITISH football rivalry has ever had a law passed to deal with its consequences. In this, and in so much else, the Old Firm of Glasgow Celtic and Glasgow Rangers is unique. This is their story. One of the fiercest rivalries in world sport, it is never dull, often kinetic and sometimes tragic – but it was never meant to be this way. One team was formed by canoeing teenagers who simply wanted to play a dry-land sport; the other by a Catholic priest determined to raise money to feed the hungry of the city's East End. This is the history of a once noble footballing rivalry poisoned by religious bigotry, which, in turn, contaminated Scotland and beyond.

There are only three things in life I hate. The experience of growing up in South Africa guarantees that discrimination of any type is on this shortlist, which is why I'm sickened that the game I love, in the city I adore, has been contaminated for so long by a sectarianism I can never fully understand.

No one has any idea how many have lost their lives or their looks over the decades in an often ugly rivalry. After one 'shame game' in 2011, Strathclyde Police assistant chief constable Campbell Corrigan told Scotland and the rest of the world:

We can't arrest our way out of this. The time's come for a wider debate. The day after these fixtures, we are literally mopping up the pieces. If anybody is so naive to think that the activity of the people involved in the game itself doesn't have a huge impact on the crowd, whether it be in the ground, in the pub, on the other side of the world, they are hugely naive.

The chief constable's comments came in the aftermath of the latest in a long line of explosive encounters. Many of the players had seen red but only three were sent off; on the sidelines, the two managers were in each other's face. Very few can recall the score, but most Glaswegians remember the trouble. After the match, police recorded a doubling of reported incidents, and, in bedrooms and living rooms, girlfriends and wives felt the full and very real pain of the loss: Strathclyde Police dealt with more than double the average number of domestic abuse assaults.

So how has a simple football match had such a traumatic impact?

I should start by saying that this is the only chapter where I will declare an interest. If I don't, others in the world of the internet and social media will do it for me. So here's my admission: I am a Celtic supporter and a season-ticket holder at Celtic Park. In politics, I wear red-rose-tinted glasses and, in football, I swap them for hooped emerald-green ones. And while there is possibly no such thing as a neutral when it comes to the Old Firm, over the next few pages I will set out to masquerade as one.

I first met the ill-fated Craig Whyte, the calamitous and short-lived chairman of Rangers Football Club, in the most unlikely of places. It was in the boardroom at Celtic Park, at half-time during a deadlocked Old Firm match. As I took the few short steps towards him to shake his hand, I reminisced in my mind that only time separated me from being one of his employees. For in the 1980s I was one of Rangers' lower-profile

Catholic signings and, at the age of just twenty-two, I was in my footballing prime. However, the only silverware I ever got my hands on was the oversized fork and serving spoon while working as a silver service corporate hospitality waiter in the Thornton Suite in Rangers' Ibrox Stadium.

Fast forward twenty-odd years and here I was, with fifteen minutes to work up to popping the question that this chapter necessitated. My target was the diminutive Craig Whyte who, by then, although he didn't know it, was already halfway through his short and controversial tenure as the Rangers chairman. He is one of the most colourful characters in the club's history. Depending on your point of view, he either took over the club as it was just about to crash into an iceberg or, less charitably, he's the guy who took over the 139-year-old institution in good health and, within a few months, managed to freeze a huge block of water before sailing the club, Titanic-like, full-speed ahead into ruinous financial administration.

But, as we met, that collision wasn't yet visible on the Rangers horizon. Once I could see that no one else could hear our conversation except my friend, the club's then director of football, Gordon Smith, I asked Mr Whyte, 'When do you think Rangers first decided on a "No Catholics" policy?' He took such a direct question surprisingly well. Perhaps because I was asking him about a Rangers from what now seems like another age. Pretty fairly, he couldn't place a date on it. For decades, his club was probably the only team in the world where the question of which foot you kicked with (Catholics were known as left-footers, for reasons I won't go into) was more important than how well you could kick. Only a few yards along the corridor, in the Rangers changing room, no one knew how many Catholics were sitting listening to the Rangers manager Ally McCoist's half-time team talk. More importantly, no one cared. On the pitch, and in the changing room at least, things had changed.

But just moments after asking my question about the birth of footballing bigotry, and not finding out when it was, I found out at least part of the answer to the question of when it wasn't. Just two steps behind Whyte, in the trophy cabinet, I saw the oldest trophy in world football: the Scottish FA Cup. As I pressed my nose against the glass cabinet like the clichéd 'kid in a candy shop' admiring the cup, I noticed what turned out to be a crucial clue in my search. It wasn't a surprise that the most regularly engraved names throughout the trophy's infancy were Queen's Park, Renton and Dumbarton. But looking down the list of winners, I noticed that next to '1909' there was a space chiselled simply with the words 'Trophy Withheld'. As the current match restarted and the bedlam of the second half engulfed everyone around me, I was alone in my thoughts, with a nagging question on my mind: 'What was it that happened in 1909 that meant it was the only year outside of a world war in which there was no winner of this ancient trophy?' The answer appears to confirm that Glasgow football didn't start off as a sectarian-inspired feud.

On cup final day, 10 April 1909, Celtic's Jimmy Quinn barged the Rangers goalie, and the ball, over the Hampden goal-line to make it 2-2. When the replay seven days later also ended in deadlock, the fans and players expected extra time. Photographs of the post-match scene show players on the pitch waiting for the referee to get the game going again. But after a few moments, the authorities announced that they would be sticking to a little-known SFA rule: there was to be yet another replay.

The fans were incensed. Hundreds from both sides of the 60,000-strong crowd poured onto the pitch. The goalposts were torn down. The pitch was badly damaged. Whisky, Scotland's national drink, was used as an accelerant to set parts of Scotland's national stadium alight. The police were attacked and, when the fire brigade turned up to deal with the blaze, some of their hoses were cut. There were over a hundred injuries but, such was the intensity of the violence, the police only managed to detain one offender. The replay was cancelled and the trophy and medals were withheld.

For reasons that could not have been understood at the time, the significance of the riot goes well beyond an unprecedented disturbance and a cancelled replay. In polite circles, the riot scandalised football. But all these years later, as I read through the archives of that day's stunned Scottish newspapers, there's something entirely unexpected; unexpected, at least, when viewed from the vantage point of those 1909 rioters' near future and with the hindsight of Glasgow's recent past. The fascinating thing is that supporters joined together to riot against authority. Despite the fury at the end of a second tense final, there are no reports in any of the newspapers – or any record anywhere – of even a single punch being aimed at a rival supporter. Infamously, the same couldn't be said in 1980, the next time Old Firm fans met on the Hampden turf. That riot, and the sickening violence of rival fans, was broadcast live after a 1-0 Celtic win. It shamed the clubs and shocked Scotland. I remember that the Murphy household was among the few in our street who saw how the riot started but didn't get to see how it ended. This wasn't because our parents didn't want us watching the daytime violence, but rather because the electric meter in our house ran out of money. Younger readers should ask an older relative what I mean.

But 1980 was a million miles from the clubs' earliest days. Celtic were born from Glaswegian poverty and an Edinburgh victory. Irishmen in Glasgow brought their culture, flags, faith and hymns to their new home and created a football club in their own image.

Many of them were survivors of the potato famine or descendants of that enormous starvation. The tragedy of the 1840s reduced Ireland's population by two and a half million and huge numbers of famine refugees came to Britain. At times during these years, there were a thousand people clambering from tiny boats on the River Clyde each and every day. Hundreds of thousands fled to America and even more made the cheaper trip to Canada. Tragically, a far greater number, one and a half million, made the journey to meet their maker. It is one of the British Empire's greatest injustices that these people died of hunger while the British government did little to support those in, what was then, its colony. Even today, the horror of the famine, including the ambivalence of the government minister in charge of its response, Lord Trevelyan, is commemorated most weeks at Celtic Park and Irish international games with the provocative and haunting ballad 'Fields of Athenry'.

The Irish influx was a shock to Scotland. The Protestant Church was a large and generous part of Scotland's welfare state in those years, but many newcomers kept their distance from the Church, fearing it was only looking to feed those who would renounce their Catholic faith. On top of this, the idea of breaking the Church of Scotland's bank account so as to feed incoming people of a different religion didn't appeal to everyone in the Church.

Many of the immigrants were deported back to their hungry homeland. The Poor Laws were reformed and welfare offices were opened in John Street and Cochrane Street to give 'hand-outs' to pay for clothes and medical treatment and fund pauper's burials. But it was nowhere near enough. Into this gathering of human desperation stepped the central figure in Celtic's history. Andrew Kerins had arrived in Glasgow from Sligo as an unemployed fifteen-year-old, although he is better known by the title given to him as a Marist priest, Brother Walfrid. After studying in France, he was posted back to the city he had left. As he took up a post in the East End of Glasgow and became headmaster of Sacred Heart School, his became a mission in what was then, without doubt, the most deprived few square miles anywhere in Europe.

Brother Walfrid wore his conscience, and his soul, on his sleeve. He lived among the thousands of underfed children, many of whose ribs were visible through their threadbare clothing. He was determined to act to free people from the nearly universal poverty of his time and their place. His inspiration for a football club came in 1887 after the avowedly Catholic Hibernian's victory over Dumbarton in the Scottish Cup final. After going along to the Edinburgh team's celebrations, he resolved that Irish immigrants in the west of Scotland should have their own team. Within a few short months, Glasgow Celtic Football and Athletic Club was born.

Immediately, it became a football club whose first priority wasn't to play football, a fact that even today gives many Celtic fans a pride that their team is a 'club like no other'. Celtic's social mission was clear long before they kicked a ball. Those who gathered that day in November 1887 for the inaugural meeting at St Mary's Hall in the Calton area of Glasgow were in no doubt over the importance of why they were there and what they were doing. The meeting resolved:

Many cases of sheer poverty are left unaided through the lack of means. The main object of the club is to supply the East End conferences of the St Vincent De Paul society with funds for the maintenance of the 'dinner tables' of our needy children in the Missions of St Mary's, Sacred Heart and St Michael's.

The founding statement also carried the club's first public appeal: 'It is therefore with this principal object that we have set afloat the "Celtic", and we invite you as one of our ever-ready friends to assist in putting our new park in proper working order for the coming football season.' The inaugural resolution then went on to suggest a religious bias in team selection that never became reality:

> We have already several of the leading Catholic football players of the west of Scotland on our membership list. They have most thoughtfully offered to assist in the good work. We are fully aware that the 'elite' of football players belong to this city and suburbs, and we know that from there we can select a team which will be able to do credit to the Catholics of the west of Scotland as the Hibernians have been doing in the east.

Thus Celtic was launched, into a crowded city of football teams that counted the fifteen-year-old Rangers among their number. The strange thing about Rangers is that most people seem to believe that they were consciously formed as a Protestant football club. Most people are wrong. It was only largely Protestant because that was the way Scotland was, and almost all teams were, at the time. Outside of Rangers circles, little is spoken about the club's formation. It may lack the philanthropic purpose of their city rivals but it is, in its own way, a footballing rags-to-riches tale. To get to this truth, I decided to meet Robert McElroy, the man who has written and probably knows more about Rangers than anyone who has ever lived.

We arranged to meet in the bar of the Redhurst Hotel, where he told me he was having lunch. After a twenty-minute wait outside, in one of Glasgow's regular autumn storms, I decided to walk into the restaurant, just in case I had mixed up the arrangements.

My arrival at the lunch was met with near-unanimous finger-pointing and what appeared to be polite amusement from the ladies, many of whom were well into their eighties. They were just about to get back into their raincoats to take on the rain that had just defeated me. Even though I was now indoors, the rain was still running down the inside of my collar and my back. By the looks on their faces, I knew I must have appeared really pitifully drenched. It was the type of dishevelledness that I could only remember experiencing once before. On that occasion, it led to a picture of me being Photoshopped with a new head on my shoulders in an election leaflet. It was a big improvement. Almost no one noticed until the *News of the World* newspaper printed both the drenched and dry pictures, whereupon, unfortunately for me, almost everyone seemed to take notice.

However, it turned out it was not my physical appearance but rather the fact of my presence at the lunch that gave these pensioners a fit of the teenage giggles. Unbeknownst to me, I had just wandered into hostile territory: the annual lunch of the South Glasgow Conservative and Unionist Association, of which Robert is chairman. It's the first and only Tory meeting I've ever attended, albeit by accident. I diplomatically beat a retreat to the bar to wait for Robert and, when he joined me, we both had a laugh and got down to the interview.

Being a Tory in Glasgow is a minority sport. McElroy carries the burden lightly and, from the moment he starts speaking, it is clear that this is a man who loves his football club. He believes that Rangers are one of the great untold sporting stories and spells it out to me in proud detail. The summary of which is its foundation as a boys' team by four canoeists, the brilliantly named Moses McNeil, his brother Peter, William McBeath and Peter Campbell. They were rowing along the Clyde and saw a group of youngsters playing football on Glasgow Green, at which point they decided to emulate that dry-land sport. For the first three years, the biggest competition Rangers faced was getting a pitch to play on. Each squad member had to take it in turn to go down to the Green at the crack of dawn with four jackets, one on their back and three under their arms, to be deployed as makeshift goalposts. This one-man pitch occupation protected the playing area until the rest of the Rangers team arrived. They would emerge changed into their kit from among the surrounding trees, the only changing room available to them.

A distant humming waitress, Robert and I are the only three people in this afternoon bar. As I finish my second Irn-Bru and Robert his second pint of shandy, he seems unsettled when I ask him about his view of romance. To save him from his own embarrassment, I quickly add that I was of course propositioning him about the romance of his football club. Visibly relieved, McElroy goes on to explain that he has been involved in what has sometimes appeared to be a lonely campaign to redress the sense that his is a club without an early emotional hinterland.

> It's difficult to put your finger on exactly why this happened.
> It's partly the club's fault because they didn't promote the
> story of the club's birth. Rangers were not at all interested in
> promoting their early days. That has all changed now and if
> you take a walk around Ibrox you see all sorts of tributes to
> the club founders.

Rangers could have continued as a team that used their coats for goalposts, had Queen's Park not refused to play these pitchless upstarts. Queen's didn't consider a rival to be worthy of a match unless they had a home to call their own. It was their quality-control mechanism to deal with the explosion of football clubs asking to play against them. Back then, there were five grounds in just one street on Copeland Road in Govan, now the site of Rangers' stadium. Rangers' second ground and first proper home was in Burnbank in the West End, on a spot now buried under a row of flats. Surprisingly, this first real home is unmarked and remains anonymous to any passersby. They were tenants there for a year before their landlord invited them to leave. They moved to Kinning Park on the ground of Clydesdale Cricket and Football Club before finding today's permanent home at Ibrox.

Rangers arrived on the footballing world with barely a whimper. They lost out in their first Scottish Cup campaign without losing a match or even conceding a goal. It sounds like a strange achievement but the truth is they failed to get their application form in on time and were refused entry into the competition. It doesn't seem to have bothered them too much. McElroy reminds me that they have won it thirty-three times since.

Their first breakthrough came in the 1877 Scottish Cup final against the Vale of Leven. Rangers were overwhelming underdogs and the media was fascinated by the fact that they prepared for the final by running through the city streets. It was around this time that the sports papers handed them their first nickname, 'The Light and Speedy Blues'. Rangers lost the final or, more accurately, they lost the third final after two replays.

Getting knocked out of the Scottish Cup without losing was to become an early habit for Rangers. 1879 was a historic year for the club: they won their first trophy, the Glasgow Merchants Charity Cup. That year they also lost the Scottish Cup to Leven after a 1-1 draw. They were furious that they had been denied what they believed to be a perfectly good and winning second goal, and simply refused to turn up for the replay. Leven celebrated regardless. It was the earliest high-profile refereeing controversy in a country that was still attracting its unfair share of them more than a hundred years later.

If Celtic are about more than just a game, then the Old Firm became so much more than just a footballing rivalry. For many people who have no religion, the Old Firm became their belief system. Too often, that faith in a footballing identity was turned against others in the name of a religion they didn't practise. Among the most vociferous in the supposed faith-based frenzy have been the people who never step inside a church or a chapel. It's a schism, but not one fuelled by established theological differences between the Church of Scotland and the Church of Rome. It has nothing to do with matters of transubstantiation, the existence of purgatory, Papal infallibility, or the biblical importance of Mary. It is a hatred of 'the other', pure and simple, devoid of any religious intellect. The majority of fans want nothing to do with the religious stuff at football, but many of those who have the sectarian chip buried in their shoulder also have it deeply implanted in their head. Most of these supporters could reel off their favourite starting eleven from years ago, although very few could name the eleven disciples who stuck with Jesus in the Bible. For years, both Churches have made it clear that this hatred has nothing to do with faith. But still it has endured.

The trouble surrounding the Old Firm has often tracked the Troubles in Northern Ireland. It has found energy from events across the water including the Easter Rising, Irish independence, the Civil War, Irish neutrality in two world wars, the Troubles of the 1960s, the hunger strikes of the 1980s and, latterly, the peace process. But now that the Queen has laid a wreath in Dublin in memory of those who died in the 1916 Easter Rising, and the Irish President has made an official state visit to the UK, then perhaps, just perhaps, trouble can also be laid to rest in Glasgow's football.

For many, it's never been about religion but about cultural identity. In a world where genealogy is all the rage, knowing that you are the latest in a long family line of inherited Old Firm affection is all the family tree many people need. Arguably, Celtic fans have a greater love for the romance of their club. When I asked a friend what Celtic meant to his Irish immigrant coal mining family, he was in no doubt when he answered, 'There are three great needs in life: spiritual, physical and emotional. Spiritually, the Church would look after us on a Sunday. Monday to Friday, the Labour Movement would protect us physically in the mines. And on a Saturday, Celtic looked after us emotionally.'

Supporting Celtic is one of the most important things in your life. It never leaves you. It's impossible to explain. No matter where you are you never fall out of love with the idea of being a Celtic supporter. It's about a sense of romance, a feeling of being the underdog even when you are on top. A unique team formed to feed starving children, it's an outsiders' club that has never felt part of the establishment. Is it right to transpose all of these emotions onto a mere football team? Will that sense of belonging ever change? Do the club's supporters believe it is unique? Yes, no, and yes – but not necessarily in that order.

The comedian Billy Connolly, who has his own seat at Celtic reserved for life, once mused:

> Celtic is important to me in as much as it's one of the only constants in my life over the years. I have changed and become various things but it is the one constant. Religion, friendships have come and gone, likes and dislikes have come and gone, but Celtic has remained.

Rock legend Rod Stewart is also a big Celtic fan. I have met him only once and spoken to him twice. It was in the changing rooms at Hampden, just before a friendly game to celebrate the opening of the new national stadium involving a team of Scotland's all-time greats. For reasons that I have never been able to work out, Rod and I were the two guest players. Hampden was full to capacity; he was in midfield, I was on the bench. Rod didn't bring any shin-guards, so in the changing rooms my first words to him were an offer of: 'You can have my shin-guards and I'll take those of whoever I come on as a sub for.' He declined my offer and explained that he never wore them. The second, and last, time I spoke to him was a few minutes later when I asked him how he was feeling as we shook hands. I was coming on as a sub for him while blood poured from the tear down his unprotected right shin.

I'm not sure if he yet knows to wear shin-guards, but he has learned to love Celtic. His private jet can sometimes be seen parked on the tarmac at Glasgow Airport on the biggest match days. He also has a permanent seat next to Connolly. Many non-football fans sing along to one of his greatest hits, 'You're in my Heart', without realising its footballing significance. In it, he serenades his two teams with the line: 'You're Celtic, United, but baby I've decided. You're the best team I've ever seen.' I'm not sure if it was playing at the national stadium, or the sight of Rod's injury, or having Kenny Dalglish shouting at me for not passing as he was running in on goal, but that night my performance in front of 50,000 fans, including my mum and dad, was far from the best they'd ever seen.

Glasgow football not only generates the odd line in a rock song, it also complicates culture and politics. Many fans have a view about who is playing right-back as well as what is happening on the West Bank. Celtic followers, even those who have never been to Ireland and whose family has never stepped foot in the country, wave its nation's flag with pride. Some Scottish Nationalist-supporting Rangers fans who would vote to break up Britain belt out 'Rule Britannia' and wave the Union flag as though they were centre stage at the Last Night of the Proms. Scottish Muslims, Jews, Sikhs and Hindus are not immune and they themselves often have a comical take on it all. As they debate their football allegiances, some of them joke about how it makes them a Catholic Jew or Protestant Muslim or vice versa. All of this probably only makes sense in one city in the world: the home of Celtic and Rangers. Match days are often culturally confusing, with Palestinian, Catalan,

Royal Air Force, Israeli, Che Guevara, Vatican, Polish and Northern Irish flags on display. In the midst of it all, there's one soul in the Celtic crowd who perseveres in waving a lone Scotland flag. I sometimes wonder who he, or perhaps she, is.

For all the intensity and complexity of the rivalry, it wasn't inevitable. In the nineteenth century, theirs was a crowded contest of underdog teams nipping at the heels of the established footballing giants. They were up against two great powers that most people outside of the country, and even some people in Scotland, have never heard of: Queen's Park, who were then the biggest team in the world, and Renton, who had their very own unique claim to fame. They had won the 1889 Scottish FA Cup and then went on to trounce West Brom, the English FA Cup holders, 4-1 in a challenge match. Rather than modestly reflecting on their easy victory, they announced to the world that their village, with a population even today of just 2,000, was the undisputed champion of the world.

Celtic quickly replaced Hibernian as the dominant Irish-inspired team, at least in part by poaching many of the Edinburgh side's top players. But Rangers' development was different: they were probably only the fourth most-likely club to become Celtic's main rivals. The 1880s was a decade of footballing bankruptcy and Rangers could have ended just as Celtic was beginning. They had lost many of their best players and attendances were tumbling. Salvation came in the form of league football. Before then, the vast majority of games played by every club were 'ordinary' games, or what we today know as friendlies. As teams were knocked out of the cup, the ordinary game was their only source of football and income. These ordinary games were the bread and butter of most teams – and the bread came no thicker nor the butter any richer than having the chance to take on Queen's Park.

They were the Barcelona of their day. Queen's were the kings of the short-passing game and stood for a much higher ideal. They believed in the total utility of amateur football and refused to join a league that they rightly felt would herald professionalism. Before the league set-up, everyone wanted the extra money that came from playing Queen's Park in an ordinary game. After the league started, no one had a spare Saturday to fit them in. As Rangers' historian McElroy believes, 'Had Queen's Park joined the league, it could well have been that nowadays we would be talking about Queen's Park and Celtic as the two major powers; who knows?'

The decline of Queen's relative to the Old Firm's rise was demonstrated by whom Queen's chose to take part in their own centenary 'ordinary' game many years later – not themselves. In 1967, they decided to invite Celtic, the newly crowned European Cup holders, to take on Tottenham. It was a painful but prosperous choice. More than 100,000 people turned up, the highest friendly attendance in British football history. The Queen's Park players and directors watched the 3-3 draw from the stand, and they remain respected, and resolutely amateur, to this day.

League football created the cauldron and the commerce that meant that, by the start of the twentieth century, the Celtic v Rangers relationship was transformed into a ferocious footballing rivalry. Crowds soared and record incomes turned them into the best of footballing enemies. Cup games that should have been won by one of them inexplicably developed a habit of ending in unexpected draws and lucrative replays. The very name 'Old Firm' came from a sense of just how close their perceived mutual financial interests were in their vested rivalry. It was first used in a satirical cartoon ahead of the 1904 Scottish Cup final, which Celtic won 3-2. The *Punch* magazine cartoon showed a man carrying a sandwich-board sign emblazoned with 'Patronise the Old Firm' above the sardonic line 'Rangers, Celtic Ltd', suggesting that, while they were two clubs, they were also a single enterprise that benefited from rivalry. It was meant as an insult, but it has in fact stuck as a nickname and collective noun for the duo.

However, the unspoken truth of their rivalry is that, from the very start, the clubs have had much more in common than subsequent decades' relationships would suggest. No one today would believe it possible, but in those early years sometimes the only noise that greeted Rangers at Celtic Park was the polite applause from home fans. There are even early records of Celtic supporters standing to applaud Rangers players and management when they went along as spectators to watch Celtic play other teams. On 28 May 1888, when Celtic needed their debut opponents, they sent for Rangers. Their fiercest rivals were also among the few who would later back Celtic against possible league expulsion. Both have now challenged the worst instincts of their supporters. They also share confusion about their respective dates of birth: the reason for Celtic's uncertainty seems clear, but the cause of Rangers' confusion will come as a surprise to their fans.

Both wear famous club crests on their shirts with their founding dates: Rangers in 1873 and Celtic 1888. For years, goal scorers have been kissing those badges in celebration, but also in ignorance of the error they contain. Celtic's badge commemorates the year of their first game instead of the date of their formation. Rangers' confusion is more complicated. Robert McElroy ponders: 'If you were to look around Ibrox or look at the club memorabilia it said 1873. Rangers have only recently admitted that they got their foundation date wrong.' All the earliest Rangers records are clear that the club started in 1872, but in the early 1920s this date was mysteriously switched to 1873. McElroy is pretty sure why this happened: it's all down to John Allen, the man who was editor of the *Daily Record* newspaper and edited the Rangers yearbook.

In Rangers' fiftieth year, it dawned on Allen that he had missed the chance to publish a lucrative book celebrating their first five decades. McElroy takes up the story:

> Somewhere about 1922, Allen realised that it was Rangers' jubilee year and thought, 'I should be writing a book so I'll change the year', and while the Rangers yearbook in 1921 states that Rangers were formed in 1872, in the 1922 version no date is mentioned – and by 1923 it was switched to 1873.

According to McElroy, Allen then brought his book out in time for the new anniversary date of his choosing – *The Story of the Rangers – Fifty Years of Football 1873–1923*. And that is the tale of how Rangers turned their clock forward. After a two-decades-long campaign led by McElroy, Rangers acknowledged their mistake and are now once again a club formed in 1872. As for Allen, he stayed on as club historian until his death in 1953 – or was it 1952?

The clubs didn't just share a confusion about their dates of birth. They also found a common cause in a controversy that could have taken both their teams' lives. Rangers won the traditional New Year's game in 1952 at Celtic Park, 4-1. Home-team hooligans responded by throwing bottles and anything else they could find at the Rangers players. After the police post-mortem, the Scottish Football Association recommended that both clubs remove 'any flag or emblem which has no association with this country or the game'. The SFA took this to include the Irish tricolour, which, since the creation of the Irish Free State, had flown at the west side of the then 'Jungle' terracing, which held the club's noisiest fans. Celtic refused to budge and pointed out that the Irish flag flew below the Union Jack, which was hoisted atop the highest pole on the ground's roof.

The SFA threatened sanctions ranging from a fine to a temporary closure of the ground – or the nuclear option of throwing Celtic out of the league altogether. Both sides in the dispute refused to back down. The SFA general council met and, under the powerful influence of their secretary, George Graham, the Sepp Blatter of his day, voted 26-7 to demand that Celtic remove Ireland's flag. Celtic stood their ground and, after a prolonged stand-off, the SFA, fearful of the financial impact of a league without Celtic, backed down. In their greatest moment of need, Celtic had an unexpected ally: among their 'group of seven' was the unexpected voice of Rangers. It's probably fair to assume that Rangers' vote in favour of Ireland's flag wasn't entirely out of cultural altruism and had more to do with the consequences of the 'Old Firm PLC' without half of the Firm. Today, the Irish flag still flies atop Celtic Park. The Union Flag doesn't.

While their rivalry has caused huge hurt over the years, it can also be an enormous well of humour. One of Scotland's funniest comedians, full-time Rangers fan and half-time Ibrox pitch entertainer, Andy Cameron, regularly tells the story about my Ibrox debut. The unlikely but true tale came about in May 2009. Rangers were generous in allowing me to help organise a charity match against a combined team of unemployed Celtic- and Rangers-supporting teenagers. My team of politicians (plus Celtic-supporting actor Angus Deayton) were the designated home team, while the teenagers played in Celtic hoops. It was as I was pulling on that famous Rangers strip for the first time in my life that I discovered the home changing room still has two framed portraits of Her Majesty the Queen. A framed picture above the changing-room door means that a youthful Queen Elizabeth II is the very last thing Rangers players see as they run out onto the pitch. In the sixty-second minute of our charity match, the unbelievable happened. I scored what I think is only the eleventh, but without doubt best, goal of my adult life. Surprisingly, it was a brilliant diving header for Rangers against Celtic.

My over-the-top celebrations in my once-in-a-lifetime Rangers strip appeared in the next day's newspapers. Two days later was a 'Helicopter Sunday' – the final league game of the season with the championship title undecided. Either of the Old Firm could lift the title, and, as a precaution, the trophy remained unengraved and hundreds of feet up in the air in a helicopter hovering somewhere between the two grounds. Celtic needed to beat Hearts at home, and hope that Rangers would trip up away at Dundee United, to have any chance of catching their rivals.

As I queued to get into a packed Celtic Park, two well-watered fans behind me shouted, 'Jim!' I didn't turn round because I'm far from being the only Jim or Jimmy in Glasgow. Next I heard a scream of 'Murphy!', but again I took no notice because it's Celtic Park and shouting 'Murphy' doesn't really narrow it down too much either. Their third attempt at getting my attention worked a lot better as they threw an almost empty beer can and its contents at me. This was in the midst of the scandal over MPs' expenses and ours was a direct and comical conversation. It ended with their question-cum-allegation of 'Murphy, we saw you in your Rangers top yesterday. Your family must be ashamed of you.' I turned away, thinking that they had finished, when they added, 'Why couldn't you just have been stealing your expenses like everybody else?' Their pre-match jibe was the highlight of my day. Rangers went into a sixth-minute lead. Very early on, the trophy stopped hovering and headed towards a Rangers victory.

Returning to the story of the clubs' evolving rivalry because, despite the occasional humorous incident , there developed a far greater horror. By the 1920s, the relationship had morphed into something altogether much more sinister, turning the Old Firm into turbulent adversaries in an often religiously charged contest. A visitor from another planet, or even another city, tuning into the debate about sectarianism might think that the football clubs invented the problem. They didn't. Football didn't create religious intolerance, but it has been used as an excuse to help keep hate alive, sustaining bigotry and providing a sectarian circus for morons. The three brothers who formed the two clubs – the canoeing McNeil brothers of Rangers, and Celtic's Brother Walfrid – would be heartbroken by the sights and sounds of their ideals being contorted. Their passions had nothing to do with other people's prejudices.

To those who doubt the pre-football existence of religious tension, and there are many, the evidence is overwhelming. After all, in 1745, long before the Old Firm, the Catholic population of Glasgow was minuscule and couldn't be considered a threat to anyone, in any way. There were only thirty-nine Catholics in the city. And yet, Glasgow boasted an astonishing forty-three active anti-Catholic organisations, more than one anti-Catholic organisation for each and every Catholic. Sectarianism existed even when there were fewer Catholics in the entire city than there are players in either of the city's top two football squads nowadays.

Tensions waxed and waned throughout the years. But in 1875 they exploded onto the streets of Partick in the city's West End. That August, thousands of Irish Catholics gathered in Glasgow Green to commemorate the centenary of Daniel O'Connell, the Kerry-born civil rights and anti-slavery politician. Today, it is the location of choice for a kaleidoscope of demonstrations. It is a vast park across the Clyde from the Gorbals where, 130 years earlier, Bonnie Prince Charlie reviewed his Highland Forces. Ironically, at the time of the O'Connell gathering it was also the home to a fledgling city football club going by the name of Glasgow Rangers. In the late light of that summer's night, marchers returned west and mass violence broke out with groups of local Protestants. It continued throughout the night and into the next day. So severe was the trouble that the Sheriff of

Partick summoned troops from the local army barracks. Above the din, he officially read, or more likely shouted, the Riot Act, aimed at 'preventing tumult and riotous assemblies as amended by an Act in the first year of Victoria'.

All of this, and much more, predates the Old Firm, and it is to the clubs' credit that, in those early years, they weren't moulded in the image of the city that was dividing around them. Neither of them had a sectarian purpose. But football isn't played in isolation and, more importantly when it comes to the travails of the Old Firm, it isn't supported in a vacuum.

Events were conspiring against the openness of Rangers' first decades and, in this, they may have Sir Isaac Newton's theorem of motion to blame. The Englishman, born almost a quarter of a millennium before the Old Firm, predicted the reality of the Glasgow rivalry in his Third Law of Motion: 'For every action there is an equal and opposite reaction.' The Catholic Church was becoming more influential and the team formed by, but never exclusively for, Catholics was becoming ever more successful. The reaction to this still influences Scotland today.

The 1918 Education Act provided public funding for Catholic schools and was an enormous boost to the faith. It was proof positive (or, for many, proof negative) of the growing influence of Catholicism. But, back then in a city of zero-sum game, a more confident Catholicism unsettled more people than it comforted. The shattering proof of deteriorating attitudes arrived in 1923 from the unlikely source of another Christian faith. The General Assembly of the Church of Scotland is effectively its Parliament. It published a report entitled 'Sectarianism', which reverberated throughout the city and has thundered down through the decades. This document, with its one-word title, contained pages of assertion that were to haunt perceptions of the Church. The tone was captured by the Reverend

William George Black when he told the General Assembly: 'Glasgow has ceased to be a Scottish city. It is very largely an Irish city at the present time.' By then, the city's Catholic population was no longer thirty-nine; the Greater Glasgow-Irish diaspora now numbered 600,000, almost a quarter of the entire populace.

Not all of the new arrivals from Ireland were Catholic, but they were singled out. The Church of Scotland declared, in an incendiary statement that focused on both race and religion, that 'they cannot be assimilated and absorbed into the Scottish race'. It went on to say that bitterness among Scots would rise when they realised 'the seriousness of the menace to their own racial supremacy in their native land. This bitterness will develop into race antagonism which will have disastrous consequences for Scotland.' Eighty years later, the Church officially apologised. All of this is a far cry from the Church of Scotland of today, which is among the most passionate advocates of the rights of asylum seekers.

At the same time, there was another force was at work. Just as Celtic were shaped by vast Irish immigration, Rangers were to be changed by a new and different type of Irish immigrant, much smaller in number but with no less of an impact. Glasgow is a city proud of its working river: at points in the nineteenth century, this waterway built a third of all the world's ships. The Belfast company Harland and Wolff saw an opportunity to expand on the industry-packed river and opened a new Clyde yard. They brought with them an experienced Belfast workforce, which was overwhelmingly, or perhaps even totally, Ulster Protestant. Many of the newcomers were bearers of a new Protestant stridency.

When I spoke to Celtic historian Tom Campbell, who has written more than a dozen books about the club, he was clear that 'the 1920s was the watershed'. Harland and Wolff's workforce gravitated to Rangers for reasons of religion and proximity, as the club played just a kick of a ball away from the enormous steel gates of the shipyards. Campbell shares the view about the importance of the new shipyard workers:

> In 1920–21, Harland and Wolff, whose base was in Belfast of course, then expanded and moved to Govan. A considerable amount of the workforce moved there. Of course, they were 100 per cent Protestant and – how should I put it? They were emphatic about Rangers. They found a spiritual home at Ibrox.

At the end of Saturday's shift, these men raced the few yards to make the 3.30 p.m. kick-off. Rangers historian Robert McElroy reflects: 'There was a need for a counterbalance to Celtic. Going back to the sporting press, Celtic were described as the "Irish team". There was a need for a Scottish establishment club and Rangers were the natural home of Ulster shipyard workers.' These shipbuilding supporters helped take Rangers on a journey from being a largely non-Catholic team to becoming a Catholic-free institution.

Back across the city, and this time to another Celtic historian, David Potter, who believes:

> … there is evidence that by 1924 Rangers fans were singing songs about the Battle of the Boyne and the Pope. There was also the absurd myth that Ulster Protestants put out about themselves, that they were the only ones who took part in the Battle of the Somme. They did do gloriously in that battle, but they tended to imply that they were the only ones who fought there.

Potter shares the general view that a combination of factors over the decade contributed to the contamination of the rivalry.

Rangers fans also sang the Scottish songs like the 'Wells O' Wearie' and 'Loch Lomond'. They portrayed themselves as the Scottish team, as distinct from the Irish team. Celtic supporters had a gripe that Celtic players weren't getting a fair deal from the Scotland selectors. In 1930, for example, when Scotland were playing England at Wembley, Scotland were losing heavily at half-time. Celtic were playing at home the same day. When the old scoreboard at Celtic Park showed that Scotland were 4-0 down at half-time, it was greeted with a huge cheer.

* * *

Some Celtic supporters believe that their club is without fault. I am not one of them. In one important area the club has been culpable: Celtic's connection to Ireland is a source of pride but the fact that so many have celebrated the IRA is a cause of shame. To sing about the club or a family's Irish heritage, as many do, is one thing. To chant about the Provisional IRA's terrorism, as too many have done, is an assault on the open-spirited sense of the Celtic ideal. The club should have made that truth clearer and stronger, much sooner than they did.

What about Celtic's signing policy? Did it ever mirror that of Rangers? Despite the proclamation from the founding meeting about being a Catholic team, Celtic has always taken the opposite approach. Celtic was formed 'by' Catholics, but, while it draws most of its support from people of a Catholic background, it has never been 'for' Catholics. The nearest the club ever got to a formal policy of religious exclusion was at the annual general meeting in 1895. A resolution was tabled and debated to restrict the Celtic team to no more than three 'non-Catholics' at any one time. It was defeated and no similar policy has even been considered since.

When I meet up with former team captain and manager Billy McNeil, he explains:

> We had the pick of the players, we took them from wherever they came from, it didn't matter what religion they were. Some of the best Celtic players weren't Catholic. Bobby Evans, Bobby Collins, Willie Fearnie, Bertie Auld, Ronnie Simpson, Willie Wallace, Kenny Dalglish, Danny McGrain. It just didn't matter to us; they were just good Celtic players. The most important game in every season for all of us was the Rangers game. For the Protestant Celtic players there was an added incentive and they got really stuck in so that no one would think they weren't trying against the team most supported growing up.

This 'not trying hard enough' label occasionally attached itself to a player. Tom Duff was one such player. He was an Orangeman but, more importantly, he was Celtic's goalkeeper on New Year's Day 1892, when the team was humiliated by Dumbarton. Some within Celtic's support claimed that, with his background, he wasn't really part of their team's effort. The truth is that he had been taking laudanum to treat his rheumatism and had drunk too heavily the night before. His doctor had told him not to mix his medicine with alcohol and, eight goals later, Duff wished he had listened to that advice.

McNeil's former teammate and fellow European Cup winner Bobby Lennox told me what is intended as a humorous story, proving his former captain's point:

> We organised five-a-side games in training and for fun we sometimes played Catholics v Protestants. One day we were short of a Protestant player to make up a team and I was put in the Protestant team. We tackled hard in training and I was getting a tough time and I remember when one tackle

flattened me. I was sick of being brought down. When I picked myself up I just said, 'I've only been a Protestant for ten minutes and already I hate you Catholics!' It was just great fun and no malice.

But for all the talk of cultural identity and lack of animosity there has been a dark, sneering sectarianism at the heart of the relationship between the clubs for nine of the twelve decades of their rivalry.

After the Harland and Wolff and Church of Scotland controversies, Rangers took a turn for the worse. No one is certain when Rangers' 'Catholics need not apply' signing strategy started. Not even McElroy, the walking Rangers encyclopaedia, can name a precise date or board meeting when the decision 'we are a Protestant football club' was made. McElroy claims:

It almost happened like natural selection, if you like. A promising Catholic footballer would choose to play for Celtic not Rangers. Once the three Catholic players in the 1900s left the club, it may not have been realised at the time that that's the last of our Catholic players gone. I don't know if there ever was a hard and fast rule that 'we will not sign Catholics'. If there was ever a firm policy decided at a board meeting, I'm not aware of it, but as Rangers became more and more identified with the Protestant establishment it became less and less likely that they would sign Catholics or that Catholics would sign for them. It becomes almost like a habit. If Rangers are the club of the Protestant majority, then is a manager going to sign a Catholic player? Is a scout going to recommend signing a Catholic player? Or is a Catholic player going to sign for Rangers?

McElroy has been able to trace a few Catholics at the club in the early years, none whatsoever for decades, and only a token number in the 1950s and 1960s. There are two ways of looking at this: a traditional argument from that time, or the truth. The former is that Rangers didn't find Catholics good enough to pull on the famous Rangers shirt. The truth is that in football, like most things in life, you can only really find something if you look for it and, in reality, Rangers weren't looking.

If the sectarian profile of Glasgow football was a process of reactionary evolution, then Graeme Souness arriving as Rangers' manager was without a doubt the game's Big Bang. At his first managerial press conference he made clear that if it was good enough for him to have married a Catholic then why wasn't it good enough for him to sign a Catholic? 'Every Rangers manager had said in the past that they'd sign a Catholic, but I meant it.' However, the player he chose to break the mould is, to this day, the most controversial signing in Scottish football history.

Mo Johnston wasn't just a Catholic, he was also a former Celtic centre-forward. He wasn't the first to make the 4.8-mile trip across the city's footballing chasm. In the century before Johnston's signing, a tiny number had made this journey: Alec Bennet in 1909; Dr Kivlichan; Tom Dunbar; and even Neilly McCallum, Celtic's first ever goal scorer against Rangers in 1888, all went on to play for Rangers. In my lifetime, only Alfie Conn and Kenny Miller have done so. Johnston wasn't the first Catholic to play for Rangers. Nor was he just a Catholic or former Celtic pin-up. He was both of those things, and something else much more important. He was a prodigal son set to return and it was announced to delighted Celtic supporters that he had agreed to rejoin his boyhood heroes.

Imagine then how the world of Scottish football was rocked on 10 July 1989 when the door opened at the Ibrox press conference to unveil Rangers' latest signing and in walked Celtic-bound Maurice Johnston. The reaction was volcanic. It helped tip the footballing balance decisively in Rangers' favour and precipitate their nine-in-a-row league championship wins. For Celtic, and their fans, it was a body blow. He was one of their own, a man who had worn the four-leafed clover club crest on his chest with pride. But, more significantly, it made it clear that Rangers not only had a new manager but also were well and truly under new management. It angered some Rangers followers and hurt almost every Celtic fan, but something important changed that day.

There has been so much written about the transfer, and so much of it rubbish, that I decided to get the inside track from two of the three men who know the most: the two managers Graeme Souness and Billy McNeil. I have always known Graeme to have expensive taste in players but, in sorting the venue for our chat, I discovered something else: he has expensive taste in other things as well. When we talk on the phone, the former Scotland captain suggests, 'Let's meet in the men's fashion department at Harrods.'

I had never been in Harrods before and I'm not sure I ever will again. As I meandered through the shop I was overcome by a wish that the very polite security man at the door had given me a map of its layout, or that I had turned up an hour early to recce the joint, because I got lost, very badly lost. Instead of the men's section, I stumbled my way through something and somewhere I had never heard of before: the Beauty Apothecary. As I read back over that phrase I'm still not sure I'm pronouncing it in the way that all those beautiful and handsome counter staff, who seemed to be staring at me, would have wished. It was a stupid thought but I couldn't get it out of my head – the image of the episode of *Father Ted* when all the priests get trapped in the women's lingerie and perfume department. Even if you have never seen *Father Ted* and can't picture what I mean, then at least I have given you a clue as to what a Beauty Apothecary is like.

When I escape into the men's fashion section, Graeme is waiting for me. He's hidden among the men's suits just outside the Italian tea room and he suggests we go for a cuppa. As we take our seats he greets the waitress in what sounds like fluent Italian, a legacy of his playing career at Sampdoria. To my surprise, Souness is an incredibly open man of confident warmth. His first revelation shows that it's not just our conversation that had an unexpected setting.

The deal was done during a clandestine meeting in the suburbs of Paris. It was the most obvious step to make: he was, along with McCoist, the best forward Scotland had. Mark Hateley could play with either McCoist or Johnston. It was for all the right reasons, the money was right, more importantly he was up for it.

Across the water in Northern Ireland, the *Belfast Telegraph* had splashed the story on its front page the day of the signing. The reward for their world exclusive? A crowd of angry loyalists outside their Royal Avenue office demanding that the 'fairytale' story be retracted. In most football clubs, rumours of a big-money signing lead to an excited crowd gathering outside the stadium and, in that sense, Johnston's signing was no different. But rarely, if ever, anywhere in world football, has a crowd gathered to condemn rather than salute a new recruit. Souness tells me that, after the most unexpected of press conferences, the head of Rangers' security, Alastair Young, told him, 'Come on, we'll go out the back door.' A determined Souness replied, 'No, I'm not going out the back door, I'm going out the front.' He adds, 'There was a couple of hundred people. Some were burning their season tickets. But I'm proud of it. I didn't do it because Maurice was a Catholic, I did it because he was a bloody good footballer and he was the right price.'

Souness illustrates the club's contrasting signing policies with a story about the man that Sir Alex Ferguson regards as the all-time greatest British manager.

> Jock Stein always said that, if there were two outstanding kids and one was Catholic and the other Protestant, he only had to concentrate on getting the Protestant kid to Celtic because he knew the Catholic kid wouldn't be going to Rangers as he knew he was coming to Celtic anyway. So he only had to put the work into the Protestant.

It was only the teenage Souness's signing for Spurs that prevented him being proof of Stein's philosophy. 'I could have been a Celtic player. For a year I used to travel from my home in Edinburgh to Glasgow every Tuesday and Thursday night when Jock was manager. It could have been so different.'

It turns out Johnston was Souness's third attempt at signing a prominent Catholic.

> I remember I went after Ray Houghton, the Irish international and he was 'Yes, yes, yes, no.' I went after the Monaco player John Collins and he was 'Yes, yes, yes, no.' They couldn't do it in the end, I think it was too much pressure from their families. But Maurice was right up for it. He was either daft or extremely brave. Maurice had to put up with a lot of shit. We ended up having to get security for him, he ended up living in my house.

Souness moved out of the house to make space for Maurice. It is a home blessed by colourful characters. It was later bought by the Royal Bank of Scotland's former Knight of the Realm, 'Fred the Shred' Goodwin.

By the time we had placed our order for tea and cake, Graeme had revealed that Mo wasn't the only one to 'put up with a lot of shit'. 'Special Branch sat down with me and asked what restaurants I went to, what pubs I went to and how I drove to work and they gave me advice.' The long arm of the law also extended into Ibrox itself. 'I was at the game one day,' he said.

> As usual I was barred from the touchline and was in the directors' box. I had a superstition that I always took my seat just after the match started. When I looked round during a lull in the game I saw it wasn't the regular people sitting round me. On the Monday I asked a club director, 'Who was that sitting next to me?' And he just replied, 'I didn't want to tell you, but someone phoned up using a recognised code word to say "We're going to shoot Souness on Saturday."'

The identity of these new supporters sitting next to him, none of whom was watching the game? 'They were all police and security officers scanning the crowd for the phantom phone caller.'

Perhaps the most unsettling thing Souness shared with me was that opposition to Johnson's arrival wasn't confined to die-hard fans but included elements in both the changing room and boardroom.

> There was a little bit of resentment among some of the players. I had to sit some of them down more than once and tell them just to get on with it and just play football. A couple of the directors were less than enthusiastic but the chairman knew it was the right thing to do.

Sitting down over our £7 cups of tea and £9 strawberry tarts, Souness is charming, but I have no idea what it must have felt like as a young player to be sat down by Souness in his prime 'more than once' and told to shut up. Souness then listed the disgruntled players and officials. Some of those he named were very prominent and some have passed away. Even now, I am still surprised by who he named. Worries about lawyers' libel letters prevent me from listing the living and, while legally I cannot libel the dead, nor can they answer back. So I'll let them rest in peace in the near-anonymity of Souness's list.

As we get up to leave, he says simply, 'It was exciting times. I didn't do it to make a point. Life was easy after that.'

In the 1980s his opposite number across the city was Celtic manager Billy McNeil (no relation to Rangers founder Moses McNeil). Years ago McNeil was the first real footballer I ever met and had my picture taken with. After that, every other player was a let-down. I was eight years old; he was the first British player ever to lift the European Cup. That year our family were on holiday at Butlins in Ayr. Bizarrely, he was employed at the camp as a football coach before going on to manage Clyde, Celtic, Aberdeen, Man City and Aston Villa. His last game as a Celtic player is the first I can remember attending as a Celtic supporter. When I look at that photo on our bookshelf today, I sometimes wonder just how that eight-year-old boy with the goofy smile got to become friends with his dad's footballing idol.

He was, and is, a gent, always above sectarianism. When we talk he confides to me that it was the two father figures in his life who helped keep him above all the nonsense. One is Celtic legend Bertie Peacock. Billy has a special word for a man who defied many of the expectations of his upbringing: 'A big Irish Protestant, he was great to me, he looked after us and kept us out of trouble. He helped me become a footballer.'

But more significant was his own father.

My old man was in the army for years. He told me that the one thing you learn as a soldier is that your life depends on the man standing next to you and you don't care whether they are a Catholic or Protestant; they're on your side. If I had ever made any remarks about Catholics or Protestants he would have battered me.

Just as well it never crossed Billy's mind, because McNeil senior was a British Army champion boxer.

McNeil was the manager for whom Johnston had pledged to re-sign. Perhaps Billy has the angel of his father sitting on his shoulder when I ask him about the Johnston saga. He simply and sanguinely reflects, 'Rangers should be congratulated for changing their policy, it was really magnificent.'

If only everyone had the guts of Graeme Souness and the good grace of Billy McNeil. Glasgow, now the most Scottish of cities, could have avoided the scars of the past and escaped the potential wounds of the future.

Chapter Three

More than Just a Club:
Real Madrid v Barcelona, 1943

REAL MADRID AND Barcelona have long been divided by geography, politics and history. No other sporting rivals have been so trapped by the multiple and often tragic identities of their country.

But, as with so many rivalries, it wasn't always so. The teams' first encounter was 13 May 1902 in the semi-final of the Copa de la Coronacion, which Barca won 2-1. But this five-team cup contest in honour of the crowning of King Alfonso XIII showed no hint of what was to follow. It wasn't until much later that the teams came to be defined by a politics that was to poison Spain.

So what is the game at which it finally became clear that Barca and Madrid had taken on wider political meaning? When did each become a rallying point for the competing forces that fought through a bloody civil war? And how does their rivalry continue to shape Spain today? Such is the ferocity of their complex relationship that not one but three candidates compete for the title of the match that, above all others, cemented an often turbulent antagonism. Each of the three games was played in a different decade and belongs to one of three separate periods in modern Spanish history. The contenders are: 1925, when a British Royal Marine band came to play; 1943, with Madrid's biggest ever victory; and, lastly, a sending-off in 1970 that never should have been.

To understand the rivalry, a basic sense of Spain's footballing history is necessary. Despite the status of La Liga today, Spanish football got off to a slow start. Its evolution was hampered. Spanish industrialisation was belated, which in turn delayed the formation of an identifiable mass working class for the football clubs to attract. The big clubs only really started to evolve into mass popular movements in the 1920s and 1930s. When they did, Barca's first main rival was Bilbao, whose formation predated both Barca and Madrid. Barca's sense of self and confidence evolved over time. It wasn't an overnight thing, it was more evolutionary than that. But by the late 1920s the sense of the cultural conceit of the Catalan club was clear.

It is impossible to separate the rivalry between Barca and Real Madrid from Spain's tempestuous political past. When I met up with the author Jimmy Burns, he summarised it well:

> If you look at the foundation of Barca, it comes into being at a time of national crisis, Spain has just lost its last colonies but hadn't found a new role. 'What's gone wrong with our nation? How have we lost our Empire?' were the types of soul-searching questions preoccupying the politicos. Simultaneously there was an awakening of cultural and economic identity and a Catalan nationalism.

Into this cross-current of sentiment walked a Swiss sports enthusiast, Hans Gamper. He was a formidable person and player. After forming FC Zurich at home, he became the inspiration behind FC Barcelona when his wealthy family had immigrated to Spain. He later went on to play for the team, scoring an average of more than two goals a game. After hanging up his boots, he became a five-time club president. The birth of the club was announced when he placed a newspaper advert. You know, the 'Players Wanted' kind of appeal that a pub team, short of a centre-back, will sometimes place in the local community paper. It was possibly the single most effective advert ever placed, and it was the start of arguably the most important football club ever formed.

Madrid's founding purpose was, in part, to challenge the power of Spanish institutions such as the Church and the army. But by the time the footballing rivalry was in full swing, Madrid found itself in common cause with a Church, an army and one of the most violent regimes Europe has ever known. Just as the sport was starting to really take off, the first of the three contenders for the 'game that changed everything' took place.

In 1925, a Royal Navy ship arrived in the port and Barca invited the Royal Marine band to perform on the pitch before the match. This was Barca pre-Camp Nou, their home was the 20,000 capacity Camp de les Corts. When the well-intentioned Marines began to strike up the Spanish national anthem, there were very few in the stadium who heard beyond the first few bars. The Marines were drowned out and not in the way that they had hoped to be, by appreciative applause, but instead by the shrill boos of an angry Catalan crowd refusing to join in with what they felt was a misplaced celebration of Spain. The military band could be seen but not heard.

There are very few people alive today who joined in that booing. But there's no one better to discuss the importance of those couple of minutes with than Jordi Pujol, Mr Catalonia. Born in 1930, he grew up in the shadow of that match. More importantly, he went on to serve as President of Catalonia for almost a quarter of a century. When I first met Pujol, it was in his presidential headquarters and he was at the height of his powers. I decided to catch up with him again, this time to talk football. I made my way to his first-floor office on the prestigious Passeig de Gracia. The set-up is paid for him by the taxpayer, in recognition of his service as Catalonia's longest-serving President. My first thought was that they must be a very grateful people. Because they have gifted him and his staff an office with the likes of Tiffany's, Gucci and Chanel as near neighbours and Gaudí's remarkable Casa Batlló as an actual neighbour. For all the designer chic, the short journey up to his office is surprisingly 1950s in its challenge. I struggled with the door in one of those dark wood panelled three-person lifts in which the old-style lift attendant would have spent his entire working life travelling up and down. For a few frustrating moments I wished he was back.

It's fifteen years since I last met Pujol. Fast-forward to our football meeting and I immediately notice that he has shrunk in that decade and a half. He has lost a couple of stone in weight and a few inches in height. As I follow two steps behind him, he slowly leads the way to his office. As we walk I notice that he has developed a slight left-legged limp. From behind and above him I can see that his suit hangs across his jagged shoulder blades as though the top of his back were an expensive wooden coat hanger. But as we settle down and he starts to speak, it's clear that his mind is still as sharp as his shoulder blades.

'Catalonia is a nation of language, culture and cohabitation. We are a country of immigration.' Interestingly, he includes non-Catalonian Spaniards as immigrants. 'We've been able to create a rather powerful economy. We are not an ethnic nation, we are not a religious nationalism.' He then deliberately repeats his theme, 'we are a country of language, culture and cohabitation,' on the off-chance that I'd missed his point. As we talk, he gives me what feels like the entire back catalogue of decades of his speeches and books.

Pujol speaks with his hands and a passion in eyes partially hidden below thick greying eyebrows. As our conversation turns away from politics and onto football, he starts with an apology, an enquiry and a statement. 'Pardon, but what is happening to Glasgow Rangers? Celtic have it so easy.' But instead of wandering onto something that is clearly of interest to him, I force us back onto the discussion of how Barca became so emblematic of the Catalan cause.

This tiny giant of a character who was jailed for three years as a subversive by Franco's feared secret police reflects:

We need symbols. We were a movement but for us it was difficult to have other sorts of symbols. Our flag was banned. We needed a symbol. The passion of the people needs to have something for the concentration of their enthusiasm and sense of identity. Especially when we have a dictatorship or a difficult situation, people need the possibility to be satisfied with something. It happened not only here. Mandela and South Africa with the Springboks, that was the sport of the white people, the symbol of South Africa. But sometimes a sports club becomes a symbol. And Barcelona helped do that because Barcelona has always been a very pro-Catalan team. Spain has had two dictatorships, both have been very anti-Barcelona with some incidents and events. In 1925 a British battleship came during the dictatorship of Primo de Rivera. He was a very anti-Catalan dictator. He oppressed our language and our culture, our institutions were suppressed. Barca had organised a match to coincide with the visit of this British fleet and the musicians of the battleship played the national anthem of Great Britain and everyone was very enthusiastic. It was then a matter of courtesy that they would play the national Spanish anthem and there was a great noise. As a consequence of that, the dictatorship closed the field for games. Sometimes when people are not able to express their feelings by a normal way then they do it in this sort of way.

So it is clear that 1925 was the first time there had been such a high-profile manifestation in the stadium, overtly connecting Barca with some sense of Catalan nationalism. But 1925 isn't the match that forged the rivalry between Barcelona and Madrid. The crowd's reaction wasn't about Barcelona versus Madrid, the football club, but instead Barca versus Madrid, the capital city and the centre of Spain's power. The outburst had little or nothing to do with the emerging footballing rivalry; Madrid weren't even the opponents that day. It wasn't football, but politics, pure and simple. 1925 wasn't, as some people suggest, the match that sealed the deal between these opponents.

A second entry in the contest for the match that made all the difference took place in 1970. You can make a more convincing case for this game because it actually involved the two teams. As the decade got underway, Europe was in ferment. There were demonstrations against the Vietnam War, strikes and youth protests. In Spain the once all-powerful dictator Franco was increasingly physically and mentally frail. The authorities were on the lookout for the next spark. In Catalonia it came in the Camp Nou and from possibly the worst performance ever seen there. What makes it all the more memorable is that it was by someone who wasn't even playing. On 6 June 1970, referee Emilio Guruceta took charge of the Barca v Real match. In one performance he managed to entrench the sense that the two clubs were playing by different rules.

There is something unique to the sport of football about the vehemence of fans' attitudes towards referees. Why is it that all the best referees are in front of the television or sitting in the stands watching the game? Of course, every sport has refereeing controversies but most are usually regarded as honest mistakes. In football, too many fans believe that only the incompetent or the malevolent get through the refereeing exams. In grounds big and small, across this and many other countries, supporters either see cock-up or conspiracy in referees' motives. For decades, Barca fans were clear where on that spectrum between incompetence and malevolence the treatment of their team was located.

In most clubs it is stories of cup victories or wonder goals that are passed from one generation of proud supporters to another. Celtic have the Lisbon Lions. Manchester United eulogise the Busby Babes and the 1999 Champions League victory against Bayern Munich. Liverpool have their 2005 comeback against Milan in the same competition. Nottingham Forest have the Clough years and Arsenal fans will always revere their 2003–04 Invincibles. In that sense Barca as a club is no different from many others. But over the years, firstly at Les Corts from 1922 and since 1957 at the Camp Nou, their fans have also passed on to their children and grandchildren a detailed oral history of refereeing injustices. In their accepted zeitgeist, the history of Spanish football is a tale of pro-Madrid referees. It's a theme picked up by Jaume Sobreques, a current member of the Barca board and the man who penned the official history of the club:

> Real Madrid was the favoured club of the regime and therefore had political backing and with it the support of the referees. There was no doubt at all that to win a championship Barca always had to catch up with the generous number of points which were fixed beforehand in Real Madrid's favour. The facts confirmed this theory.

It's in that spirit that those at the 1970 match claim to have seen the decision more clearly than the referee Emilio Guruceta chose to. That is possible because people in the stands certainly seemed closer to the incident than the ref. It was the second leg of the Spanish Cup quarter-final. Madrid were 2-0 up after the first game. Both were desperate to win the consolation prize of the cup after losing out in La Liga. Barca were 1-0 in the match and had all the momentum as well as eleven determined players on their side. But in the fifty-first minute, Madrid's Velazquez bumped into the home side's defender and future manager Joaquim Rife. Guruceta blew his whistle, gave a penalty and in doing so he entered Barca's pretty packed hall of infamy.

Even by current pampered standards of near non-contact football, the penalty shouldn't have been given. To this day, Barcelona officially describes it as 'the famous false penalty'. I've seen the replay of the award. I watched the YouTube clip over and over again and I can't see any infringement, nothing at all. It's two players chasing after the same ball and one falls over, the other doesn't. There is no referee in the world who should put the whistle in his mouth for that. It's hard to imagine just how, in the 'rough and tumble' era of the 1970s, the ref's conscience allowed him to make that eccentric split-second call. What's worse is that, looking at the replays, he is so far away from what he decides is an infringement that he doesn't make it into the long-range camera shot. The entire Barca team protested; some fans threw cushions onto the pitch; some of the players including Rexach and Reina refused to play on and walked off. Once Amancio converted the penalty, Barca's Eladio was sent off for sarcastically applauding the Madrid goal after telling the ref, 'You're a Madrid stooge, haven't you got any shame?'

What happened next is part of Barca folklore and always will be. While some of the players wanted to leave the pitch, many of the supporters decided they wanted to go onto it. Local author Manuel Vazquez Montalban famously wrote about it for *Triunfo* magazine. He wrote in a style that would seem ludicrous if it wasn't about Barcelona. But such is the romance attached to the club, it must be the one and only time a pitch invasion has been written about in what feels like poetry. The Communist Party member Montalban is quoted in Jimmy Burns's book *Barca: A People's Passion* thus:

> Guruceta continually stops play and orders the latest wave of cushions to be removed. It becomes increasingly difficult to do so. Twenty, thirty thousand cushions fill the night with strange colours, and behind them the first of the fans begin to advance towards the pitch. Mr Guruceta is beginning to look worried. No one has touched him, but now that some five thousand fans are surrounding him, someone must have said something to him because suddenly he is running against the stop watch and he is running as fast as Juan Carlos used to in a good match, not caring how much of the pitch he has to cover or about the steps into the changing room. Now the pitch belongs to the people, five, six, ten thousand people parading with their Barca flags, shouting the name of the club, marching towards the presidential box. The spectacle is bigger than any match you've ever seen – the colours of summer, the enthusiasm of countless bodies, the green turf, the cushions like so many poppies, the dark blue night, fireworks, Barca flags, and an intimate, total, collective satisfaction, so much so that even the middle classes with their cigars are shouting at last, at last... Today is a fiesta. You can breathe freedom, and the night has the most favourable of colours. The public shout, clap, sing, 'Barca, Barca, Barca' ... and then some secret bugle must have warned that things are going to change. The rectangle is plunged into darkness and there follow other noises, other shouts ... The colours have changed. The first of the fires appear ... the straw of the slashed cushions is flaming, setting fire to the advertising boards ... The cries have turned bitter ... The public disperses ... But strange angers have been born ... A group of fans pass by me, shouting, 'Barca, Barca, Barca'...

Outside the stadium, some Barca fans fought and lost running battles against riot police. But the response of the Barca board marked a renewed confidence and resilience at the football club, despite Franco still being in power. The Barca president, Agustin Montal, announced:

> For too long the College of Referees, the Spanish Federation and all the other official bodies have allowed things to happen that should never have been allowed in our football stadia ... The members and supporters of FC Barcelona felt profoundly hurt and insulted by the shameful and unjust role played by Mr Guruceta...

One of the reasons this match is on my shortlist is that it is one of those moments when the Barcelona fans themselves announced, 'Enough is enough.' There's an added significance because an important part of the allure of the FC Barcelona story is the conceit that there is something unique about their supporters or Culés. Many clubs carry that sense of exceptionalism about their followers. The thousands of Dortmund fans crammed onto the Schwarzglben, Manchester City supporters who stuck with the team throughout the dreary years before the Sheikh Mansour's millions are part of their club's folklore. But the true stand-out fans are surely the small number of thousands who turn out most weeks to watch the Rochdales, Montroses and Scunthorpes of the world. These supporters can and most will go their entire lives without their team ever winning anything other than three points. By contrast, most big football clubs are backed by enormous overseas Diasporas. Admittedly, my experience of this is mostly about getting together in sometimes dingy bars in the seedier parts of adopted towns. I remember going to watch a game at the Chicago Celtic Supporters Club straight off the plane from O'Hare airport. The worried taxi driver checked with me time and again that I really did want to be taken to that particular pub at seven o'clock that summer Sunday morning. Years later, when I joined Barca expats at the London Barca Supporters Club or 'penya' he would have had no such worries. Not for them any old pub; instead their home is their very own barge on the River Thames.

I met up with them for the second leg of the Champions League semi-final against 'ugly' Chelsea. They weren't really thinking of it as a semi, more like a warm-up for the inevitable Munich final. Barca have always had a global émigré following. London's penya has regularly been boosted by history and economics. The history of Franco's rule forced thousands of Catalans to London in search of safety. The financial crash of 2008 brought many more Catalans looking for work.

It has to be one of the most picturesque settings to watch the prettiest football team the world has ever witnessed. I sat with 200 Barca fans opposite the Tate Modern Gallery, with the lights of Big Ben and the London Eye reflecting alongside us on the night-time river. The barge's top deck must have officially been classed as 'outside'. That's where the smokers unappreciatively watched the game to escape from the anti-smoking laws I had helped pass in Parliament, just a few hundred yards further down the river. I was guided below deck to a low-ceilinged single dark room that stretched the length of the barge. I joined chairman Eduardo and his committee at the only reserved table. For a moment, it felt a little like that bar that my Chicago taxi driver had sped away from; except for the port holes, the almost even balance of youthful men and women and the gentle rocking every time another boat motored past. I took a seat next to Robert and his pregnant wife Tanya from Turin. It was clear pretty quickly that this Italian lady was going to nervously watch the game from behind her hands; in the way that I remember first 'watching' the shower scene in the original *Psycho* movie, as Norman Bates butchers Janet Leigh.

Whether upstairs or downstairs, the Catalans cheered the two early goals and laughed at John Terry's red card for stupidly kneeing Alexis Sanchez in the bum. After Ineista's forty-fourth-minute goal, the penya treasurer began to make Munich plans on his iPhone. 'How will we get there? Should we try to book the hotel now to beat the rush?' It was a conversation with himself that lasted barely two minutes. Ramires' goal catapulted Chelsea back into the contest. The second half could be summed up by nine of the most unlikely words ever used to summarise the outcome of any football match – 'Messi misses a penalty and Torres scores the winner.' As I went back upstairs to leave, no one was smoking because there was no one around, the disbelieving fans had disappeared into the London darkness.

But despite all the anger from these fans' parents' generation, 1970 wasn't the game-changing match. The truth is that the moment that confirmed the depth of the animosity between the capital of Spain and the capital of Catalonia's main clubs came much earlier. 1970 may never have happened at all, or certainly not with such a ferocity, if it hadn't been for an even more dramatic encounter in 1943. The Guruceta-inspired pitch invasion was an outpouring of almost three decades of bottled-up angst that had been building since a cup tie played during the Second World War.

To fathom what happened in 1943, you need to understand something about the one event in Spain's history that has influenced politics, the nation's football and culture for decades. For those who lost family it's the heartbreak of modern Spain. For many football fans it's the emotional backdrop to the Barca v Madrid rivalry. In his brilliant book *The Spanish Civil War* Antony Beevor wrote of the conflict that 'It is perhaps the best example of a subject which becomes more confusing when it is simplified.' Read his book to see what he means.

In early 1936, Spain had a democratically elected left-wing Popular Front government. It was rocked by an attempted military coup that summer by its right-wing opponents. The plotters had pockets of success in bloody battles. But in both Madrid and Barcelona the government's supporters made up of militias, socialists, anarchists and trade unionists held firm against the military plotters. After that initial stalemate the civil war raged for three years. When the war broke out on 18 July 1936, Barcelona were on a break from playing. Their Irish manager, Patrick O'Connell, who had played for Sheffield Wednesday, Dumbarton and Manchester United as well as captaining Ireland, was abroad. As the war ebbed and flowed, the anti-Franco militias won control of both cities and purged Atletico and Real Madrid of Franco followers. Eight of the twelve First Division teams, including Real and Barca, were soon in Republican-held territory. The temporary war victors asked permission for both Madrid clubs to play in the non-Franco Catalan league. Barca said no.

But these battle successes were temporary because there was a massive imbalance in military capabilities. On the one side were the Nationalist authoritarian, centralising powers under General Franco. They were violently supported by Hitler and Mussolini and celebrated by the Catholic Church in Spain. On the other side were the disparate and often divided groups of anarchists, socialists and Communists. They were strengthened by the bravery of the volunteers of the International Brigades of committed men and women, who travelled from all over the world. The Soviet Union under Stalin succeeded in appearing to support while also manipulating and dividing Franco's opponents. The Soviets sided with the anti-Franco forces, at least in part because they couldn't abandon a coalition that included their Spanish Communist Party comrades. But the Soviets were also cautious. In the 1930s, Stalin was a strong man at the head of a weak state. He was worried that significant Soviet intervention would provoke a violent reaction from Hitler.

And he didn't want to unsettle Britain with the prospect of victory and a Communist-orientated Spain.

The UK and most other democracies stayed on the sidelines of this curtain raiser to the Second World War. Hitler provided Franco with significant support and was only exceeded in his enthusiasm for Franco by Fascist Italy. The Nazis provided Junker fifty-two aircraft, Heinkel fifty-one fighter-bombers and the men and material to make them operational. Germany also deployed anti-aircraft gun batteries and the fearsome Condor Legion.

Faced with this huge Nationalist arms influx, the Republicans could only initially count on Mexican rifles and Czechoslovakian machine-guns. And what of the 'Great Powers'? The US, tied to a non-intervention agreement and lobbied by American Catholics, refused to aid the Republicans. France provided them with limited and poor-quality support. Even after Hitler and Mussolini got involved militarily on Franco's side, Britain sat it out. Looking back from a post-Second World War vantage point, many find it puzzling that Britain refused to back the anti-Fascist Republicans. Even as late as 1938, Republicans hoped that Britain would side with them. But there remain accusations that Britain via the Royal Navy, possibly then still the most effective sea-based global fighting force in the world, pushed the boundaries of neutrality beyond credibility – in favour of Franco. They provided his forces with crucial communication support via Gibraltar. The Germans believed that the Royal Navy were actively blockading Soviet attempts to ship weapons to the Republicans.

On top of that, British companies, more than any other, owned the greatest share of Spanish business. Many British and American enterprises seemed to have a renewed enthusiasm in their trade, as long as it was with Franco's Nationalists.

Ask many older Barca supporters what they think of Real Madrid and they will describe them as General Franco's team.

It was the actions of the General in associating himself with Real Madrid that turned many neutrals into Barca fans. Like most people in their mid-forties, I don't remember Franco's government but I do remember when he died. The death of the dictator was big news in Spain and so, too, it would seem in at least one house in Glasgow. It's one of the first memories I have of anything happening any further away than my own street. The eight-year-old me scribbled in his school news jotter on 10 November 1975: 'General Franco is very ill and he is being kept alive by a cidny misheen.' And two weeks later my spelling hadn't improved, nor had the dictator's health, as I wrote: 'General Franco is dead. He was bireed yesterday.'

It's not that I understood Spanish politics, but I put it down to the eight-inch mini-sombrero hanging on the wall in our home's tiny hall. My uncle and aunt had just come back from Spain. They were the first in our family to ever get on a plane or travel abroad. This little hat was our only connection to the great extravagance of foreign travel. For the eight-year-old me, Franco was the dead guy from the sombrero country. I still have that tiny hat.

That day a thousand miles away in Barcelona, the imposing bust of the dead dictator was given the same treatment meted out to every toppled autocrat's statue. In the heart of the stadium that he had forcibly renamed, the club's chief secretary Joan Grandados tossed it across the room in what we have to assume was a mix of anger and relief. It disintegrated into tiny pieces.

So just how did Franco become so associated with Real Madrid? It's generally understood that FC Barcelona rapidly generated a political and cultural purpose rooted in their region and to a certain extent the sentiment of Catalan nationhood. But Madrid developed early their own unique identity and it was a million miles away from being Franco's plaything of the future. As a footballing institution, they are much more complicated than many of their critics are willing to give them credit for. For the unthinking many, there is a sense that Madrid the club was founded by the forefathers of fascist neanderthals. There's also the parallel assumption that Madrid the city was a building block of Franco's civil war coalition. Both assertions are as ignorant as they are popular. Madrid the city, like Real the club, is lazily misunderstood. The war truth is that Madrid fought fiercely against fascism during a painful three-year city siege. It wasn't until Madrid succumbed to Franco on 1 April 1939 that the war came to an end.

Despite the sense of the club later being nurtured as Franco's team, Madrid were formed by a group of liberal intellectuals. Not for them the sense of muscular Christianity of the Edwardian British footballing pioneers, quite the opposite. Instead, Madrid's founders wanted to dilute the influence of the Catholic Church and the Spanish armed forces. They were determined that their new team would help liberate Spain from what they saw as the suppression of the people by the Church and the military. In fact, during the Civil War, Real Madrid, like Barca, were 'collectivised'. Despite there being some debate about the motivations for these boardroom revolutions, the owners affiliated their clubs to socialist trade unions. Perhaps counter-intuitively, Real raised and donated money to anti-Franco forces.

But the complexity of the club's identity is multi-layered because it is also the Real of the president that gave their famous stadium its name and helped give the club its eventual political identity. In 1943, Santiago Bernabéu took over a struggling institution, which had just finished in the bottom half of the league. He helped transform their fortunes on and off the pitch and stayed on as president until 1978. But Bernabéu was close to the victorious regime and had volunteered for Franco's forces in the civil war. He helped Francoist acolytes serve on the club's board and refused to let his players join a trade union. He was inventor and then cheerleader in chief for Franco's 'Real as an export commodity' plan. Under his leadership, the club built a physical legacy that their fans are rightly proud of. But he also left a political identity that many still mourn. Always a controversial character, he reflected in the 1970s, 'I took sides in the civil war and later I regretted it.' The families of many of the victims rightly doubt the sincerity of his four decades' delayed non-apology.

But Franco hadn't started out as a Madrid supporter. Surprisingly, Franco's club was the Basque club Athletic Bilbao. In many ways he considered the Basque region as the real Spain. He saw them through the prism of a romanticised history, as a pure Spanish race that existed before Iberia and had survived the Romans and the Moors. Even though he went on to oppress Basque identity, for him Bilbao was the symbol of the Spanish fury, guts and the conquistadors.

The answer to 'Why Madrid?' lies in the timeless truth that dictators crave association with popular sporting success. And in Real, Franco had handed to him the most wondrous footballing icon to hitch himself to. The 1950s was a sparkling era in Spanish football; and nowhere was it brighter than in Madrid. The beauty of their appeal is that it wasn't the triumph of systems but of a fluency and a fresh footballing flamboyancy. They won playing exquisite football with stars and a chemistry that had never been seen before with players like Puskas, Di Stéfano and Pento.

While the world watched footballing greatness, Franco saw political opportunity. Back then, Spain's two great exports were people and oranges. The dictator couldn't believe his luck and grabbed it. His was a regime that had successfully turned his country into the bogey man of Europe. Spain and its government were ostracised by most of the world. But now out of the blue, Franco suddenly had this extraordinary power of the appeal of the greatest team on earth. He purred as Real travelled around Europe presenting a different image of a post-civil war Spain.

And for the first time, the genius of Madrid was being celebrated in record numbers thanks to the new middle-class 'must have' gadget of the black and white television. Across Spain, the government controlled the media and ensured that, whenever football was on television, more often than not it was Real. In Britain, families who got their first television to watch the Queen's coronation could now see the majesty of Madrid in their own homes. The British public were fascinated by television and entranced by Madrid. Almost overnight, football or, more accurately, one football team became an instrument of the government's foreign policy. The Spanish foreign minister under Franco, Fernando Maria de Castiella, famously boasted that 'Real Madrid is a style of sportsmanship. It is the best embassy we have ever had.' I have spoken a lot about this with Barca aficionado Jimmy Burns and he explained Franco's motives. 'This was Spain's great export and you would have been mad if you're at the head of a government not to try and identify with it or make it part of Spain's great national enterprise, which is what Franco did. They become Spain's and Franco's great export.'

Franco was nothing if not a persistently ruthless and occasionally astute dictator. It was a combination that helped keep him in power for so long. He recognised that by the 1930s, even in Spain, football had morphed into a mass movement. It had even come to rival that most Spanish of pastimes, bullfighting. But the Madrid government didn't shut Barca down. To close them down may have provoked rebellion. Instead, he curtailed activity on the pitch and clamped down on what the supporters did off of it. They weren't allowed to display the Catalan flag in the stadium. He seemed to take the view that he would rather have Catalans in the stadium supporting their team under a tamed leadership than outside on the streets demonstrating against him. The Fascist Franco appeared to mimic the Communist Marx's slogan of 'Die Religion ... ist das Opium des Volkes' (religion is the opium of the masses). He hoped that football in Barcelona would be the faith that would blind the people, if not into full acquiescence, then at least into distraction. It didn't always work. In 1951, the club played a high-profile role in the first post-war demonstration. When Barca played Santander in Les Corts, a mundane protest against increased tram fares led to leaflets being distributed around the stadium. Huge numbers of fans joined in the protests by refusing to take the trams laid on by the authorities. Instead, they walked home.

Then and, even now, Catalans didn't need any convincing of Franco's affections for the capital's team. It's a sense that is felt throughout the club right to the very top, including Sandro Rossell. I've met Sandro a few times over the years. To many people in the world of football, he is infectious company. If Rossell hadn't got involved in running the football club, many in the media thought he would be trying to run Catalonia. Over lunch, when I told him about this book and his beloved Barca's place in it, he instantly agreed to be interviewed. I had a sneaking suspicion that he would have been a bit disappointed not to have been asked.

So he suggested that we meet up again deep inside the heart of the Camp Nou. By chance, it was perhaps one of the most poignant places for us to talk about the heritage of the club. Because while of course it's rude to look over the shoulder of anyone when they are talking, especially the guy who runs the joint, I couldn't help but notice that just a few feet away on the wall behind him was the roll of honour of all the FC Barca presidents. At the top of the list is Gualteri Wild, whose actual name was Walter Wild, the English footballer who served as the club's inaugural president. There in the middle is Josep Sunyol, the assassinated president. My interviewee, as the incumbent is last on the list. Rossell is clear that, from minute one, Barca were about much more than football: 'You have to look back to history, it was founded in 1899. It started as a football club but immediately it was converted into a social institution of Catalonia.' He reflects that the club played a crucial role in Catalan resistance during the civil war and beyond.

> During forty years that Franco was the dictator of Spain and he was not in favour of Catalonian culture, the language, the books, music, etc. etc. Then it was FC Barcelona that was the tool for the Catalonian people to express themselves publicly. In a way people were using the football games. During the games they were expressing what was forbidden to express outside the football games and this is why it became more than a club.

Times and circumstances have changed but there are always causes at the Camp Nou.

As we spoke everyone around us was making increasingly rushed preparations for kick-off, which was less than an hour away. After seventeen minutes and fourteen seconds of the game, thousands of supporters stir into a chant demanding a referendum on Catalan independence. 1714 is the year that many Catalans believe they lost their nation status. With twenty-seven minutes and forty-six seconds to go in the second half, they repeat the act. Although it sits uneasily with UEFA's decree of not mixing football and politics, for the fans there's nowhere better than the stands that stood against Franco to make this, the most modern of democratic demands.

There is one event during the war that every Barca fan born after 1936 seems to have been born aware of. But when it comes to the history of Barca, fact and folklore are sometimes conflated. Sunyol's death is the best illustration of one being mistaken for the other. The young Catalan was president of FC Barca and an idealist. He lived out his dreams through football: 'To speak of sport is to speak of race, enthusiasm, and the optimistic struggle of youth', and 'to speak of citizenship is to speak of the Catalan civilisation, liberalism, democracy, and spiritual endeavour'. He didn't live to see his dream. Barely a month into the war, he was executed by troops loyal to Franco. It wasn't until sixty years later that academics published an account of his fate. Sunyol was murdered on the road from Madrid on the outskirts of Guadarrama. In much of Catalan folklore, the Barca president was killed because he was the Barca president. The reasons have often been disputed but what seems more likely is that Sunyol was crossing a guarded checkpoint where he mistook foes for friends. Believing the armed men to be opponents of Franco, he offered them a republican greeting. It's probable that single act of self-identification as a Republican led to his murder. His memory is an eternal part of the spirit of FC Barca. His body has never been found. As I stood in the Camp Nou interviewing Sandro Rossell, I could see the name of the murdered president carved onto the list behind him.

Sunyol is but one of the many 'disappeared'. And as the war ended, Franco threatened even more violence by boasting 'the war is over, but the enemy is not dead'. And what followed was forced labour and prison populations running at twenty times the pre-war levels. He also unleashed industrial-scale firing-squad executions. The city of Barcelona was subjected to a grotesque revenge. FC Barcelona shared in the punishment.

The Catholic Church, my church, played a soulless role, driven by a sense of morally corrupt self-justification. It was of the type that decades later I saw the Protestant Dutch Reform Church practise in South Africa while defending the race hatred of apartheid. Pope Pius XII celebrated: 'Lifting our hearts to God, we give sincere thanks with your Excellency for the victory of Catholic Spain.' Not only did the Catholic Church act as cheerleaders for a Christian nationalism, which they believed was facing down Godless Republican Communists. But they also went on to tolerate the relentless killing of prisoners. Some captured Republicans were forced to attend Mass and those who refused were manhandled into chapels. At Castellón de la Plana, some prisoners who refused to kneel in church were taken out and executed.

As the Nationalists gained the upper hand, they assailed Catalonia with an overwhelming force of more than 300,000 troops, supported by hundreds of aircraft. They marched into a Barcelona unrecognisable today. It wasn't the crowded fashionable Ramblas and the metropolitan cafes now so loved by the eight million tourists who visit this beautiful sea-side city every year. Instead, this bustling city felt and looked like a ghost town. Residents had fled or were in hiding fearful of reprisal from the advancing troops. What happened after the city fell to Franco proved that they were right to do so.

Ten thousand local people were executed in a few blood-crazed weeks. Street names were changed and the Catalan language was banned. Barca's stadium was given over to the regime to host a cleansing ceremony. A group of Spanish players were turned out in the Barca colours to be humiliated 9-1 by the Athletic Bilbao's youth team. The government even changed the club's name from Football Club Barcelona to Barcelona Club de Fútbol. It may seem trivial but it was a highly significant switch to Spanish away from a name that had recognised their English and Swiss heritage. Those on the club committees with left-wing or republican sympathies were purged. And ominously, from this point onwards Franco's feared secret police were to vet each and every new applicant before they could serve on the club board.

Men like the textile industrialist Enrique Llaudet were appointed to keep Barcelona Club de Fútbol out of politics and in with the Madrid government. And as if to proclaim to the world and Catalonia that the purge of the club's culture was complete, a sign was mounted in memory of Franco's allies and supporters who had perished in the civil war. It proclaimed simply 'For Spain and for God'.

And what of his Republican opponents who had perished? There was to be no such tribute to them at the club that many had loved. They were rounded up. And in what has become the vogue for dictators the world over, many were then crammed into football stadia and executed. It is hard to imagine but 200,000 were murdered by firing squad over the next four years. As a thousand a week were killed by their own government, the world, which was busily limbering up for the Second World War, again adopted a 'nothing to see here' attitude. Some opponents who survived were sent to labour camps. And in this, too, Franco seemed in tune with Hitler's twisted sloganeering. At least one of his labour camps boasted 'redemption through work' in a chilling homage to the Nazis' 'Arbeit macht frei' or 'Work makes you free' slogan erected over the entrance gates of Auschwitz-Birkenau. Hundreds of thousands of anti-Franco refugees also poured across the French border. But in 1940, after Hitler conquered France, ten thousand of those Republican fighters were sent to the Nazi concentration camp of Mauthausen. They were emblazoned not with the Star of David but with Blue Triangles.

The depth of the conflict between Barca and Madrid was exposed in a post-civil war game played during the Second World War. The contest also confirmed the philosopher Unamuno's insight that the dictator would 'conquer but not convince'. The club, its supporters and officials were stamped on by Franco but they stood firm. When the teams met in 1943 in the semi-final of the Generalissimo Cup, a competition named in Franco's honour, Barca travelled to the capital with a 3-0 lead. This despite a refereeing performance that seemed to give Madrid the benefit of every doubt. By this point, things had become so lopsided against the Catalans that even their new pro-Franco board officially protested. But the Madrid media reported that their anger was motivated not just by football but by the clear intention of 'attacking the representatives of Spain'. Before the return leg, angry Madrid fans were incited into a frenzy. Barca's fans were banned from attending the match. After travelling from their hotel in the south of Madrid, their team was booed as they arrived at the stadium. To help create a din, the home fans were given a free whistle with their match ticket. The capital's newspapers joined the noisy chorus. Mariona Gonzalvo, a Barca player who turned out internationally for both Spain and the Catalan XI, revealed 'five minutes before the game had started, our penalty area was already full of coins'. The crowd behind Miró goal were screaming 'Reds!' and 'Separatists!'

The Barca team received an uninvited guest just before kick-off. He carried an even more unwelcome message. There are various accounts of who the shadowy figure was, with some players suggesting it was a member of the armed forces. But in Jimmy Burns's book *Barca: A People's Passion*, he records that no less a character than the Director of State Security, the colourfully named José Finat y Escriva de Romani, the Count of Mayalde, visited a bewildered Barca team. According to Burns's account, the Director warned them: 'Do not forget that some of you are only playing because of the generosity of the regime that has forgiven you for your lack of patriotism.' In a country gripped by the vengeance of post-civil war reprisal, there was little left to the imagination in the Count's reminder. Raich, Escola and Balmanya, the three Barca players who had fled the country during the war, would have expected at a minimum to be the subject of fresh police investigations. Hardly the best pre-match team talk. But as a motivational speaker the Count appears to have hit the mark.

Within half an hour, Madrid were three goals up and Barca were a man down after Benito Garcia was sent off. According to contemporary accounts, the crowd bullied the referee – although many Barca fans probably believed he needed little, if any enticement – into sending Benito off. If the game hadn't already been settled by the uninvited team talk, it certainly was now. Madrid added to their tally and Barca's humiliation before the break with goals in the thirty-third, thirty-fifth, thirty-ninth, forty-third and forty-fourth minutes. It is quite possibly the most intimidating atmosphere at any game in Europe's footballing history. Barca physio Angel Mur said: 'An armed police lieutenant spent the whole game calling me a Catalan dog and a red separatist, and all the rest of it. When I got up to treat an injured player, he grabbed me and told me to sit back down again.'

At half-time, Barca had had enough and didn't want to come out for the second half. There is some confusion about who came into the away team's dressing room and when. According to one of the Barcelona players in an interview years later, a Spanish army colonel popped in without warning. The defender Francessc Calvet, who played at Barca for thirteen years and who was capped by both Spain and Catalonia, said of the terrible day, 'He threatened us and said literally, "Go back out on to the pitch or you're going to jail."' It's not clear if there was one or a second dressing-room intruder or whether the players were understandably confused by the terrifying tactics.

But even though they went back onto the pitch they didn't play. It finished 11-1 to Madrid. Barcelona scored their solitary goal in the final minute. I spoke to the English football journalist Sid Lowe who has written the book *Fear and Loathing in La Liga*. As part of his meticulous research, he interviewed the only living member of the defeated squad. On the day of Madrid's biggest ever win and Barcelona's second biggest defeat, Fernando Argila was Barca's reserve goalkeeper. He heard and saw everything from the bench. When asked by Lowe about how this match affected the clubs' rivalry, Argila told him revealingly, 'There was no rivalry. Not, at least, until that game.' Quizzed as to how a 3-0 win could be transformed into the 11-1 defeat, he says simply, '*Pues, politicamente*. Politically, politically, it was something.'

We don't have to take Argila's word for it. Juan Antonio Samaranch is a name known to sports fans of a certain age the world over. He was head of the International Olympic Committee for two decades up until 1981. What is less well known about him is that he was a staunch ally of Franco's regime as it tried to crush the spirit of Catalonia, the land of his birth. In those days, this future global sports ambassador was, more often than not, little more than a mouthpiece of the regime. But even he, surprisingly, found his own voice after the squalid 11-1. As an occasional reporter, he wrote in *La Prensa*:

> If Barca had played really badly, the result would have been different. But it was not a question of playing badly or well. Barca simply ended up by not playing at all. Individual players were fearful of making even the most innocent of tackles because of the crowd reaction and therefore hardly touched their opponents ... It was frankly sad having to watch the spectacle of Barcelona forcefully reduced to impotence by the coercion of the crowd...

In their readiness to believe in a Franco/Madrid collaboration, Barcelona fans are and were motivated partly out of truth, but also out of excuse. There was enough evidence of the association between the government and club for it to become a Catalan fact. But it was also a way for Barca fans to explain away Madrid's golden era. How else can they account for the stratospheric success of their rivals? 'They must be benefitting from preferment at the feet of the dictator' was the most comforting way for many Culés to rationalise it.

And the perceptions of Franco's favouritism to Madrid continued long after the war. For anyone who doubted a continuing 'hand of government' in favour of Madrid, then the remarkable story behind the transfer of Alfredo Di Stéfano to Madrid more than a decade later helped to convince them. Because, despite having agreed to sign for the Catalans, he somehow became a Madrid player.

He scored on his Madrid debut in a friendly against French side Nancy, just five hours after he and his family got off the train from Barcelona. But the entire episode of football intrigue, probable espionage and certain double cross is the enduring proof many Barca fans needed to cement their sense that Real belonged to Franco.

But like many of the great events affecting Barca, the truth is more complicated than it appears on the first telling. Because of a footballing strike in Argentina, Di Stéfano was registered with two clubs in two countries, Argentina's River Plate and Millonarios in Colombia. Adding to the complication was the undeniable fact that Barca were ineffective negotiators. They allowed a Catalan lawyer, Ramon Trias Fargas, who empathised with Barca and understood Colombia to handle the negotiations. In a spectacularly ill-judged process, Barca offered to pay just $10,000 for Di Stéfano's services, while the Colombians wanted something closer to $40,000. As the move to Barca stalled, Madrid jumped in. They were far more decisive negotiators. But they also seemed to have a helping hand. What followed was an episode in subterfuge that wouldn't have been out of place in a Cold War spy defection novel.

Fargas was so concerned about Francoist influence in the transfer that he went to extraordinary lengths to conceal the deal from the government and Spanish football authorities. He went as far as to use code words in his Argentina-bound telegrams. The depths of his worries are revealed in one clandestine telegram where he informed the recipients that

> Football in our country has become a very important issue, as it is the only way we can collectively convey our regional aspirations. Therefore the Di Stéfano question is a national problem. We know for a fact that our telephones are being bugged by the government of Madrid, which claims to be defending the integrity of the Spanish state.

While both teams scrambled for his signature, the Spanish footballing authorities changed their procedures to introduce a ban on the signing of any foreign players. The rushed review of rules was designed to guarantee that from that moment on the government would have more of a role in any and all future footballing imports. For reasons that don't stand up to even the most superficial of scrutiny, Di Stéfano was the only player exempted from the new law. But there was a peculiar caveat to the distinct treatment of Di Stéfano. For no obvious reason other than to spike Barca's move, the Spanish FA decreed that Madrid and Barca would have to share the player. They made clear that he was to be a Madrid player first in 1953–4 and then would swap sides every season after that. Both club presidents agreed. But such was the reaction of Barca directors and supporters it was a compromise that cost the Barca president his job. At the end of the affair, Barca rejected the player-share idea in its entirety. Di Stéfano headed off to the Bernabéu as a full-time recruit. As soon as the dust had settled, Barca had immediate reason to regret the move. In Di Stéfano's first season, Madrid won their first league title in twenty-one years. He scored a brace in his first El Clásico and would add another sixteen goals to the tally against his initial suitors. More importantly, he became the catalyst for an unprecedented golden era of silverware, celebrated in Madrid and manipulated by the government.

Di Stéfano, playing alongside Puskas in Real's frontline, scored a club record: 216 league goals in 262 games. He was European Footballer of the Year in 1957 and again two years later. His forty-nine goals in fifty-eight European games stood as a record for almost half a century until another Madrid striker, Raul, surpassed it in 2005. Andriy Shevchenko and Ruud van Nistelroy did the same a year later.

With Di Stéfano mesmerising defenders at home and across Europe, Madrid were the first to win the newly created European Cup competition when they defeated Reims 4-3. They were also the second, third, fourth and fifth team to win the trophy. As unbelievable as it sounds, Madrid won the premier European trophy in every one of its first five years. And so another one of Di Stéfano's records is unlikely to be ever wrested from him, which was his feat of playing in five consecutive European Cup finals. To appear in five in a row seems improbable. To score in five consecutive finals sounds as close to impossible as you can get in the sport. But that is exactly what Di Stéfano did, including a 1960 hat-trick in the incredible 7-3 defeat of Eintracht Frankfurt at Hampden. Not to be outdone by his strike partner, Puskas scored the other four goals. The irrepressible Di Stéfano was also capped by a hat-trick of countries: six times for Argentina, twice for Colombia and thirty-one games for Spain.

Nowadays, Barca maintain their Catalan imagery and cultural expression. Real Madrid have changed and changed for the better. Of course, they long ago ceased being the liberal social movement romanticised by their idealistic founders. But long ago they also stopped being the plaything for fascist followers that many sensed them to have been over those four decades until the 1970s. Today's Real fans are a real mix. While there is still a tiny dwindling old guard of Franco followers, they are vastly outnumbered by people from across the world who just love football. They include a younger generation who have never heard of a fascist called Franco. Sadly the spirit of the old Madrid still sometimes haunts the Bernabéu. Too many visiting black players are still confronted by racism pouring down from the stands that once saluted Franco.

For some, however, old habits die hard. And while it's accepted that the old Madrid is part of a terrible period of dictatorship, there is a sense among some in Catalonia that the club now represents a new and different elite. I wanted to learn more about this claim for myself. In many parts of Britain, the best place to listen to the nation's pulse is in the local pub. In Barcelona, fashionable cafés seem to fulfil the same role. So I invited four Catalans to come and have a drink with me on Avinguda Diagonal in one of the many Restaurant Fargas. They were a supremely well-informed, although not strictly representative, group.

Ernest Maragall is an economist and ex-education minister of the Catalan government. Pere Vilanova, Professor of Political Science at the Universitat de Barcelona and former Director of Strategic Affairs and Security Division at the Defence Ministry. His father and grandfather fought in the civil war and ended up in Franco's camps, or what he provocatively calls 'concentration camps'. Jordi Muñoz, from the Political Science department of the Universitat Autónoma. My final guest is Mr Victor Terradellas, Secretary for Foreign Affairs of the nationalist Democratic Convergence of Catalonia.

They have never met as a group before. But it's clear that when it comes to politics every Catalan has a lot to say. Maragall is first: 'Now, Catalonia is the most interesting political society in Europe. It's where things are happening. Significant proportions of the people are dynamic, creative and know what they want.'

Vilanova, a former Marxist, starts talking about Spain's journey from civil war to the perpetual impasse between Barcelona and Madrid and quips, 'Spain was first a tragedy and now it's a joke.' He describes FC Barcelona as 'an emotional anchor', which he adds 'takes on a bigger role during a period of the dictatorship because there is a symbolic emotional importance because normal democracy doesn't exist'.

As the political debate tapers off, we stumble into a discussion about Catalan role models. It's a reflection of the power of the club that none of them suggests a pop star or politician as the ideal Catalan icon. Instead, surprisingly, to me at least, they appear to arrive at a consensus that Pep Guardiola is the man. Three of my guests compete in their eulogies about the former Barca coach. Muñoz keeps to his own opinion. But the others describe him interchangeably as the 'perfect Catalan young man', 'almost perfect' and as 'every Catalan mother's favourite son-in-law'.

Talk of Guardiola takes us into football. As soon as it does, they quickly gallop through the roll call of the grievance greatest hits. It's clear that much of it is now programmed into their DNA; the oppression of the club by the 1923 dictatorship, the killing of a club president by Franco's forces, the malevolence of the referees and the Di Stéfano signing. Maragall adds a new dimension to my research on the transfer saga. 'This is a real thing. In the early 1950s, Barca every year was contracting a new big player. First was Kubala, then Barca tried to contract Di Stéfano.' Intriguingly, he claims, 'I saw Di Stéfano play with some of the Barca players in that summer, I was there, I saw him.'

As I force them to talk about Real Madrid, what is refreshing is that they are genuinely respectful of their capital rival's origins. Less so of Atlético Madrid and their military heritage connected to the Spanish air force. But that doesn't mean that they have a soft spot for the Madrid of the post-civil war years or even today. 'Why is Real Madrid's economy still something? Why?' one of the guests asks in his third language of English. Immediately he answers his own rhetorical enquiry, suggesting without any evidence that there were unusual arrangements at play that allowed Madrid to fund the Cristiano Ronaldo transfer.

Having gone through the established injustices they went on to update it with what felt like a new addition to the list. Vilanova announces, 'It is said the main decisions in economic business roles are made in the Bernabéu Stadium ... every Sunday in the stadium.' He's not alone in his view because one of my other guests excitedly interrupts him: 'Decisions are made there!' Terradellas even appears to have compiled a cast list of the Bernabéu's business who's who – 'the seventy people that you really need to meet if you want to do business in Spain are there every Sunday, petrol, construction...' Before he can add to his no doubt long list, someone else shouts over him and at me, 'You're going to the wrong stadium, Jim!'

In the absence of any Catalan, I thanked them and jumped in a taxi to the 'wrong' stadium to meet the club's president. But somehow, as I headed through the city and the rain to the Camp Nou, it didn't feel that way. It's difficult for any true football fan not to feel at home or at least in a second home in that footballing cathedral.

Sandro Rossell has a more subtle approach to Catalan identity than some of his predecessors. One of them announced in the main hall of the city at a reception in the team's honour, 'I am proud of this city that shares the name of my club.' He acknowledges that, while Franco is dead and buried, Barca's identity is very much alive. 'It started, I would say, in a somehow political way, but it is converted now that there is a democracy, it was converted to more than a football club by other activities such as the Charity Foundation,' and in what I take to be a pretty clear kick at the £80 million Cristiano Ronaldo and £85 million Gareth Bale signings he continues:

> ... the fact that we dedicate more money in creating our players than buying our players. We dedicate a lot of money in trying to explain the values of the club and this is something that altogether we can simplify in one sentence and must conclude it's more than just a club.

With just ten minutes until kick-off, he acknowledges that if Barca is more than a club then the matches against Madrid were, and still are, more than just a game.

> Real Madrid represented the central government and we were representing Catalonia as a country and then it was, let's say this, a fight during the dictator period; there was this controversy that the dictator did not want Catalan culture to be seen, so yes in a way it was. Now it's more a football thing and a question of two cities. They want to be the best city in one state; in one Spain. But now it's more a football rivalry rather than a political rivalry that it used to be.

Shortly after our interview, a new name was carved into the presidents board at FC Barca. Rossell had to stand down in controversial circumstances. If you haven't heard of the story, type the words 'Rossell, €40 million, Neymar transfer, emergency board meeting, Judge Pablo Ruz, payments to Neymar's father's company' in any random order into any internet search engine. After that list, you probably don't need to search any further. Rossell vigorously denied any and all allegations.

So have the scars of 1925, 1943 and 1970 fully healed? Historically, many Barca fans have traditionally supported the semi-official Catalan XI and whoever Spain were playing against. Others made a real point of trying to ignore the national team altogether. There were some commentators who had hoped that the 'anyone but Spain' sentiment had been defeated by one David Villa goal in Africa's only World Cup. Spain's first ever World Cup victory was no ordinary win. A World Cup in Africa was history. A tournament in post-apartheid South Africa was dramatic. Unprecedented in any tournament was that every goal scored by the winners came from one single club – Barcelona. The scenes of jubilation in Catalonia were as widespread as they were unexpected. In places Spanish flags flew spontaneously.

Drunk on the moment, some hoped or even thought the victory would help heal a divide. Naively, they thought the World Cup triumph could achieve what Franco's bombs, bullets and militia failed to do – to make many more people in Barcelona feel at home in Spain. There's a little aside that has always intrigued me, which is where do people find flags of the nations they have no connection with and no affection for? Think about the scenes in Tehran and ask just where do they get those Israeli and American flags to burn for the TV cameras? Of course, Spain isn't Israel and Barcelona isn't Iran but the point is the same. Why did people who want nothing to do with being part of Spain have the country's flag gathering dust in a Catalan cupboard?

But the more sober truth is that, even in the apparent unity from the reflective afterglow of the Johannesburg victory, there was a message in the small print of the flags. It should have kept the optimists in the realists column. That night one of the popular images was the Spanish flag and printed on top of it in the corner was the Barca club insignia with the Catalan flag. It was a reminder not everyone was supporting the concept of Spain but instead were only supporting Spain with Barcelona.

Anyone who doubts that the spirit of 1925 lives on should listen to the Nou Camp. There's unlikely to be a military band. But as the match clock strikes seventeen minutes and fourteen seconds you will hear the sound of Catalonia's history being celebrated.

West German captain Fritz Walter clasps the Jules Rimet trophy as he and controversial coach Sepp Herberger celebrate Das Wunder von Bern.
© *Press Association*

Chapter Four

Das Wunder von Bern:
Hungary v West Germany, 1954

IN 1954, IT was Europe's turn to host the World Cup. For the first competition on the continent since the Second World War, FIFA opted for the decidedly neutral Switzerland as their venue. And while there were sixteen teams in the event, there was only expected to be one winner. The Mighty Magyars of Hungary had come into the tournament carrying a Puskas-inspired twenty-nine-game unbeaten run stretching all the way back to the May of 1950. They had taken on and defeated all-comers with a flamboyancy that no team could combat. And as they prepared for the final, only the unfancied and unseeded West Germans stood in their way.

Switzerland was Germany's first time back from their post-war pariah status, after having been excluded from the 1948 London Olympics and the 1950 Brazil World Cup. In what is probably the biggest ever turnaround in a World Cup final, the underdogs recovered from an early two-goal deficit to be crowned champions. Bern was then, and remains still, the most important World Cup final in history. Because, for the victors, it was also something much more significant than a first championship win. Franz Beckenbauer, the man who would go on to win the World Cup for West Germany, both as a player and manager, believes that, after their success, 'suddenly Germany was somebody again'. And reflecting the

103

experiences of his own childhood he knew how an eighty-fourth-minute winner by Helmut Rahn changed Germany's view of itself. 'For anybody who grew up in the misery of the post-war years, Bern was an extraordinary inspiration. The entire country regained its self-esteem.'

In 1949, the West German population seemed strangely unattached to their new country. Perhaps it shouldn't have come as a surprise; after all, their nation was defeated, divided and occupied. A surprising number were willing to blame all three predicaments on the victorious Allies. Too many seemed captured by a collective amnesia about the Nazi regime's culpability. There was ambivalence about living in a state that had almost ceased to exist. As late as the 1945 Yalta conference, when the war was finally being won, the Great Powers – the UK, the US and the Soviet Union – were undecided as to whether Germany should be allowed to survive as a country at all. France wanted to break its foe up into a group of smaller nations, in the expectation that some would be immediately reliant upon a newly dominant France. Stalin publicly talked about eliminating 'forever its ability to function as a single state in the centre of Europe'.

The chances of an economic recovery were being stolen as the Soviets plundered factory equipment, a surprising amount of which had survived the Allied bombardment. Distrust among the population was rampant. A process of de-Nazification led to concerted efforts to expose and punish Nazis who were hiding in the anonymity of plain view. But the anti-Nazi policy proved to be largely ineffective – a lesson that many of the same Allies failed to learn in time for the second Iraq War's de-Bathification programme against followers of the ousted Saddam Hussein. The Americans were the keenest to uncover former Nazis. They distributed an enormous number of 'Fragebogen' asking people to inform on their neighbours', families' and workmates' recent Nazi past. The 'Fragebogen' process divided the population into five crude categories ranging from the major offenders to the entirely innocent. An impossible-to-process 1.3 million forms were returned.

Nazi teachers were sacked and pensioner ex-teachers dusted down their teaching skills to replace them. The West German World Cup-winning manager should have been caught up in it all but wasn't. Josep Herberger had joined the Nazi Party in 1933. The de-Nazification committee classed him as a 'Mitläufer', which roughly translates as: 'Yes, we know you were a Nazi member but not really an active one.' Or more accurately, 'Yes, we know you were a Nazi but you are the best manager we have, so don't do it again and now go and win us the World Cup.'

Public opinion was confused. There was a craving for the very latest American consumer goods such as jeans, but an aching wounded patriotism seemed willing to sentimentalise the recently defeated strident nationalism. Anyone with eyes to see or ears to hear could also sense the public mood. The US and others had easy access to the public's mind because the Office of Military Government in the American Zone conducted opinion polling. The results offered disturbing insights into the population's attitudes. The findings exposed a tolerance of the former regime that had just taken their country to the brink and beyond. In 1949, 59 per cent of West Germans thought that Nazism was a good idea that had been badly implemented. Three years later, more than 40 per cent still believed there had been more good than bad in Nazi ideas. Only 4 per cent thought there was reason to recognise 'certain guilt' for 'Germany's actions' under Hitler.

This malaise meant there was no inevitability about the 'Wirtschaftswunder' or the economic miracle. Mary Fulbrook argued in her book *The Two Germanys* that 'success could not be predicted with any certainty'. Before the war, the German economy was second in size only to that of the US. But post-war Germans were suspicious of the occupier's plans to cap their economy at 1932 levels. The victors were determined to hinder Germany's production of metals and heavy engineering so they could never again sustain a war effort. But how did the German economy go from a clumsy attempt to transport it back in time to the creation of the German Miracle. The historian Richard Overy knows that the turnaround wasn't down to any traditional sense of the inexplicable. 'Not a miracle in the sense that defied explanation,' is how he put it. Of course, it wasn't down to a single act of Divine Intervention. There were many factors that allowed West Germany to fulfil the pre-war united Germany's role as the dominant European economy. The 1948 introduction of the new Deutschmark currency, the government giving banks large currency deposits and the bank's lending to the burgeoning small business sector all helped. Personal income tax and corporation taxes were cut. The post-war opening up of world markets pressed surviving German factory equipment into action to meet the rising global demand.

Businesses kept their costs down and workers' wage demands stayed low. Hitler had decimated the trade unions, meaning that, in the immediate post-war period, workers lacked a voice. Even as the trade union movement rebuilt, they limited their wage ambitions for fear of inviting the return of the hyperinflation that in 1923 had led to a pound of bread costing 3 million Marks. The country also turned the national humiliation of being blocked from reinvigorating their armed forces into an economic virtue; they simply invested elsewhere. On top of all this, the established companies such as Klockner and Mannesman became more nimble as power seeped away from the founding families towards a new breed of middle managers and shareholders. Industrially, they resumed a pre-war advantage in electrical, chemical, engineering and car manufacture.

Rationing ended in Germany in 1948; news that astonished Britons, who struggled on with food restrictions until 1954. The pace towards partition of Germany into two separate countries quickened as the three Western powers of the UK, France and the US failed to find common cause with the Soviet Union. Major disagreements included the direction of economic policy and demand that Germany pay compensation for the costs of the war. Nor could they see eye to eye on whether there should be one strong single German central government. On this the Americans and Soviets had the same expectation but opposite policies. The Americans, who opposed it, and the Soviets, who supported it, did so for the same reason. Both believed a single central government would be more prone to Communist influence. In domestic politics, the German Chancellor Adenauer made a highly publicised visit to Washington just eight years after American troops had helped free Germany. He was re-elected in a landslide.

By 1955, a five-day working week was introduced. Cities were being repaired, satellite towns on their periphery were being built. One hundred and fifty thousand officials who had been sacked as part of the anti-Nazi purge were reinstated. Consumer goods including televisions and cars were being snapped up by a powerful and growing middle class. Record numbers of Germans could now afford to pay for holidays that had previously been beyond their reach. Some even began to compare these years to the boom times of the American 'Roaring Twenties'. An unanticipated boost also came from the new spending power of women as independent workers and active consumers. New laws meant that women no longer needed their husband's permission before taking up paid work. The post-war shortage of men led to more single women living busy single social lives. Each was important but the aggregate consequence was that, within just eighteen years of Germany's war defeat, West Germany was the most powerful economy on the European continent.

But still, West Germany felt uncertain about herself. When the Allies gave the green light for them to modernise her armed forces, it connected to the nations' sensitivities. Dr Richard Jaeger, a member of the Parliamentary Security Committee, summed up the mood of many: 'Germany had in the past a good army. Today, we doubtless have the start and development of a good democracy. But we in Germany have never had at the same time a good army, a good democracy and a balanced relationship between the two.'

Participation in the 1954 World Cup followed the established pattern of European domination. There were more participants than in any of the previous tournaments in Uruguay, Italy, France or Brazil. The Home Nations had stayed away from the first three World Cups as they continued to stick their heads in the footballing sand.

Europe dominated the line-up with ten of their eleven slots filled by West Germany, Scotland, Italy, Yugoslavia, England, Belgium, Czechoslovakia, Austria, France and the favourites Hungary. Turkey was counted as a European qualifier. The Americas had two places, which Mexico and Brazil secured. Asia was restricted to the lone representation of South Korea. On top of that, Europe's numbers were boosted by the hosts Switzerland automatically joining the holders Uruguay in the tournament.

The 1954 competition was littered with the type of rules that just wouldn't be tolerated today. Top of that list would surely be the two Finals places guaranteed to British teams. Younger readers won't remember that Wales, Northern Ireland, Scotland and England played an annual Home Nations tournament among themselves. As well as giving bragging rights at home, the tournament also doubled as the British qualifying process for the World Cup. Impossible to imagine today, but the winners and runners-up both went straight into the Finals. England won all three games to take first place in the 1953–54 Home International tournament. Their reward was a place in World Cup group four alongside Switzerland, Italy and Belgium. Scotland qualified by beating Northern Ireland and drawing with Wales. The runners-up in the now defunct tournament were drawn against the now non-existent Czechoslovakia, Austria and the defending champions Uruguay.

Scotland, and to some extent England, may have wished they'd continued with their World Cup boycott for a few more years. The Scots lost 1-0 to Austria. They were then overwhelmed 7-0 by Uruguay. Scotland went home early from their first World Cup without a point or a goal to their name. In the quarter-finals, the Uruguayans completed a British double by disposing of England 4-2.

Scotland's defeat by Uruguay was one of many high-scoring and one-sided matches in a competition of 140 goals. Today the tournament averages 2.3 goals over each of the sixty-four games. Back then the stridently attack-minded form-ations and the likes of Hungary's Puskas, Probst of Austria and Switzerland's Hugi banged the goals in. Defences were pulverised into an average of almost five and a half goals every ninety minutes.

Hungary went to the competition as Olympic gold medal-lists. They had won twenty-seven and drawn four games in a four-year unbeaten run. West Germany only had to beat Norway and Saar to qualify for the fifth tournament. The latter was a peculiar footballing anomaly, as a French protect-orate territory, which a year later voted to join West Germany. The two eventual cup finalists were teamed up together in group two with seeded Turkey and unseeded South Korea. In a strange set-up, teams only played two others in their group instead of all three of their group opponents. A draw after ninety minutes automatically went to extra time and only then, if the scores were still level, were the points shared.

Modern-day goal difference calculations hadn't yet been introduced so a win was a win, regardless of the margin.

Bafflingly, West Germany progressed to the knockout stages by only beating a single team – Turkey. They defeated them 4-1 in a one-sided group contest. Boosted by self-belief from that unexpected win, the Germans decided to field a weakened team against the rarely beaten and seemingly unbeatable Hungarians. They were ripped apart. The squad found it hard to cope with their humiliation. After the defeat, coach Herberger didn't put it down to any sort of footballing hard-luck story. Instead, he poured a mountain of stinging salt into their gaping emotional wounds. Peculiarly, he didn't look in the mirror in search of the culprit in their calamity. The morning after the defeat, he sat the squad down and forced them to listen as he read out the overnight telegrams of condemnation from back home. For one player it was the end of his World Cup. Paul Mebus was one of the squad players drafted in for the match. Moments after the defeat, Herberger found the midfielder singing in the shower. Mebus never played another minute for Germany while Herberger was in charge.

Tied on points with the Turks, they then had to play each other again in the second-place playoff. The unseeded Germans thumped the seeded Turks 7-2. So, bizarrely in a four-team group, they played three games but didn't meet South Korea. West Germany went on to beat Yugoslavia 2-0 and Austria 6-0.

Hungary progressed unbeaten from the group to then defeat two of the three Americas representatives. While the Germans had emerged from their post-war pariah status, the Hungarians had their own more recent battle to shake off. In the quarter-finals, they knocked Brazil out 4-2 in an infamously physical encounter. I haven't seen that 1954 contest. The roughest game that I've ever watched is the Sweden versus Israel contest at the 1970 World Cup. I saw a violent re-run of the 0-0 draw in the Heathrow departure lounge while I waited for my flight to the 2010 South African World Cup. As the minutes ticked by and the assaults piled up, I increasingly felt that the broadcast should have come with an age restricted 'Fifteen Certificate'.

But that 1970 encounter must have seemed like a friendly compared to the 1954 match refereed by Englishman Arthur Ellis. It's reported that, after one incident, several journalists and cameramen had to be forcibly cleared from the pitch by police. It was an ill-tempered match in which the whistler from Halifax awarded forty-two free kicks, two penalties and four cautions. He also handed out three red cards, which at that time was a World Cup red-card record. It remained undefeated until 2006 when Portugal overcame Holland 1-0 in Nuremberg. In that game, the Russian referee Valentin Ivanov showed an unlikely ever to be beaten sixteen yellows and four reds. In Britain, the *Daily Mirror* said of the Hungary versus Brazil events: 'It was more than bad. It was disgusting – and a disgrace to all the other competitors in the tournament.' The *Daily Telegraph*'s front page reported: 'scenes reminiscent more of the bull-ring than the football field...' The *Times* reporter was even more graphic: 'Never in my life have I seen such cruel tackling, the cutting down of opponents as if with a scythe, followed by threatening attitudes and sly jabs when officialdom was engaged elsewhere.'

Surprisingly, one of the most detailed reports of what happened after the final whistle in this incendiary encounter was in the Norwegian paper *Verdens Gang*. The tabloid reported that Puskas, one of the finest players that Hungary or any other nation has ever produced, attacked the Brazilian team with an empty bottle during a brawl in the Wankdorf Stadium's changing rooms. The next morning, one of the Bern papers, *Der Bünd*, told its stunned readers: 'The fight was stopped by the military police ... Both [Hungarian] federation officials appeared on Sunday, after the job was finished, with bandages on their faces. The injuries seemed to come from bottle fights.' Only *The Times* found a slight slither of a silver lining in this thunderously dark footballing cloud. Their report used it to encourage comfort and conceit in Scotland and England's status as tournament 'also-rans' by suggesting, 'Praise be that this was not the final...' and, taking aim at the Hungarians, argued '...and so far as old domination of the game is concerned if this is what it breeds then the British Isles are well out of it.' After overcoming Brazil, Hungary went on to defeat Uruguay, the reigning champions in a 2-0 semi-final.

By contrast, West Germany journeyed towards the final with a growing sense of momentum with the unexpected tail wind of German public interest at their back. As soon as they had clobbered Austria 6-1 in the semi-final, the country sat up and took notice. Sections of the intelligentsia and some newspapers like *Frankfurter Allgemeine Zeitung* determinedly stood outside of a growing national enthusiasm. In the UK, if the coronation of Queen Elizabeth was the first big television moment, which it was, then, for Germany, this football a year later became their big first television event. Although very few West German families had their own televisions, many arranged to watch the match at neighbours or in pubs; others simply peered through the windows of the growing number of TV shops.

Two club teams dominated the two international finalists. Eight of the Hungarian squad played for Honved; five of the German starting eleven were teammates at Kaiserslautern. The now mighty Bayern only had one player, Hanz Bauer, an unused member of the 22-man squad who didn't kick a ball throughout the entire tournament. Dortmund fared little better with second-choice goalie Heinz Kwiatkowski being their lone representative. His only involvement was as part of the weakened team in the group stages Hungary humiliated when he picked the ball out of the back of the net eight times. By contrast with the unfortunate Kwiatkowski, the German first-choice goalie, Toni Turek, had established himself as a real match winner. He had kept his team in the tournament during the earlier rounds to such an extent that the best-known German radio commentator Herbert Zimmerman had to formally apologise to religious leaders after he proclaimed on air, 'Toni, you are a footballing God!'

At times, it seemed as though Germany were playing with two goalkeepers; not just because of Turek's shot stopping but also the effort of a special defender. Time and time again, throughout the tournament when forwards got the better of Turek, he was saved by his left-back. In the match against Yugoslavia, Werner Kohlmeyer acted almost like an auxiliary goalie. In a team that went on to be celebrated as stars, one of the rarely mentioned successes was the outspoken Karl Mai who marked the Hungarian record scorer Sandor Kocsis. He prevented him adding to his astonishing eleven goals in four tournament games. But, for all the glory granted to Turek and Rahn, the man who arguably did more to win the tournament was another Kaiserslautern player and a tough tackling centre-back, Werner Liebrich. He played for his club for two decades and was capped by his country sixteen times. Liebrich's competition-winning contribution didn't come in the final but in the 8-3 drubbing in the earlier head-to-head between the finalists. His tackle on Ferenc Puskas helped change the destination of the trophy.

Puskas, Kocsis, Bozsik and Hidegkuti had been deployed as an untrackable attacking four. In 1953, the year after they had been crowned Olympic champions and the year before many thought they were destined to be World Cup champions, Hungary travelled to Wembley to take on England. The match was to be the clash of styles and the two most formidable records in the sport.

England had never lost on home turf to any team beyond Britain and Ireland. Even considering the interruptions for two European wars, theirs was some achievement. Most of the 105,000 who turned up expected England to prevail. When the visitors scored in the first minute, England should have adjusted their match plan, but didn't. Within an hour, Hungary had scored six in a 6-3 triumph over old world football. The teams went on to meet in Budapest the following year in the countdown to the World Cup. England hoped to prove that the Wembley defeat was a one-off fluke. But in an England team that included the famous Billy Wright and Tom Finney, their hopes were misplaced – they were battered in a 7-1 defeat.

The beating heart of that unbeatable Hungarian side was Ferenc Puskas. During his time at Honved, he was one of those rare players who scored more goals, 352, than he played games, 341. Despite this, some commentators were dismissive of Puskas, sceptical over whether he was the real deal. After all, they thought, he was only scoring against Hungarian backwoodsmen. But when he signed for Real Madrid that all changed because he went on to almost repeat the trick; netting 156 goals in just 180 games. He served his club career with two teams and did the same internationally. He played for his country of birth in the 1954 and 1958 World Cups and after moving to Madrid he turned out in the 1962 finals for Spain.

Puskas had been destined to be the star of the 1954 show. In the first two games, he got off to the expected flying start with two goals against South Korea and one against West Germany. But Liebrich's tackle on Hungary's number ten fractured his ankle and sidelined him for the next two games. Puskas returned for the final but was still hurting. Despite scoring the final's first goal, he wasn't capable of being his usual mesmeric self. The footballing records show that Puskas went on to manage twelve clubs across six continents. But what the records don't detail is that I played for the thirteenth team that the great man was unlucky enough to take charge of. My experience proves that, while the Brazilians discovered that he may have been handy with an empty bottle, I was to find out that he was also pretty influential with a full one.

In the 1990s, the MPs' football team was invited to travel to Budapest to take part in a charity football match against Hungarian MPs; and before anyone shouts at the book – no, it wasn't on expenses and the British taxpayer didn't pay a penny. The game was partly to commemorate our host's victory over England but also had the serious purpose of raising money from businesses to help alleviate the impacts of deadly floods that had swept the country. It was all quite a big thing and our exploits were broadcast on Hungarian television. But there was more to it than anyone watching on TV or at the game could ever have believed.

We were due to play at a packed Ferencávros then Népstadion, the venue of England's 1953 humbling. My nerves were under control until we arrived at the British embassy for the pre-match hospitality. The formal introductions to our manager for the day unsettled me. As soon as I walked through the door, I vaguely recognised the elderly small man that was the centre of everyone's attention. It was Ferenc Puskas.

But in a surreal footballing episode, Puskas played a part in spiking his own team. He deliberately helped overfeed us on Hungarian goulash and overwater us with local port. I was the only teetotal vegetarian MP in Parliament at the time and I did my usual of asking for the vegetarian option. In the absence of Irn-Bru, I drank diet coke. But some others in the team tucked in. I only realised how much some were enjoying the hospitality when I bumped into one of my fellow midfield-playing MPs; or should I say he bumped into me. He said something like, 'I don't feel right.' We both knew that it wasn't down to his pre-match nerves. It makes me smile even now to think how such a global footballing icon had spent the entire lunch at the embassy cajoling our team to eat, drink and be merry. While no one was actually drunk, the combination debilitated a team that had little mobility to start with. Our Hungarian hosts had already won the game before we had boarded the bus for the one-hour journey to sleep off the lunch.

We lost by a score that I can't remember. As we struggled to get the ball in that first-half onslaught, I remember looking over to our dugout for guidance – but it was empty. 'Our' manager had taken up his place in our opponent's dugout!

As the 1954 final approached, the Germans wanted rain, and lots of it. They would have been forgiven for performing an unlikely Germanic rain-dance. The Hungarians, particularly Puskas and Hidegkuti, were technically superior and among the world's best on the ball. The German hunch was that heavy rain and a sodden pitch would hinder their creativity and help, in a sporting sense, to make it more of a level playing field. Mud also suited the German Fritz Walter's style of play. They also had a fantastic faith in their own late game fitness, if they could only keep the contest alive until then. As the Germans left their hotel to head to the stadium, the first heavy drops of what was to become a deluge began to fall out of the sky.

In addition to the rain, the Germans also had science on their side. The precursor to a well-known German advert of the future came into play. The 'Vorsprung Durch Technik' or 'Advancement Through Technology' slogan of a renowned German car company came to their aid. Have you ever wondered where the name ADIDAS comes from? Well the answer is a Bavarian shoe maker by the name of Adolf Dassler. 'Adi', short for Adolf, and 'Das', an abbreviation of Dassler, earned his reputation by providing technically superior running shoes for Jesse Owens at the 1936 Berlin Olympics. The company was also one of the first to develop stud technology for football boots. And Herr Dassler's innovative spirit certainly helped as the Germans seemed to adapt better to what their coach described as perfect 'Fritz Walter weather'.

If the West German team were playing today, there's no doubt whose picture would be all over the back and, for that matter, the front pages of *Die Welt* and *Der Spiegel* – Helmut Rahn. So enormous was his impact that Franz Beckenbauer, the inspirational German footballer that they called 'Der Kaiser', thought that the forty-times-capped player 'shaped an entire nation'. A former coal miner, Rahn was a minor during the war. Too young to fight, he was evacuated to Czechoslovakia. He grew up to be one of the original bad boys of German football with offences including what at the time was a scandalising conviction for drink-driving. The national coach considered the outside-right 'a genius at positive improvisation, who never ceases to surprise us'. But so fractious was his relationship with the football authorities that the 'genius' wasn't even in the manager's original pick for the tournament. Instead, Rahn travelled with his club on a tour of South America. It was only after news of his extraordinary performances on tour reached home that Herberger repented and Rahn was hurriedly called up to the national squad.

When the squad was announced for the final two weeks later, he was the only one of the German goal scorers from the earlier 8-3 defeat against Hungary to play. The other scorers, Richard Herman and Alfred Pfaff, didn't make the cut. But it didn't seem to matter as Hungary sprinted into an early lead. After little more than five minutes, the ball fell to Puskas who struck it home left footed from the corner of the six-yard box. The weather was the only good early news for the West Germans. After just eight minutes, Zolthan Czibor made it two after an amateur-hour mix-up between the otherwise outstanding Turek and defender Kohlmeyer. Just as the Germans looked on course for another 8-3-style humiliation, Helmut Rahn took control. More than any other player it was Rahn who, with three magic moments, hauled them back into a game that already seemed lost. His tenth-minute deflected cross set up Max Morlock to slide in to score from close range. It was game-on again. Just eight minutes later, Rahn ghosted in from nowhere at the back post catching the entire Hungarian defence by surprise to make it 2-2. With less than twenty minutes gone, the sodden crowd, hiding under umbrellas and makeshift head coverings, couldn't believe what they were seeing.

The momentum swung back in the Hungarians' favour and they did everything but score again. They hit the bar, had a certain goal cleared off the line and, in goalkeeper Turek, they were up against a worthy contender to Rahn for the man of the match award. With just six minutes to go, the irreducible Rahn sealed what is arguably the biggest upset and comeback in a World Cup final's history. And his brace of goals emphasised why he was known as 'The Cannon from Essen' or simply 'Der Boss'. He received the ball twenty yards out. Having watched the game online, it looks like he has delayed for far too long before getting his shot away. As he makes his way into the box, he shifts the ball from his right foot to his left. To the German fans, it must have looked like the moment and his chance had gone. But, as three fatigued Hungarian defenders bore down on him, he fired powerfully into Grosic's goal.

The German radio commentator Herbert Zimmerman celebrated live on air. 'Schäfer delivers a cross into the box. Header cleared. Rahn should take a deep shot, Rahn shoots. Goal! Goal! Goooal!' Then he paused in a wasted attempt at calming himself down. 'Germany leads three to two, five minutes before full-time. Call me mad, call me crazy!' And as the final whistle sounded he uttered the most famous words in that nation's sporting history announcing, 'The game is over! Over! Over! Germany is world champion!!! And beats Hungary three goals to two in the final round at Bern.' The match was turned into a hit box-office movie, but it's Zimmerman's radio commentary that Germany remembers most. His one minute and fifty-nine seconds of excited joy has become a popular online download.

The director of *The Miracle of Bern* movie, Sönke Wortman, dedicated her work to the match changer, Rahn. He is loved across Germany and revered in Essen. There, a life-size statue stands on the street that also shares his name near the Essen stadium where he played 201 games. The movie was seen by six million Germans. The storyline captured Germany's desire to understand its post-war past. Cinema-goers followed the story of a soldier returning home from a Soviet POW camp. The footballing story of German triumph helps to bring the Lubanski family and the German nation back together. It becomes compulsory for politicians and important for players to have seen it. The German Chancellor (equivalent to the British Prime Minister) almost seemed boastful that he had cried not once, but twice in the cinema. He was joined by the then German coach Rudi Voller who admitted, 'I've seen it three times. Boy, I really had a cry.'

But for Rahn, like George Best, Paul Gascoigne and a minority of other genuine footballing superstars, their genius and its accompanying attention weighed heavily on his shoulders. For the last twenty years of his life, he lived in seclusion with only his wife, Gerti, for company. He rarely ventured beyond their front door. When he did, it was usually to attend church or to go along to Friesenstube, his local pub. He never did see the film. He died the day after the movie's review screening. His 2003 funeral took up a full two hours of the schedules on national television broadcasts. The state's Minister-President acted as mourner-in-chief, declaring, 'Helmut Rahn achieved something extraordinary. He belongs to the story of our reconstruction, forever embedded in the nation's consciousness.' In a lovely obituary of the time for *The Guardian* newspaper, Barbara Smit suggested some people believed Germany had three founding fathers: Adenauer for independence, Ludwig Erhard for the economy and Fritz Walter for self-confidence.

The eulogised goal scorer is far from the only '1954er' to be celebrated. Morlock, the man at the end of Rahn's cross, is adored in Nuremberg where he scored 294 goals in 472 club appearances. So beloved is he by the locals that in 2006 fans voted to change the name of their stadium to the Max-Morlock Stadion. But, so far, there's not been a happy ending to their efforts. At the same time as the vote, the City authorities completed a commercial deal with a local bank, a part of which included the naming rights of the EasyCredit Stadion. Today there's a new commercial deal. So now the fans walk through Max Morlock Square as they make their way to the clumsily branded Grundig Stadion.

The most popular German footballer of all time was also a 1954 hero but surprisingly its neither of the goal scorers, Morlock or Rahn. Instead, it's Fritz Walter, the team captain, who was handed the Jules Rimet trophy by the FIFA president Jules Rimet. The winning captain's popularity is no longer just a matter of opinion but an accepted truth. When UEFA celebrated its fiftieth anniversary, they asked all of its members to nominate their most outstanding player of the previous five decades. The BDF proposed Fritz as their Golden player. His life was a collection of coincidences and narrow escapes, without which Germany would never even have heard of him. Throughout the war, Josep Herberger, the national team coach, was determined to keep as many of his squad as possible out of harm's way. Not for them any frozen and deadly attempted march towards Moscow or even a hazardous bombing raid over Britain. Herberger's sense of his patriotic duty meant he stretched many of the rules to do so. The coach cashed in most of his favours with an air-force friend, Hermann Graf, to have some of his stars, including Fritz Walter, transferred to the relatively cushy role in air-force ground crew. But it was a plan that spectacularly backfired when the Americans overran the base and captured Walter's unit. Things took a further treacherous twist when his captors decided to transfer them into Soviet hands. A certainly tough and undoubtedly short life awaited him in Siberia; that was until he entranced the Ukrainian guards at a transit centre with his footballing skills. It appears that he survived the war to make it to the World Cup after the camp commander was convinced that he wasn't German, but French.

In so many ways, the 1954 tournament was groundbreaking. It was the first to be televised. And it was also the first time that brothers had played in a final – and won. Despite the coach's dubious political judgement, he had a great sense of how to match players and personalities. Undoubtedly one of his successes was blending the two Walter brothers into his starting eleven. Ottmar Walter was Fritz's younger brother and, like so many in the team, he had been lucky to escape the war. His ship was sunk and he was taken to a British Prisoner of War camp in Derby. He agonised that 'My entire body was full of shrapnel', but he recovered enough for it to be rumoured that Derby County wanted to sign him. But instead, he returned to Germany to score ten goals in twenty internationals and 321 times in 336 appearances for Kaiserslautern.

There's now a contemporary and, perhaps inevitably, less romantic theory doing the rounds about the German comeback. If it can be proven to be true, it certainly demolishes any sense of a miracle. In 2010, Professor Erik Eggers, from Berlin's Humboldt University, claimed that the players may unknowingly have been drug cheats. There's little dispute that the team management arranged for their players to have injections. The players believed what they were told, which is that the syringes contained nothing more than the entirely legal energy-boosting Vitamin C. But Eggers's contention is that it's possible the German comeback was super-charged not by innocuous vitamins but by injections of methamphetamine, a drug administered to German troops during the war. If Eggers' version is ever proven to be true, it has come too late to rob the 1950s population and team of the sense of 'Germany being somebody again'. But, for some cynics, it might explain how the most powerful footballing nation on earth that had rushed into an almost immediate two-goal lead was eventually humbled by the unseeded underdogs.

In a brilliantly researched analysis, written in painfully perfect but convoluted English of the type that only comes from having an impeccable mind and English as a second language, the sports historian Arthur Heinrich described the impact:

> This was the first post-war German victory worthy of that description. Until now there had been multiple millions of individual German successes as the economy of the vanquished outperformed the economies of most of the victors. But here on a football field in the Swiss city was the first collective experience of success for Germany, either East or West.

Der Spiegel newspaper reported, 'Never before in Europe … did the Germans' collective feelings sparkle so exclusively for nothing other than their football team.'

Heinrich thinks that 'The triumph of Bern served to make West Germans feel secure about where they were located and who they were. It signified – nine years after the end of a criminal regime and dreadful war – something like a re-entry into the world, this time in a civilised fashion.' Across world capitals, even among those who were uncertain about football, there was a real sense of relief that Germans at last could be patriots without being aggressive nationalists. *Der Fortschritt*, the German publication, said:

Since sport towers above any other institution of public life when it comes to popularity, any triumph in this area powerfully increases national prestige. That's why our football players in Bern ... have accomplished a feat filling us with confidence that we Germans, in peaceful competition among the nations, have surmounted the shadows of the post-war period, and that – in the spirit of that ideal to which the classical athletes of yore once paid tribute to Olympia – we are there again.

The German sports historian also thought, 'The World Cup gave the Germans and the rest of the world a new experience – that it was possible for German self-confidence to be kept to an environmentally compatible normal level.' In other words, football wasn't war by another means. For many West Germans, Bern was the first time they had felt emotionally connected to being West German. Those who were unsure about the new state and resented the occupation at last had their own success and belonging. This was their victory, achieved without, or, in some people's minds, despite, the occupying forces.

In a nation terrified of the birth of new demagogues, the players were idolised. The team captain, Fritz Walter, was transformed into the poster boy for the remarkable turn-around. Walter, like many of the team, was a former soldier of the non-Nazi 'I was only following orders' variety. Many of the German team were stalked by the experience of war; some were physically scarred by it. First-choice goalkeeper Toni Turek had a shell splinter lodged in his head. Karl-Heinz Metzner suffered a hand injury that affected him throughout his life. In their euphoria, the 'Weltmeisters' or World Champions were determined not to look too far over their shoulders into the recent past. As a football and war veteran who made his international debut in the second year of the conflict, Fritz Walter asked the public: 'Let's not talk about war, let's talk about football.'

As the victors made the long train journey from Bern to Munich, they were greeted by tumultuous crowds hundreds of thousands strong. At each tiny station or railway halt, hundreds of fans crammed onto the platform to steal a glimpse of their new heroes. Not for these fans the unruly norm of latter-year football crowds. In a very German way, they bought platform tickets and behaved impeccably. Fans tossed presents at the players. The team must have expected it, because they had left a carriage unoccupied as a storage cupboard for the gifts. They had even consulted and settled on a formula on how to divide between them whatever was thrown. Albert Heinrich wrote: 'Whether in Kaiserslautern or Cologne, Nuremberg or Fuerth, Dusseldorf or Essen, everywhere there was a joyous inferno' made up of 'ecstatically excited, raging, screaming, laughing and weeping crowd'.

Some in the media were more cautious in their coverage, deliberately dialling down the rhetoric for fear of unleashing a new nationalism. There was a real worry that the euphoria might stumble back into a sense of German exceptionalism. Sincere concerns were aired about a throwback to Nazi rhetoric echoing '… embarrassingly of certain mass rallies from the thousand-year Reich', as one correspondent in *Der Spiegel* argued. The newspaper *Frankfurter Rundschau* reported:

It was feared that a bunch of people would recast our football victory … as a national event, along the lines of some shibboleth-like: 'We lost two world wars, but now we've triumphed after all.' Little could they have realised that the 'bunch of people' they were anxious about would turn out not even to be German. Instead it was to be the supposedly good humoured idiocy of groups of England fans, who decades later got themselves into the habit of taunting Germans about victory in 'Two world wars and one World Cup.'

But those who were worried that victory on the football field would be linked to a sense of injustice from the battlefield didn't have long to wait or far to look. Only a couple of days after the win, it arrived with an equal balance of vengeance and embarrassment. The Munich beer festival celebration in honour of the team in the Lowenbraeu cellar was a huge occasion, carried live on German radio. Not long after taking to the stage, the head of the German Football Association inexcusably announced that the victory was 'representative of the best of Germandom abroad'. He then followed the standard formula of thanking the twelfth man; which of course is the standard routine the world over to reach out to supporters. But, bizarrely and deliberately, he thanked someone who hadn't been anywhere near Bern forty-eight hours earlier – Wotan, the German God of War. That homage to a mystic war god was the last thing that people listening at home heard. In a state of panic, the radio pulled the plug on the broadcast. But he hadn't finished. In the unlikely event that the Bavarian beer had robbed the cellar audience of their ability to understand his point, he sledgehammered his message home by loudly eulogising the 'Fuhrer principle'.

The episode highlighted one of the understandable concerns about the militarisation of footballing success. Of course, the truth is that dictators crave association with sporting prowess. In Germany, despite the 1954 outpouring, that sense of football guilt by political association was pretty marginal. The main reason Nazism wasn't as closely associated with the sport as others lies in the simple fact that Germany's footballers had never won anything. While they had come third at the 1934 World Cup, they were eliminated earlier in 1938 and were no more successful at the 1936 Olympics. It's thought that Hitler only ever attended one German match, he left early from a game Germany lost 2-0 to Norway.

Bronson Long, the professor of History from Indiana University, has researched how, in the parts of the defeated Germany controlled by France, the French authorities

> ...banned sports they associated with militarism such as shooting, fencing, gymnastics, boxing and martial arts. The French were especially suspicious of gymnastics, which they viewed as having a long association with German nationalism and Nazism. And on that they were right. Arthur Heinrich described German gymnastics as a form of 'proto-military training'.

At the end of the nineteenth century, the Deutsche Turnerschaft, Germany's gymnastics organisation, dominated the nation's exercise; there were 650,000 members in 6,500 clubs. Other sports were portrayed as somehow 'unGerman'. Football was considered by many Germans to be an 'English weed'. Consequently, in 1946, leagues for what were deemed as neutral sports, such as football and hand-ball, began to reappear throughout the French zone of occupation.

It's generally thought that football didn't arrive in Germany until the 1870s when it was taken there by arriving Britons. The Deutscher Fussball-Bund (DFB) or German Football Association was formed three decades after the sport's import. Football spread and there was nothing that the angst-ridden Turnerschafts could do to halt its growth among the middle classes. As in other countries, after the First World War, social reforms especially the introduction of the eight-hour day gave the working class the energy to play and the time to watch football. During the post-First World War Weimar Republic, football became the nation's number-one sport. By 1931, the DFB had dwarfed German gymnastics with more than a million members. By the 1950s, football's dominance meant that events on the pitch could easily have national symbolism off of it.

There was also anxiety about how the West German fans greeted the 1954 victory. They sang 'Deutschland, Deutschland über alles', which was the old national anthem's first verse. After the war and the creation of West Germany, the authorities had switched the old anthem's discredited 'über alles' first verse with what had been its less aggressive third verse. The opening of the newly sanctioned West German anthem now started 'Eingikeit und Recht und Freiheit' (translated as 'Unity, Justice and Freedom'). But, wherever the team went, they met adoring crowds singing the former first verse 'von der Maas bis an die Memel, von der Etsch bis an den Belt' (meaning 'from the Meuse River in Alsace-Lorraine to the Memel in Lithuania, from the Adige in Northern Italy or Southern Tyrol to the Belt or Straits of Denmark'). With the benefit of all these years, it's easy to claim that those who were alarmed in the 1950s were panickers. It's a jibe that has some merit. 1954 surveys show that most West Germans had no idea whatsoever where any of these rivers were. In all likelihood, this wasn't a renewed war ambition but a misplaced sense of nostalgia.

But even intelligent people were worried. The author Seitz spoke of 'high nationalist waves' and thought that victory in Bern was a 'symbolic second helping following the energy reserves missing at Stalingrad' and that some hankered after a nation that was 'some kind of chosen people after all'.

I wanted to get a sense of modern Germany's take on the Bern miracle and arranged to meet Christian Sachs in his office at Behren Strasse in Berlin. He is the head of the office of the German Olympic Sports Federation. I overestimated how long it would take to get to Behren Strasse and arrived forty-five minutes early. Rather than hang around outside his office, I went into a nearby cafe that was obviously popular with students. It was packed and, uncomfortably, I had to take a seat next to four young strangers. Instead of wasting the opportunity, I decided to involve these two couples of twenty-something men and women as part of my research. I studied German for two years at school, the only legacy of which is that I've got a microscopically small under-standing of the correct use of various personal pronouns. I had absolutely nothing at all that could be of any use in a normal conversation about football. But, ignorantly, I interrupted one of the pauses in the two couples' conversa-tion to ask if they'd ever heard of the Miracle of Bern. 'Yes, every German has,' said one of the young women directly. The others hardly looked up at me. There was no further response. I drank up and left. I was still early for my meeting with Sachs. But when I met him in his clinically minimalist office I was immediately glad I'd made the journey across the city.

My aim wasn't to prove Eggers's theory but I asked Sachs about it nevertheless.

In '54 we had a discussion in a scientific level, we had the conversation more or less about the technical advantages that they maybe had over the Hungarians with the new football boots from Adi Dassler. Then of course you have the discussion that maybe there was some performance enhancing drugs involved. There's not really any scientific evidence on that but some players afterwards got yellow fever, which could be connected to some kind of injections, but of course there was no anti-doping scenario at that time.

More important was what he had to say about the win giving the new nation a much-needed shot in the arm.

There are historians who have really concluded that this victory, this world championship in '54, was in many ways the first for the fairly young Federal Republic of Germany to appear on the world stage in a major international sports competition and actually win. Germany had never won before. In the 1930s, the efforts to win the World Cup had been rather disastrous. It was a surprise due to the dynamics of the tournament. After losing 3-8 in the preliminary round no one really expected the team to be in the final. It was the first time in a way, the moment when Germans were able to be proud again of the effort on the international stage. That's why some historians have concluded that maybe this is in a way the birth hour of the Federal Republic of Germany. Because in 1949, when the Federal Republic was built, it was a product that was half self-produced and more or less half-produced by the Allies.

Talking about the victory in 1954 and other footballing successes since then, Sachs reveals:

Those were the days, from my point of view, that Germans realised that they could be patriotic without being xenophobic or nationalistic. That was the first time that people from my generation but also the older generations were willing to pull out the German flag and wave it without thinking about...

He finishes off his sentence by euphemistically referring to the Second World War as '...the historical context'.

But his awkwardness about 1954 doesn't really matter. Because West Germany were back on the world stage and had passed its first big post-war test. A relieved world could breathe easily again.

A jubilant Nelson Mandela with the World Cup trophy. Football became a rallying cause for many anti-apartheid prisoners incarcerated on Robben Island.
© *Getty Images*

Chapter Five

Football on Africa's Alcatraz:
Bucks v Rangers, 1967

33 48 DEGREES south and 18 22 degrees north must be the unluckiest place on God's earth. Nowhere else can ever have been put to so many different and terrible uses. And yet it's the home to what may very well be the most inspiring and least-known football tournament ever played.

It is now a World Heritage Site, but a more pitiful place is surely impossible to imagine. The Dutch owned it and turned it into a prison camp in the mid-sixteenth century. By 1795, Britain, with ingenuity befitting the then only global superpower, found three different misuses for it. A prison, an offshore asylum for the City's 'deranged' and for ninety years, until the 1930s, a leper colony. After British rule, it regained the contempt that comes from the familiarity of its being returned to its original role as a prison. As if this three-square-mile plot hadn't gathered enough misfortune over the centuries, it also had a strangely magnetic attraction to passing ships that crashed upon its unlit, razor-sharp, rocky shores. Perhaps its only saving grace is that it was the home of Second World War air defence batteries.

This place is Robben Island, Africa's Alcatraz. Whoever ran South Africa ran Robben Island. The Colonial Dutch, the British Empire and apartheid South Africans used it to collectively punish and isolate whoever they deemed their 'undesirables'. It is the peak of an undersea mountain and

131

is made of 4,600-million-year-old Precambrian metamorphic rocks. But it was the eighteen years that prisoner number 466/64 spent breaking some of those rocks in its quarry that catapulted it into the world's attention. Nelson Mandela was the 466th prisoner to arrive on the Island in 1964, imprisoned as an enemy of the state that three decades later he would lead.

The story of Nelson Mandela is well known but the history of Robben Island's Makana Football League has been a secret to most football fans. It deserves to be celebrated; it helped bring down apartheid, shape a country and change African football forever.

I should have known about it long before I did; because, to the extent that the prison had neighbours, I was one of them. We lived in probably the third closest house to Robben Island. If there was a contest for the most picturesque bus stop in the world then the one in De Plessis Road would win every time with its spectacular view across Table Bay. It was here at 7 a.m. that I stood every morning. It was at this spot that I waited in my whites-only area, for my whites-only bus to take me to my whites-only school. This was South Africa in 1980 at the high point of apartheid.

Here, beyond the dolphins surfing in the Atlantic waves, was apartheid's Island home for those that South Africa deemed their most dangerous prisoners; men like future Presidents Nelson Mandela and Jacob Zuma.

But it wasn't just my morning view of Robben Island that proved apartheid's existence. When I first arrived in South Africa aged twelve, I immediately stumbled into the despicable rules of apartheid recreation. Just off the plane, my disorientated family knew no one. We invited the first person we met, the airport driver and his family, to come with us to the beach on our first weekend outing. When the day came we went to the shop and bought biltong (dried ostrich meat) and a cheap football. You know the type: the lightweight ball with yellow and black hexagon-shaped patterns that move in strange directions if you kick it too hard.

Despite the strange ball and the even stranger food, I was looking forward to my footballing debut on an African beach. But while the Cape has an array of beautiful flat sandy beaches we ended up on an uneven craggy pebble stretch on the Atlantic. Why? It was all because our driver and his sons, aged just nine and ten, were what South Africa termed 'Cape Coloureds'. Unbeknown to us, they were banished from the best beaches and this hazardous stretch was one that apartheid permitted them to use. My family were the only white people there. Football was impossible and the terrible currents meant swimming was difficult for anyone but the strongest swimmers. Apartheid gave the black majority the minority of beaches that were too dangerous for white people to swim at safely.

Life on Robben Island was as brutal and unforgiving as it was remote. Nelson Mandela believed that it was 'without doubt the harshest, most iron fisted outpost in the South African penal system'. He and many of South Africa's political prisoners were exiled there with hundreds of common criminals; the aim was to cut them off from a growing rebellion on the mainland.

The Island is only seven miles across its Atlantic Bay from Cape Town. It shares the city's climate, warm in the summer and cold and wet in the winter. The wild Cape Doctor winds battered the unprotected island and its exposed prisoners. It was an island of almost no escape and very few ever risked their life to even try it. The English Channel is three times wider than the Table Bay crossing and has been swum almost a thousand times but in the Island's entire history there are only a couple of documented escapes. The boat *Autshumato*, which today takes some of the maximum 1,800 permitted daily tourists to the prison, takes its name from one of the few successful escapees, dating back more than 300 years.

As ever more prisoners made the journey by prison ship, many arrived with nothing more than a shared passion for politics and football. Their politics took them to the Island; incredibly their love of football was to help them leave it intact. The new arrivals brought with them fresh memories of Manchester United under Sir Matt Busby and emerging South African teams like Orlando Pirates.

The Island was the living, breathing symbol of the hatred of apartheid. None of this should have come as a surprise in a British Commonwealth country whose future Prime Minister was previously detained for supporting Hitler. Many of the wardens treated the inmates as creatures worth less than the Island wildlife. Some guards openly displayed swastika tattoos and joined the South African Nazi movement, the Ossewabrandwag.

When I began researching Island football, I drew up a shortlist of who I really should try to speak to. At the very top of that list was Dikgang Moseneke, the man who served as chairman of the Makana League for many years. While he has the confidence to stress that it was a team effort, he was the man more than most that made it happen. Dikgang was the Island's very own Sepp Blatter.

Back in the early 1960s, just at the age when youngsters the world over are planning their social life and starting to think about a future career, fifteen-year-old Moseneke was kicking a ball about in the dusty streets of a Pretoria township and getting involved in anti-apartheid politics. He must have been a phenomenally quick learner because within a year the state had found him guilty of a 'conspiracy to overthrow the apartheid government'. He was transported on the long journey south to Robben Island. He has more reason than most to know the law and not just because his teenage violation of it made him a decade-long resident on the Island. This softly spoken, thoughtful man went on to be one of Africa's most senior legal minds and serve as the Deputy Chief Justice of the Republic of South Africa. Moseneke is highly regarded at home and much sought after abroad. When I dialled his Johannesburg number in the hope of speaking to him, a charming lady, Lesley Elworthy Grobler, picked up the phone with a welcome in that unmistakable strong South African accent, 'Justice Moseneke's Chambers, good day.'

After a surprisingly short delay, a man's voice said, 'Good morning, Jim.' I had been told by his office staff that his mind may not be on football as he was preparing for high-profile legal speeches he was about to give in the UK and US. When we first talked, he spoke with such caution that it was as if he was in a crowded court of law. As if he was carefully cross-examining every one of his own chosen syllables just in case it held a deeper meaning or a wider implication. But as our discussions switched from politics to football, this Arsenal fan came to life. I could almost sense that in his own mind he was clambering out of the constraints of his judges robes and jumping into his football gear. So animated did he become that at points he sounded more like the twenty-something Robben Island footballer of forty years ago than his ultra-respectable 63-year-old persona he had become.

Thinking back to the early times, he confided, 'The first few years on Robben Island were quite vicious. The prison warders had decided they were going to create a little hell out of the Island.' And he explained, 'Our priority was not how to gain physical comfort, our priority was how to make sure our brain and mental being survived. That was the real challenge, how do you survive imprisonment?' He kept his now famously inquisitive mind fit by reading.

I read *Das Kapital* by Karl Marx and it was also where I read *The Wealth of Nations* by Adam Smith. We read about English soccer, read about England's victory in 1966. I was on Robben Island and read about it because we couldn't hear about it on the radio.

And he is in absolutely no doubt about the crucial importance of football in the prisoners' lives. It was football, he says, that 'kept hope alive'. He adds: 'It suggested that there was a world other than a prisoner world that required their thoughts, accomplishments and achievements; that's what it did for me. Soccer was one of the array of means we used to fight back – to ensure that you survived imprisonment.'

Some of the maximum security prisoners, like Mandela, were banned from playing and watched the games from afar. He was locked away in a tiny isolation cell measuring just six foot wide. Think for a moment just how small a world that is to live in. Think of it as a footballer and particularly as a goalkeeper. Compare it in your own mind with the size of a football six-yard box. How could anyone live contained in such a space? The next time you see a football pitch on the TV, look at the size of the six-yard box. Better still, the next time you play the game, stand in the six-yard box by yourself before the game kicks off and count out eighteen seconds. Look around your feet at the size of the six-yard box and then think again; because Mandela's eighteen-year prison life was lived in a cell a tenth of that size. As the future Nobel Prize winner lay down on his straw mattress, his head and feet pressed against the damp walls at either end of his tiny cell.

The Island regime had a clear purpose, which was to rob individuals of any sense of self or faith in their future. It's impossible to overstate the daily humiliation of this 'living hell'. Imagine the scenes from all those movies depicting the 1960s US Deep South prison work gangs such as *The Shawshank*

Redemption and *Cool Hand Luke* and let your sense of perspective run away with itself because this was nothing like that. It was much, much worse. An island jail in an imprisoned country. A paradise that if it were anywhere else would be populated by Saudi princes and 'A-list celebs' and be too expensive for normal tourists to dream of ever visiting. In reality, it was a racist, isolated, hard labour camp intended to be without end. And, while most inmates dreamt of leaving, many feared they never would.

Mandela and other Section B prisoners were woken at 5 a.m. every morning with the shrill Afrikaans command word '*Wakker! Stanan Op*', meaning 'Wake up! Get up.' Breakfast was at 6.45 a.m., lunch at 12 noon and dinner at 4 p.m. Lights out was at 8 p.m. The rest of their day was spent breaking and lifting rocks in the quarry. Mining for lime was an escape of sorts. As they hacked away at the calcified residue, they were able to look across to the final major shipping stop at Africa's tip, the beauty of Table Mountain and the city on its slopes.

Twice a year they were permitted a single letter and a single visitor. They waited for their letter in the way that an expectant father awaits the birth of his first child. But correspondence from loved ones was often so censored that it was robbed of all meaning. Tragically, one such letter brought to Mandela the news that his son Thembekile had died in a car crash. The authorities refused his request to attend his funeral.

Less prominent, lower-category political prisoners were squeezed into larger cells with thirty other men. It seems that they were allowed an extra half-hour in bed before the sound of the iron bell broke the silence. Prisoners sometimes washed and shaved in the chilly Atlantic water. Many were regularly whipped, stripped naked and subjected to a full and humiliating body search. They spent eight hours toiling in the Rangatira Bay quarry. Warders broke the monotony of their own day by beating prisoners at random, taunting them and threatening them with attacks by their Alsatian dogs. Prisoners had nothing whatsoever to look forward to; each passing hour brought them closer to the end of today's work, but also nearer to the start of tomorrow's. There was no respite, Christmas Day was the one day in the year they had off. It's miraculous that any human spirit survived to even think about football.

And there was no break from apartheid either. Even on the Island, the real-life discrimination of the mainland was ever present. The warders lived on the West End of the Island, while the prisoners existed in the East. A West versus East divide is commonplace in many British cities not for reasons of race but of income. Many eastern districts have previously been the preserve of the poorest. In Britain, it was down to the prevailing westerly winds dumping Industrial Revolution pollution onto parts of cities that the middle classes could afford to avoid. On Robben Island, it was down to racist separation that had survived Harold Macmillan's Cape Town 'Winds of Change' speech.

Asian or 'coloured' prisoners were less unequal than the black prisoners in almost every way. Black prisoners were forced to wear shorts and rubber sandals without socks. The coloured and Asian prisoners fared slightly better as they were given a top, long trousers, socks and shoes. Nelson Mandela was the only black prisoner who was given long trousers. Just a fortnight into his 936-week term, a pair of long trousers mysteriously appeared in his cell. To the astonishment of the authorities, he refused to put on what he had previously demanded, until all of his fellow African prisoners no longer had to wear shorts.

It's in this environment that a Wolverhampton Wanderers fan first played football on the Island. Tony Suze was football-mad and knew that the many hushed football conversations while crushing rocks in the quarry 'gave one strength to survive experiences of Robben Island'. But he didn't want to just whisper about it, he wanted to play his game again and so he started the first ever football game – in his prison cell. The cell walls provided makeshift goals, the ball was his prison shirt which he tightly rolled up into a loose ball. Soon many others joined in. The warders couldn't crack down because they knew nothing of these silent matches. When the warders did arrive to search the cells the footballing shirts could quickly be pulled apart. In the evenings, the cell blocks soon became a hive of five-a-side and eight-a-side matches. One of the prisoners always stood aside, not as a referee or coach but as a look out for the vindictive guards who were always searching for new reasons to punish them.

But pretty quickly, the excitement of kicking their shirts around wasn't enough for the inmates. They wanted to play proper games of football. To do so, they knew would need the consent from the harshest prison regime in the world. It was never going to be as simple as just knocking on the chief warder's door and asking permission. The Island operated around a series of tight regulations; all communal activity was prohibited, prisoners weren't even permitted to gather together in public and nor were they allowed to talk to one another. Those were the rules. They knew that playing the game they loved violated all three.

But the prisoners found one rule that would allow them to break the others, and in so doing make the joy of playing football possible. They managed to use South Africa's Prisons Act to, in former prisoner Marcus Solomon's words, 'turn the whole thing round'. When I first spoke to Marcus, I was immediately struck by this pension-age youth worker's mix of modesty and humour. Not for him any self-important boasts. Back in the '60s, this rugby-playing primary school teacher was found guilty of plotting to overthrow the state by military means, a plot that he insists never got off the drawing board. When I ask him about his capture while travelling in a car with Winnie Mandela, he finds many different ways to proclaim, 'It was no big deal.' He even tries to persuade me that the fact that he is one of a very small band of people locked up on Robben Island not once, but twice was something quite routine.

But of his decade on the Island he says, 'The first year was a terrible time for the first inmates because of all the brutalities; people were buried in the sand and there were terrible living conditions, but we survived. So I can talk to you today.' There are thousands of youngsters in the Children's Movement, which he runs in Cape Town today, who are thankful that he did.

Long-established apartheid prison procedures stated that the prisoners should be allowed to exercise once every three days in the open air. Until now, exercise had amounted to just wandering aimlessly around the dusty prison yard. Solomon still remembers how 'We eventually turned the whole thing around. We used the Prisons Act to begin the fight back against the Department that several times had violated their own Act.' Once a week, prisoners were allowed to approach the prison governor to make '*klagtes*' or complaints. In public parks and on street corners all across the world, Saturday morning is for recreational football. On Robben Island, it was to become the weekly fixture to make a '*klagte*' about not being allowed to play the sport. Traditionally, the complaints were about physical punishment or withdrawal of food. Chief warder Theron didn't hear and wouldn't listen. Before the complainant was halfway through, he would usually shout, '*Volgende!*', which meant 'Next' in Afrikaans. He would then ignorantly wave away the complaint and its owner as if he was swatting fresh air.

But the prisoners were getting nowhere and decided on a new tactic – teamwork. From December 1964 onwards, the prisoners decided that from now on every Saturday they would all make the same simple complaint; that they be allowed to play football in the open air. Theron, a man straight out of apartheid central casting, couldn't decide what he was more furious about; that the prisoners had conspired without his staff detecting it or their having the temerity to subject him to such an insolent campaign. Some prisoners like Suze were punished and had their food withdrawn for the entire week-end until the Monday morning's breakfast. Soon more and more prisoners sacrificed their food for football.

While Theron and other prison staff have never admitted it, I suspect that the sports-crazy guards may have developed a simmering respect for their football-inspired campaign. In a tightly controlled country, the bans imposed by FIFA, the International Olympic Committee and other sporting bodies was the only sense that many white South Africans ever had that the rest of the world was repulsed by their nation's apartheid politics. It shouldn't come as a surprise to anyone that a supposed sporting prowess was part of the country's sense of virility; sport is so often iconic to despots and total-itarian regimes. Hitler celebrated the supremacy of an Aryan ideal at the 1936 Olympics in Berlin, only tempered by the four gold medals won by the distinctly non-Aryan Jesse Owens. For apartheid's rulers, it hurt like hell that they couldn't compete against other white nations. They resented the years they were left with no one of note to compete against, except teams of has-been mercenaries who were happy to break the international sporting boycott.

I am in a minority as a Scot who likes five-day cricket. It is about the only cultural legacy I have from my time living there. But I remember, back then, being bemused that crick-eters were among the worst sanction-busting culprits. Graham Gooch led a 'rebel tour' in 1982 that recruited Geoff Boycott, Bob Woolmer and many others. Mike Gatting headed a later mercenary tour. I remember watching the South African state broadcaster elevate the cricketers who took the apartheid shilling to a quasi-Test Match status. The 'England' players got what they wanted – handsomely paid. They also got what they deserved – a three-year ban from international cricket.

On the Island, the prisoners' food and clothing suddenly improved, and some were even given sewing kits. The cause of this turn of events wasn't the prisoners' campaigns but an impending inspection by the International Red Cross. They had been spurred on by international media coverage exposing island conditions. But the prison put on a show. And it worked. Shamefully, in a report that marks a low point for such a highly regarded body, the IRC pulled its punches and the prison carried on regardless. Football was no closer.

After this false dawn, an unlikely hero took centre stage in the prisoners' struggle, Helen Suzman. She was the only anti-apartheid MP in the whites-only Parliament. She was suspected, bugged and tailed; and she knew it. So much so, that when she was about to speak on the phone she would first stand up from her chair, then using all of her energy fill her lungs to bursting. She would then blow a referee's whistle down the receiver. Those listening from the state security service, BOSS, then couldn't hear her conversation for the ringing in their ears.

In 1967, this remarkable politician seems to have been the first woman to visit the Island in 150 years. I haven't exhaustively researched every soul who ever set foot on the Island but, it's also entirely possible that she was also the first person to ever choose of their own volition to go to Robben Island.

In Dutch, the Island's name means 'Seal Island'. But it really should have been given the universal name of 'Out of Sight, out of Mind Island' because regardless of which country governed the Island that was to be its timeless purpose. Over the centuries, it's hard to think of anyone who had chosen to make the short sea trip. Certainly not those locked up as lepers, the hundreds locked away in the asylum or the thousands who were imprisoned by different countries. The Red

Cross visited after media interest. Those who worked there did so because they had to. Helen Suzman came to the Island because she wanted to.

In his autobiography, Nelson Mandela marvelled at the bravery of this tiny stranger. 'It was an odd and wonderful sight to see this courageous woman peering into our cells and strolling around our courtyard,' and reflected that 'she was the first and only women ever to grace our cells'. Mandela and Suzman were to become close friends. She would send classical music to the Island at Christmas. After his eventual release from prison, he welcomed her to his home, where she cheerfully chastised him for his occasionally chauvinistic attitudes.

Later to be made Dame Suzman by the Queen, she would make regular return prison trips. Her visits forced the International Red Cross into doing the same. Spurred into action, there were no more soft balls from them as they demanded improved prison conditions and to know why football was banned. For the first time, the authorities and the entire apartheid government, the most powerful military force on the continent, had lost the initiative to a group of undernourished prisoners on a barren rock in the Atlantic. Empty excuses rather than reasons were given to the IRC such as a lack of facilities or that it might be bad for prisoners' health. And without doubt the most bizarre excuse offered by the authorities was that they didn't have a football on the Island to play with!

But finally in December 1967 the chief warder, under pressure from a bewildered government in Pretoria, relented. After three full years of the campaign, it was official; they had won. They could play football.

Judge Moseneke shared with me the importance of what that moment meant:

We got the better of the apartheid prison system by actually creating an internal system of our own. We had an education system where we taught each other how to read and write. We had a bridge club in there, a chess club sprang up and there was a drama society. People started doing Shakespeare on Robben Island, *Waiting for Godot*, people did a variety of plays.

And when I ask him for his fondest memory of this period, his enthusiasm is clear:

> The best teams would give out so much joy and near absolute escape fully dressed up in their soccer kit. For me it was the antithesis of what the apartheid government sought to do because we managed to get out of the prison clothing, get into clothing used right around the world and play. My own joy was when my fellow prisoners, comrades and colleagues in the struggle stood there and they were basically liberated from this only to get back into prison clothes an hour later.

From now on, the prisoners could do what millions the world over take for granted: play football. And for half an hour on a Saturday morning, that's what they did. For many, it became the most important thirty minutes of the week. Former inmate Lizo Sitoto spoke for many when he later told the *New York Times* that 'football saved many of us. When we were outside playing, you felt free, as if you were at home.'

Years after many of the men had first been brought to their windswept island prison, this victory marked their first real step to freedom. The prisoners named their league in honour of the great Xhosa Warrior-Prophet Makana who had died a martyr in 1819. His boat capsized while fleeing the Island. He had been banished there for fighting against British colonialism.

The all-important official inaugural Island match took place between Rangers and Bucks. It was a gusty warm December summer morning as the two teams from cell block four took to a bumpy uneven pitch surrounded by a tiny group of spectators and under the ever-suspicious glare of the heavily armed guards. Every football fan knows that our sport's history is cluttered with games that don't meet the pre-match hype. Games like the 1998 World Cup final between France and Brazil. Ronaldo, one of the greatest players ever to put on a pair of boots, was excluded from the team an hour before the game only to be reinstated at the last minute. His body turned up to play but his mysteriously distracted mind didn't. And neither did many of his teammates. It was a massive anti-climax for football fans the world over; except in France. The first Island game fell into this category – the result isn't even officially recorded.

The Bucks v Rangers match stumbled into the twin categories of historic and disappointing. But on this occasion there were genuine reasons. It wasn't because of any overpaid prima donnas who just didn't fancy the conditions. Nor was it the endless tactical planning of over-cautious coaches too scared to lose, leading them to be too unambitious to win. In truth, what could really be expected when the players' bodies were wracked with pain from rock-breaking duties, while their diet meant they lacked basic strength, and they hadn't run or trained since they were landed on the Island. The pitch was a bumpy, stony piece of ground. Many played in their exhausted bare feet.

But the most influential league ever played was now underway. For all the money of the Premier League, Serie A or Bundesliga, none has had as big an influence on their nation as the Makana League has had on South Africa. In fact, there were three leagues on the Island. Each league accommodated the imbalance of footballing talents including those who had never played football before, such as rugby-playing Marcus Solomon. When I caught up with him, he talked me through why they developed A, B and C Leagues. 'If it was going to be soccer, everyone had to play. Soccer is a very competitive game, people play to win. There was an agreement eventually that people of the same skill level more or less played against each other. It was to ensure that everyone played.'

A league that started as a cause became a sporting passion and a way of Island life. It gave them back a little of what the prison tried to rob them of – their dignity. Another former prisoner, and FIFA Committee member, Tokyo Sexwale, said when he returned to visit the prison years later:

> What kept us together here? Loneliness from home, from our children, from our wives, fathers, mothers. We came here young, with our feet and eager to play sport. We were not allowed to play any indoor or outdoor games but in the end the spirit of survival prevailed.

Having constructed a league, the players then set out to build a decent playing surface. They went to incredible lengths to do so. They made a cement water tunnel and drainage system to deal with Cape Town's spring showers and winter deluges. They secretly installed a water tap to sustain the grass in the baking summer sun. The pitch they nurtured was as good as any played on by British village teams.

Facilities and kit gradually improved. Friends and family bought and sent football strips. In the most isolated of leagues, the players cannibalised whatever they could. Goalposts were shaped from washed-up debris found on the shores, and football nets were hand stitched from second-hand fishing nets. And it was at this spot, years later, on Nelson Mandela's eighty-ninth birthday, that football's good and great gathered. Pelé, Eto'o and many others took turns to take one of eighty-nine shots at these rickety old goals and their tired nets.

The men now had dual identities; one given to them as prisoners and one forged by them as footballers. Slowly but surely, they improved their standard of play and began to organise secret training sessions in the bathrooms of their cells. During the day, they tried to take it easier in the quarry. At night, they exhausted themselves in training sessions with running on the spot, press-ups as well as dribbling, passing, shooting and tackling. Even now, a single player would nervously sit out the sessions to listen for the footsteps of the ever-vengeful guards.

And long before it became vogue they developed their own footballing retreats. Spurs were one of the first to get away from it all when they stayed at the Royal Hotel before the 1901 FA Cup final. Today top clubs think nothing of jetting off to the sun to recharge mid-season. The more ambitious countries spend a couple of weeks isolated together preparing for a World Cup. But it's a sign of the seriousness with which the player-prisoners took their Saturday mornings that on Friday nights they would take part in what is surely the most clandestine football camp ever mounted. Just before lock-down, players sneaked out of their own cells to swap with others so that each team could be together overnight to talk tactics and plan playing formations.

That they were able to get away with this showed once more the casual racism of the warders. They paid so little attention to the prisoners' appearances that they never noticed this pre-Bosman inter-cell free transfer system. They didn't really distinguish between one black prisoner and another; they took a head count not a roll call. And on an island world where the only woman to ever visit was Helen Suzman, there were no WAGS to distract the players.

The players did nothing in half-measures. They established an almost obsessive footballing bureaucracy of the type that we are all too frustrated by here at home and seems to make FIFA proud. To be fair to the much-maligned world footballing body, they took the Makana League to their heart. They officially recognised it, the only non-national association ever to receive FIFA recognition.

The Makana authorities didn't have football blazers but they did follow a footballing formality, not for its own sake but as a means of governing and respecting the new mini-society they were creating. This is where Moseneke came into his own. He was, by his own admission, an enthusiastic trier as an old-fashioned outside-right. But his real skill was as a football administrator; so much so that his fellow inmates repeatedly elected him chairman, despite his being one of the youngest on the Island. I remember posing the stupidest of all my questions, when I asked him, 'How much of your time did it take up organising the league?' I'm almost too embarrassed to include his polite put-down of the type I suspect his courtroom opponents have become used to over the years. He simply replied, 'For a prisoner, time didn't matter much, did it?' Fortunately for me, he then rescued my stupidity by responding to my query:

> It took quite a bit of time because you played over weekends, never midweek because you had to go to hard labour. But we had to prepare fixtures, we had to allocate referees, you had to receive match reports after every game, you had to require the Disciplinary Committee to take action against any infractions that may require it.

Moseneke's weekly 'To Do' list highlights the enormous effort that went into the non-playing side of the game. Each club had its committee and office bearers; protest and misconduct committee, a referees committee and a disputes committee. The Referees Union acted like a police force for the league. Each ref had to pass the FIFA refereeing courses before they could take charge of a game. The rules of the league were that players should elect their own president, secretary and officials. Committees were to run both the clubs and the overall League Association in a way similar to the Football

Association or the Federation Francais De Football. I can't be the only one that can see the beautiful irony of men who were imprisoned for their campaigns for the right to vote now organising elections and exercising that right under the noses of their jailers. The prisoners on Robben Island now voted more regularly than any other black people anywhere in the whole of South Africa.

The men took months to draw up the new rules for the Association, which would mimic FIFA's. By this time, the book most sought after on the Island was *Soccer Refereeing* written by the Birmingham MP and future British sports minister Denis Howell. *Irish Times* journalist Keith Duggan wrote that the players 'wanted to imagine that their private league could aspire to the rules and regulations of the world beyond that island. They wanted to abide by the same rules as Pelé and Charlton and Cruyff, as the best in the world, wherever they were.'

Football was the one way that the prisoners were in control of how they were governed and they were determined to do so with a discipline that would prepare them for life after apartheid.

> It was a matter of pride to the prisoners to show the authorities they were capable of self-regulation, that they could remain in control of themselves and others when the passions ran high, that they were able to deal with problems and broker solutions in their own community.

The new framework for the league was to foreshadow the constitution of the new South Africa, which in many ways it was a precursor to. The founders of the league wanted to enshrine the concept of freedom at the heart of everything they did; except in one crucial area. They knew there would be more than just footballing chaos if they permitted a free-for-all in players swapping clubs on a whim. And to avoid this, there were long and complicated rules on how players were to be registered and minute details on how players could transfer from one club to another. To outsiders, it may seem pedantic but in reality it was compulsory for reasons far beyond football. In all their dealings with the prison authorities, the inmates had to maintain one thing above all else – unity; it was what gave them the strength to challenge the system. It's not an overstatement to say that a transfer merry-go-round would have jeopardised that collective spirit.

Think for a moment about the most controversial transfer involving your own club and how it made you feel. Think back to Sol Campbell moving to Arsenal from Spurs and being labelled 'Judas', Mo Johnston signing for Rangers on the same day he was meant to sign for Celtic, causing anger on both sides of the Old Firm for different reasons, Luis Figo making the switch between the fiercest rivals of Barcelona and Madrid or Carlos Tevez being 'welcomed to Manchester' as he left United for Manchester City. The impact of a transfer on a city can be incendiary. But in a world were football is the only freedom, the impact of player-prisoners constantly on the move could create feuds that would last for years. Easy transfers could unilaterally surrender power back to the prison authorities. It had to be avoided at all costs.

For all its successes, Island football didn't proceed without its difficulties. Initially, tribal and ethnic tensions were present. The seven clubs that made up the league were originally 'ethnically pure'. They were Bucks, Hotspurs, Dynamos, Ditshitshidi, Black Eagles, Rangers and Gunners. They were a reflection of the type of South Africa that apartheid's supporters claimed would inevitably befall the country if there was a democratic election. But Tony Suze changed all that. He set up Manong FC, an all-conquering team, the Island's very own Brazil. They had two simple rules for their new club. Firstly, players were to be selected irrespective of party allegiance and, secondly, everyone was entitled to be a member of the club.

There were other problems to overcome. When a new regime took over in early 1967, they were angered by the testimonies about prison brutality from recently released prisoners. So they then set out to hinder and frustrate the games. They cancelled matches at short notice and prevented other prisoners from watching. Instead of allowing the authorities to dictate when they could play, the players seized the power. They decided not to play at all. Instead, they launched an audacious football strike. Only occasional matches took place over the next two years. It was a peculiar strike. They wanted to play more football but their protest meant that they had to stop playing football. But it worked. Everyone on the Island knew that the International Red Cross would be back and would demand to know why there was no football. When the government appointed a new prison regime in 1969, they relented and in a trial of strength the prison authorities lost out to the Makana authorities; not for the first, nor the last time.

So football prospered through a combination of prisoners' determination, the visits of Helen Suzman and the Red Cross, and the coverage in the international media. Once the league took hold, it was British football above all else that inspired the way many played the game. As they ran with the ball at their feet, they mesmerised themselves into believing that they were scoring the winning goal at Wembley or the home of British teams they had adopted without ever having seen them.

The inmates were already seduced by the glamour of the English and Scottish leagues but a chance discovery gave them a new window on the outside world. Among all the second-hand fiction books with ageing and missing pages in the third-rate prison library was an unlikely treasure trove that kept them entertained for months – old copies of *Shoot* football magazines from Britain. These teenage football mags, which I remember buying with the money from my first job as a paperboy in a Glasgow housing scheme, became a wonderful footballing kaleidoscope for the prisoners. In their imaginations, they were magically transported 6,000 miles and sharing in the experiences of the British players; the transfers, the tactics and their fashions.

Once caught, the British bug was contagious. The discovery of the mags was immediately followed by official requests for the prison library to buy and stock British football books. They were hungry for every detail about their new and flamboyant heroes such as Denis Law and Tommy Docherty. But on a pedestal they placed one player above all others: the man who Nelson Mandela's fellow Rivonia-accused Ahmed Kathrada, thought of as 'a radical who rejected authority'. Their footballing superhero was the midfielder still celebrated today by many Leeds fans as their greatest ever player: the tough-tackling, red-headed Billy Bremner.

It wasn't just the British style of play that inspired them. Three of the teams, the Hotspurs, the Gunners and Rangers, shared their names with British teams. Rangers played in royal blue and gold, Gunners were black and white, and Hotspurs lined up in green and white. As a Celtic supporter and in the interests of balance, I should mention that the future South African President Jacob Zuma was a rugged, uncompromising centre-back and captain of Rangers.

The cross-party and non-sectarian Manong were champions at a canter in their first year. In the middle of this first league campaign, a final footballing demand was made: to allow more inmates to attend the matches. And, once the authorities relented and allowed non-playing prisoners to leave their cells on match mornings, then the truth of football the world over was also true to the Island. Each team attracted their own supporters clubs in the prison, dedicated to following them.

Their loyalty was never tested by long journeys to either home or away matches. But they displayed their affection by designing banners, devising chants and generating a sometimes raucous match-day atmosphere.

One of the practical problems to overcome was how to source all of the team strips. It was solved in an unprecedented way that was totally outside of apartheid orthodoxy. Instead of relying on the prisoners' families to haphazardly search for replicas, the prison authorities found a single supplier in Cape Town and had them shipped across the Bay. This thaw in football strip diplomacy was one of the first instances of cooperation between the prisoners determined to destroy apartheid and the prison authorities employed to protect it. It was a small but significant sign of what might be possible in a democratic South Africa.

Despite this, one group of prisoners was banned from playing or spectating: the highest-profile Section B prisoners. So desperate were the authorities to cut them off from the rest of prison life that when they thought Mandela may be watching from his cell they built a new wall to block his view. Despite this, many Section B prisoners adopted a team. Such was the importance of football, they found out the scores through scribbled notes smuggled in to them by other prisoners.

The men who lined up for Rangers and Bucks in that very first official game had kicked off a process. It was to help take many of these brave Island footballers right to the top of South Africa. Zuma the player followed in Mandela's footsteps into the top job. Steve Tshwete took his love of sport into politics to become the nation's first post-apartheid sports minister. Tokyo Sexwale became leader of Gauteng, South Africa's most important province. Many more, such as the Makana League's first secretary, Indres Naidoo, went on to become MPs and ministers. Countless others are among the most senior people in academia, science and business and in many other chosen fields.

And, fittingly, the last word about the enormous role Island football played in weakening apartheid should go to Justice Moseneke, the man who built the league that led to the authorities building an ever higher wall around Nelson Mandela. 'We understood more than the wardens did and more than the prison officials did and the prison governor that we were drawing enormous strength out of the comradely competition and the togetherness that came out of it.'

And, as I started to interrupt him, again he spoke over me to say, 'I want to add that it was the great escape [and he said 'escape' more as though he was shouting it than speaking it] from imprisonment. I don't think the governor and wardens understood the full meaning of the football that they allowed us to play.'

Very few people came out of Robben Island broken, very few. And some went on to become leaders.

Chapter Six

The Soccer War:
El Salvador v Honduras, 1969

HAVE YOU EVER heard of the El Salvador, Honduras War of 1969? Most people outside of the two countries haven't. It's better known as the 'Soccer War'. The first shot in the conflict was fired by Honduran Roberto Cardona. The second was by an El Salvadorian, a young woman by the name of Amelia Bolanios. Cardona was the Honduran striker who scored his country's winner in a first-leg 1-0 win over El Salvador. Bolanios had watched the match on television. After the final whistle, she went in search of her father's gun. So distraught was she about the defeat that she took aim at herself and committed suicide.

This is the story of the brief and bloody conflict between two Central American neighbours. How a shortage of land and abundance of anti-immigrant anger drew the two dictatorships to the brink of war; and how a World Cup playoff helped push both over the precipice.

Before telling the story of the World Cup War, it's important to reflect that Central America isn't the only troubled place where, or 1969 the only volatile moment when, football has been caught up in the threat of conflict. Far from it. After the 2014 Russian military takeover of Crimea in Ukraine, the home nation's troops were determined to regain their bases. They marched towards the occupying forces at Belbek airport.

155

The Russians were well armed, while the Ukrainians, determined not to spark a fire-fight, had laid down their weapons. But tensions were escalating terrifyingly. The international news channels were poised. The world held its breath. The Russian aggressors fired warning shots over the heads of the oncoming Ukrainians. The unarmed soldiers reacted in an extraordinary way. They took from their bags one of the few things they were still carrying – a football. They then organised themselves into two teams and played the sport they loved right there under the noses of the confused Russians. Theirs was a potent act of peaceful defiance. The Russians scrambled for fresh orders from Moscow on how to respond. The impromptu kickabout had won the Ukrainian cause new supporters.

But on occasion football has been the catalyst for dreadful state violence. The match between Dinamo Zagreb and Red Star Belgrade on 13 May 1990 is another such game. Trouble started on the terraces of the Maksimir Stadium and spilled onto the pitch with such ferocity that, at its height, it included acid attacks and stabbings. Football had never seen anything like it before, nor thankfully since.

Zagreb were backed by the Croatian hooligan 'Bad Blue Boys' group; Belgrade had their own infamous renegade element going by the name of 'Delije', which charmingly translates as 'heroes'. When the rival thugs clashed on the pitch, one player, Zvonimir Boban, sealed his place in Croatia's heart and earned a six-month footballing ban. Instead of running for cover, as the other players understandably did, he went to the aid of one of his supporters being brutalised by the police. His aerial flying kick against the uniformed assailants is the iconic image of resistance of this abandoned match. The next time many of these feuding hooligans were to meet was in the battles of the Balkan Wars.

When the old Yugoslavia fell apart, it didn't break up, it disintegrated. Often characterised as Serb v Croat v Muslim, in truth the battles of the former Socialist dictatorship defied so simple an explanation. What followed was a series of savage wars that engulfed the crumbling federation for a decade. The spectre of ethnic cleansing and genocide, mass graves and crimes of war returned to Europe with a vengeance. All the while, UN peacekeepers failed to stop the bloodshed.

In the end, Yugoslavia's collapse was complete. Over those bloody years and in the peace since, the old Socialist federation gave way to the new independent nations of Serbia, Bosnia and Herzegovina, Macedonia, Montenegro, Slovenia and Croatia. They were joined by the tiny ethnically Albanian state of Kosovo, liberated by a determined NATO bombing campaign.

Rightly or wrongly, many Croatians see the events surrounding the Zagreb versus Red Star match as the first violence of their war of independence. In case readers think this is just the author's creative mind reading too much into the Maksimir mayhem, any visitor to the stadium is in no doubt. A statue stands outside the ground declaring 'To the fans of the club who started the war with Serbia on 13 May 1990'.

I remember travelling to Sarajevo a few years after the war that tumbled out of the collapse of the old Yugoslavia. Bosnia was a country dreadfully divided but precariously at peace. Mass graves were still being discovered and war criminals still being uncovered. I went to meet three groups of politicians, Serbian, Croat and Bosniak, whom I'd been told might not enjoy the experience. So just how could I at least get these groups in the one room to talk? I turned to my old ally – football diplomacy.

I have always believed in the power of football to break down barriers but most rules exist to generate their own exemptions and this was one. My idea was for the three groups of politicians to take on the Brits; simple enough an idea, you may think. How could it possibly go wrong? Easily, I was in the Balkans. The city where the First World War began is a complicated and painful place, and I was up against groups of politicos who could design inventive and unheard-of new ways not to get on.

As we arrived at the basketball hall to play football, the Serbs were first to burst my bubble. One of their older players sidled up to me and, with one of those really loud theatrical whispers that are designed to be heard by all, shouted, 'Why don't the Serbs and the British play against the Croats and Bosniaks?' I gently explained that that wasn't the idea of the event. Next up was a Croat who enquired, 'Jim, why don't we and the British make it two on each side?' And to complete the set a Bosniak then approached me with his question; well, I don't need to explain – you get the picture, I'm sure.

It was pretty obvious the game wasn't going to be a success from the start. But it went ahead as planned, Three versus One in what can be best described as a drab Stalinist-style indoor basketball stadium. There were only eight spectators; all from the British embassy and each cheering and holding tiny Union flags on the end of little white plastic sticks. Curiously, most of these flag-waving British patriots weren't British but Bosnians who worked for the embassy. I can only really remember two things about the match. Firstly, the exceptionally talented ambassador Matthew Rycroft felt the need to pass to me, his minister, every time he got the ball, no matter where I was on the pitch. The second is that one of his improbable passes led to me colliding with a teammate and taking home a two-year injury. I can still feel that moment; my knee bending at an angle it was never designed for. Even now, I see it all in full colour and in slow motion. But it wasn't really the ambassador's fault; it was more down to the misdiagnosis of my knee ligament damage by a Serbo-Croat doctor. (At least I think that's what he was; he certainly was Serbo-Croat. I'm not so sure about the 'doctor' bit.) As I lay in agony in a Sarajevo bed, he prescribed, through a translator, that the best cure was strenuous exercise. Six weeks into my 'doctor'-directed recuperation regime, I bumped into the Arsenal manager Arsène Wenger. I explained my injury and he told me he thought my footballing career was now almost certainly over. Despite that, I've stumbled on, which is more than can be said for my Sarajevo football diplomacy.

A match involving feuding politicians at the tail end of a civil war, Her Majesty's ambassador, an unorthodox and misunderstood doctor and a walk-on part and diagnosis by Arsène Wenger really should be the strangest game I ever played in; but it's not, not by a very long way. That honour goes to a match just a couple of stops on the District and Circle Underground line from the House of Commons. It started simply enough when a few months after the second Iraq War our team of MPs was invited to play against some Iraqis.

The morning of the game was slightly less violent in Iraq than what had become the tragic and bloody norm; one car bomb and five mortar explosions in Baghdad. The MPs' football team is a side full of serious people who don't take their footballing flaws too seriously. We usually take on any willing amateurs for charity and our big matches are played at places like Stamford Bridge, Celtic Park or Wembley. We thought it would be a good thing to play against assorted London Iraqis who no doubt had been through a lot. As I turned up to our usual venue at the rain-sodden Royal Hospital Chelsea's pitch, I was starting to have second thoughts, not about the game but about the venue. I felt slightly guilty that we hadn't, in a sign of respect, tried to play the game at a more prestigious venue.

Our team doesn't train and we don't warm up. The exertion of the hundred-yard jog from the wooden changing room to the pitch often serves as our pre-match exercise. And halfway there, just as many of our team started to get out of breath from the medium-paced jogged slow walk, I couldn't quite believe what I thought I was seeing. There ahead of me was a team that played in what turned out to be the strangest and most one-sided game I have ever played in or read about.

Our opponents looked like the fittest and fastest team ever to step onto the Royal Hospital Chelsea. It wasn't, as I had been promised, a team of Iraqi politicians at all, but the official Iraqi national football team in their first ever post-war tour of Europe. The idea was dreamt up by the Iraq and British governments as a way of showing our nations' newfound friendship. The Iraqis seemed to be as annoyed to see us as I was stunned to be playing them. As far as I could work out, their anger wasn't down to any lingering anti-war sentiment. I didn't get to hear their views on that or anything else as they appeared to be under pretty stringent instruction from their management not to mention the war. While, of course, they will have had strong views one way or the other about the conflict, that morning's anger was because they had been told they were coming to London to play in a prestigious goodwill tour. But here they were singing their national anthem on a rain-sodden, uneven public pitch staring at the strangest-shaped football team they had ever faced. Out of the corner of their eye, they couldn't have missed what I was seeing: the two white-haired elderly ladies walking their two elderly white-haired poodles just twenty yards from us at the side of the pitch. One of the poodles was relieving itself. I had to clench my eyes closed, grind my teeth together and curl my toes up inside my boots to hold back from laughing out loud during the Iraqi anthem at the entire bizarre episode.

I was astounded by how well we did, and I put it down to what one of my Iraqi opposite numbers told me at half-time. They had expected to stay at the English FA's five-star Bisham Abbey training complex but had been put in a grubby two-star B&B near Heathrow Airport. The first half was closer than I imagined it would ever be; we were only 11-0 down at the break against these sleep-deprived, dispirited but friendly Iraqis. Neither goalie made a save. Theirs didn't have to; ours couldn't.

The football was the least peculiar thing about the game. I couldn't help noticing that here was the official national team without a team doctor to look after them or an interpreter to speak to the media on their behalf. Instead, they had a ready-made supply of ominous-looking hangers-on masquerading as supporters. This was the team that had been beaten by Saddam's sadistic son Uday whenever they lost and I felt sure that the Iraqis on the sideline who seemed to have little or no necks had played some part in those punishments. Among the silent fans that day was Hussein Saeed, a former hired hand of Uday who stood alongside Ahmed Radhi the former Iraqi FA vice-president. Radhi's term of office came to an abrupt and early end after a failed grenade attack against the home of his fellow spectator Saeed. As I chased after footballing shadows, what seemed strange to me was that none of their fans spoke to one another. Nor did they cheer or even seem to notice any of the Iraqi goals, which were going in at a rate of one every four minutes in that lopsided first half. Either way, it's easy to get the picture about those ninety minutes on that May morning in 2004.

It was only later that I realised the full extent of corruption around the team and the incompetence behind the tour. All of which contributed to my going down in history as playing in one of the first ever teams to take on the post-Saddam national team. The result wasn't in doubt, but if it had been I had already thought about another first – to throw the game and lose intentionally to save the Iraqis from their own supporters who thought it was OK to throw a grenade. I decided not to do it but it never came to that. The second half was officially recorded as much closer and again their keeper didn't have a save to make. In truth, just like all those endless kickabouts from many of our childhoods, no one kept the score.

This mismatch is a footballing footnote (although it is covered in detail in Simon Freeman's enjoyable book *Baghdad FC*). But it does prove again that, at a time of war or peace and anywhere in between or after, football is rarely far away.

But enough about the amateur antics of the parliamentary football team. Let's get back to the story of the 1970 World Cup, which was a special tournament in so many ways. Throughout the footballing world, the tournament is known as the year where a young man with a long name – Edson Arantes do Nascimento; alias Pelé – stole the show. But in El Salvador and Honduras the tournament is known for starting one of the shortest wars. By the time the tournament was over, Brazil were champions; by the time the hundred-hour war ended, 3,000 were dead. More people were violently displaced than were in the Azteca Stadium to see Brazil beat Italy 4-1 in the cup final.

Tensions were already running high. History and heated arguments about immigration and land reform meant that these were two nations spoiling for a fight. Amid this stand-off, they were paired in the playoffs for a place in Mexico. It seems a strange decision; it would be like asking Scotland and England to play home and away during the Wars of Scottish Independence. Perhaps we can count ourselves lucky that FIFA and their eccentric fixture processes weren't around in 1603. FIFA's rules would surely have decided on a two-legged winner-takes-all playoff between a William Wallace XI and a King Edward XI.

For El Salvador and Honduras, playing for the chance to get to the tournament was their final. Neither team had ever qualified before. Both had made it through the preliminary rounds and, in a quirk of the qualifying process, the two now had to face one another for the right to take on Haiti in the last qualifier. While it is one of the biggest Caribbean nations, Haiti were undoubtedly one of your standard footballing minnows. Both teams knew that whoever got through their tie would be expected to beat Haiti with something to spare. So, even in pure footballing terms, regardless of any cross-border tensions, the two-legged affair between El Salvador and Honduras was the most important match in either country's history.

Going into the tie, 'Los Catrachos' of Honduras were probably the underdogs. El Salvador had a longer footballing pedigree and an established league that was two decades old and already influenced by a smattering of imported foreign managers and players. By contrast, the Honduran league was still in its infancy in only its fourth year.

A week later, Honduras took their 1-0 lead into the return match in San Salvador's Flor Blanch Stadium. But an already troubled mood had taken many turns for the worse over those few days. The second-leg hosts were furious as the persecution of Salvadorian peasants in Honduras gained momentum. Tales of the first-leg pre-match shenanigans by Honduran fans keeping the Salvadorian players awake and the post-match violence against visiting supporters infected the Salvadorian public mood.

But the focal point of the nation's soul searching was the funeral of Amelia Bolanios. The entire government turned out in tribute to someone who up until that point had been a loved but anonymous teenager. The generals at the head of the government skilfully manipulated the soccer suicide into a state occasion and an emotional tribute to family, football and flag. The funeral service and procession were carried live on state television. And there among the mourners and ministers was the entire El Salvadorian football team. El Salvador was hurting over Amelia. Her death became a powerful proxy for the fury that so many of their own were at that very moment being brutally victimised in Honduras.

In the middle of this maelstrom, Honduras travelled to El Salvador. Their arrival was greeted with an angry public and a hostile media. Both countries' broadcasters and newspapers had become an echo chamber of their government's policies: loud, nationalistic and aggressive. Faced with increased immigration and anxiety at home, the Honduran government turned on the visitors in their midst. Nothing seemed off limits in the demonisation of their neighbours. Often, it was deadly, occasionally child-like. The Honduran Minister for Foreign Affairs alleged that Colgate toothpaste manufactured in an El Salvadorian factory increased cavities in Honduran children's teeth. Less dramatically and even more infantile, El Salvador made the puerile claim that Glostara hair cream, imported from Honduras, deliberately caused El Salvadorian dandruff.

If it had ended there, we would have thought nothing more of this playground diplomacy by two unpopular dictatorships. But it didn't. Both governments were desperate to distract attention away from their own mistakes and problems. In Honduras, teachers were on strike, driven at least in part by an experiment in replacing classroom teachers with classroom televisions. On top of that, there was student violence and general trade union unease. Honduras is the original banana republic; a nation overly reliant on that single fragile crop. But in the late 1960s the harvest had failed. And when the major companies took their business elsewhere, in particular to Ecuador, local unemployment spiked to 7 per cent. By contrast, El Salvador was reliant on two things; an underperforming coffee crop and an ominous attachment to military governments. Eight out of ten of their governments between the Second World War and the 1969 war were headed by the Salvadorian military.

On the eve of the second match, relations between the two countries were so hazardous that many media reports suggest that the visiting team had to be escorted for their own safety by the Salvadorian military. In his book *The Soccer War*, the Polish reporter and author Ryszard Kapuscinski describes just how poisonous the pre-match atmosphere had become. 'During the playing of the Honduran national anthem the crowd roared and whistled. Next instead of the Honduran flag – which had been burnt before the eyes of the spectators, driving them mad with joy – the hosts ran a dirty, tattered dishrag up the flag-pole.' Inevitably perhaps, El Salvador won the return leg 3-0. In that environment, the score wasn't a surprise. But what was unexpected was that, despite the off-field hostility, the match was physical but clean. There was only one bit of rough and tumble and it was the treatment of Enrique 'The Rabbit' Cardona, the scorer of two of the home team's goals. 'I got a boot right in the chest. I've played in Spain, in England, in Ireland and it's never happened to me since.'

Nowadays, the score would be reason enough to celebrate a tense but decisive 3-1 aggregate win. But back then goal difference didn't count. Despite the gap in goals, FIFA rules meant it was technically one win each and therefore a draw. Worryingly for everyone who cared about football and anyone who wanted to avoid war, the teams had to do it all over again. The playoff was set for a week later on 22 June. The Salvadorian captain, Salvador Mariona, confirmed that the players discussed how best to block out the emotions that had engulfed their nation and were contaminating the tie.

> We chatted about it in the team and we said to each other that we shouldn't let the pressure get to us. We have to win on the pitch but were not going to cause a fight with the Hondurans. If we do, we will get sent off and that will give them the chance to beat us.

But any attempt to cocoon themselves from their wounded nation's ambitions would be tough for most people, in any profession, on both sides of the dispute. Mariona also revealed that it was to become impossible for the Salvadorian players because 'General Hernandez, the President, invited us into his house. He told us we had to win, we had to beat the Hondurans and that our victory would be for all the Salvadorians who had suffered in Honduras.'

One of the finest stadia in the world was chosen as the neutral venue for a game that increasingly felt like the sporting curtain-raiser on a military conflict. Mexico's Azteca stadium, with its capacity of over 100,000, is the perfect setting for a World Cup final; perhaps that's why it's the only ground to have ever hosted the final twice. But it was an eccentric setting for the last of these three Central American get-togethers. Just 15,000 fans made the journey to watch a game played in torrential rain. Tight security prevented any repeat of the previous off-field play-off violence. But the thousands of Mexican police ringing the stadium couldn't silence sections of the El Salvadorian support. They screamed, *'Asesinos! Asesinos!'* – meaning 'Murderers! Murderers!' – at the opposing players and fans.

El Salvador lived up to their billing as favourites as they went into a two-goal lead. But Honduras pulled back level forcing the extra game into yet more extra time. El Salvador re-took the lead late on to seal the 3-2 victory. Understandably, it was a strike that delighted Salvadorians in the tiny crowd and cavernous commentary box. I've listened to the live Salvadorian radio of the moment the goal went in. It is a far from neutral, joyful expression of celebration: 'Goooaaalll El Salvadorrrrrr!' The winning captain reminisces, 'I remember it so well. One of our midfielders passed the ball to our centre-forward, Pipo Rodríguez who slid in across the wet turf and beat the goalie to the ball and slid it home.'

Mariona wasn't sure whether Pipo had actually scored. I find that surprising that he couldn't hear the radio commentator's wild celebrations or see the half-dozen or so photographers rushing onto the field to join in the jubilation, while taking close-up pictures of the match winner.

I was in the centre of the pitch and couldn't actually see if it was going in or not, it went in so slowly. If the surface had been any wetter it might not have gone in at all. But it did and that's when all of us at the back rushed forward and piled on top of each other, hugging and celebrating, because we knew then we had won the game.

In a corner of the stadium and in every home in the land, Salvadorians were jubilant. There's no record of what the Salvadorian peasants in Honduras thought. I suspect it was a mix of delight at the result, and fear of the inevitable revenge from the militias who had been terrorising them. But on the field the winners tried to console their opponents. Captain Mariona went up to the Honduran players, some of whom were on the ground crying. Mindful of the border tensions, the triumphant captain did what he could to keep the triumphalism to a minimum.

As the Salvadorian team offered a hand of reconciliation, their government continued with their iron fist of all-out military mobilisation. Hours after beating Honduras, El Salvador broke diplomatic relations with their neighbours and officially withdrew their ambassador. War now seemed inevitable.

In El Salvador, the man who scored the decisive goal and so many others for his country is known simply as Pipo. His real name, Mauricio Alonso Rodríguez Lindo, wouldn't fit on the back of a football top. He is the only person I interviewed in the book by email. While his English is much better than my non-existent Spanish, we decided it would be easier to translate if we spoke via our keyboards.

> The El Salvadorian national team, for Salvadorians, forms part of their sporting identity, for whom it is always important, but in the case of 1969 the means of communication added another dimension to the elimination, giving the encounter almost the importance of the dignity of the whole country being in play.

Not only was Pipo a celebrated goal scorer, but he also went on to be an accomplished manager. As a player, he was at the 1968 Olympics in addition to the 1970 World Cup that his goal secured. After retiring, he spent the next decade as a manager and took El Salvador to the World Cup in 1982. But thinking back to those playing days of 1969, he knows that, while they tried to stay out of the politics, both teams had unknowingly become potent symbols of their nations' pride:

> The feeling among the team was very stressful because of the importance of playing for a position in the World Cup in Mexico in 1970. It was overloaded by external social-political events; national pride had been loaded on our backs, thus feeling a greater responsibility.

The night before the match in Tegucigalpa, groups of local people disrupted the visitors' sleep by playing loud music and setting off fireworks. The compliment was returned before the return leg when the Honduran team tried to get a good night's sleep in their San Salvador hotel.

This disruptive eve-of-football tactic has been repeated over the decades. The night before a 2012 Portugal v Germany international, opposition fans caused a racket outside the Portuguese hotel. Knowing that the brilliant Cristiano Ronaldo was tucked up in bed, they tried to disrupt his sleep by chanting, 'Messi! Messi! Messi!', the name of his greatest rival for the mantle of being the best player in the world. The following year, when Arsenal were on Champions League duty in Turkey, Fenerbahçe fans disrupted Arsenal's eve-of-match rest. It didn't go unnoticed. The Arsenal midfielder Jack Wilshere tweeted a picture he had taken of the late-night disturbances. The next day, he tweeted: 'Getting ready for tonight! Had some visitors outside our hotel last night! Atmosphere tonight will be amazing!'

Next up for the victors was Haiti, who had just knocked out the USA. El Salvador beat Haiti, again over three matches. They won 2-1 away, but after losing 3-0 at home they were forced into another playoff. A Juan Raman Martinez extra-time goal saw them through. There seems to have been something about the Salvadorians and trios of matches. Having played three games to get past each team in the qualifiers, they only managed the same number of games in total at the Finals, losing to the Soviet Union, Mexico and Belgium.

Nothing, including football, lives in a vacuum. These tensions didn't begin or end because of football. There have been disputes along the 210-mile border ever since Spain first drew up the map of Central America. The frontier between the two countries has never been a clear line but more like a disputed grey area. Disagreements have festered since the sixteenth century and weren't finally settled until a 1992 ruling by the World Court in New York. The *New York Times* reported, 'It took fifty judicial sessions and close scrutiny of reams of old documents to resolve the most complex case in the court's history.' So intricate was the judgment that it took the presiding judge, Jose Sette-Camara, of Brazil, a full three hours to read it to the Court.

But it wasn't the exact location of the border that brought the disagreement to life in a way that was to cause so much death. Instead, it was the mass-scale northward movement of Salvadorians across the border into Honduras that proved so explosive. As a consequence of this informal, prolonged shift of Salvadorian peasants, there was a violent Honduran response. Soon there was to be a second El Salvadorian incursion. Only this time, it wasn't families in search of land or work. Instead, it was men in uniform, determined to capture land and protect those who had crossed before them.

Both nations were run by dictatorships. At their head were two military strongmen: General Fidel Sanchez Hernandez in El Salvador and General Oswaldo López Arellano of Honduras. They took their populations into a war that should never have happened and that bemused many international observers. Both were members of the Central American Common Market, which bound them as well as Guatemala, Nicaragua and Costa Rica into a shared prosperity project. The shared market was aimed at boosting economies that were too reliant on bananas, coffee and cotton production. The established theory of influence is that countries that share a Common Market don't fight wars against one another. For the generation who lived through the Second World War, this was part of the credo of the 1957 European Common Market; former foes locked into a shared economy where each has a selfish and joint interest in one another's financial success. The terrible events of 1969 shattered the 'no war within common markets' rule. But the cocktail of border tensions, racism and government malevolence proved to be stronger than a shared market.

The governments in Tegucigalpa and San Salvador had seen Castro take power in Cuba and watched on in horror at the conflict in Guatemala between the military and Leftist guerrillas. They were determined to quash any hint of copycat actions in their own countries. This was a time of Cold War paranoia about supposed Communist takeovers. Back then, the USA along with NATO were locked in a static stand-off in Europe against the Soviet Union. But in Central America, both the USA and the Soviets were limbering up for a series of bloody quarrels in which they would back violent and rival sides. The region was beginning to become the world centre of 'the ends justify the means' type of superpower-sponsored militaries and militias.

Honduras is five times bigger than El Salvador but has a smaller population. El Salvador had a shortage of land but a surplus of people. The obvious tensions about access to land to farm on was aggravated by the land-hoarding wealthy. In Honduras, land has traditionally been monopolised by a powerful group of fourteen families. Across the border, a different exclusive group in the shape of US banana companies dominated much of the land. El Salvador had mechanised their farming techniques creating an army of unemployed peasants desperate for work. This unemployed army were the first to cross into Honduras to settle on unfarmed land. The historian David Goldblatt said of El

Salvador that it was 'the most grotesquely unequal distribution of land in a grotesquely unequal part of the world'. On the eve of the first playoff match, there were 300,000 Salvadorians in Honduras. Put another way, one in eight people in Honduras had come from across the border.

The Honduran government could no longer put off a decision on land reform. The pressure was intense. All that they had to decide was what type of reform. The choice was either give peasants and their families the right to settle or roll over to the demands of the big landowners. By the time new laws were passed in the early 1960s, they had succumbed to the landowners' agitation for their property rights to be protected above all others. The implementation of the new land laws blatantly appealed to a sense of Honduran griev-ance and deliberately incited hostility by giving fresh rights to Hondurans, while displacing Salvadorians. Just in case they were in any doubt, the president of the Instituto Nacional Agrario (Honduran National Agrarian Institute) even wrote to immigrant settlers to tell them that the law was to benefit those who were 'Honduran by birth'.

As hostility gathered pace, the new law gave a green light to the sense that it was open season against the Salvadorian minority. Rampaging Honduran militias targeted the peas-ant immigrants. By May of 1969, the death toll among Salvadorians in Honduras was mounting. Ignoring pleas for protection, the Honduran government callously looked the other way. The anti-migrant backlash gained a devastating energy. No fewer than 25,000 migrants were terrified by the gangs back northwards across the border.

El Salvador complained to the Inter-American Commission on Human Rights alleging that a genocide was unfolding. The Salvadorian government was clear: 'The government of Honduras has not taken any effective measures to punish these crimes which constitute genocide, nor has it given assurances of indemnification or reparations for the damages caused to Salvadorians.'

Within days of the footballing victory, their military build-up was complete. On 14 July, El Salvador invaded Honduras. The BBC's Latin American football correspondent summarised that moment: 'It's impossible to believe that football is the underlying cause for the conflict but it's also difficult to see how the tension could have become a military stand-off without the inflammatory effects of the playoff with a chance to get to the 1970 World Cup.'

This is far from the only time football has been tangled up in matters of life and death. A game in Derry featuring Eusebio's Benfica came perilously close. Derry in Northern Ireland has a football team that takes its name from the City. But they play in a league in another country. The *Sunday World* journalist Hugh Jordan, who is one of the most talented in his trade in the whole of Ireland, tells the story of one of the highest-profile club matches ever in Northern Ireland, how it was almost postponed and the absurd way in which it was saved.

Derry City had pulled out of the Irish League (which is the Northern Irish football association) many years before as a result of the Troubles – a huge sectarian riot in 1974. In 1985, the club was resurrected, but this time round they joined the League of Ireland, which operates in the Republic. In September 1989, Derry were due to play Benfica coached by Eusebio. The city, which was down in the dumps back then, was abuzz with anticipation.

Jordan takes up the story:

On the afternoon of the match, a bomb was discovered in a beer keg which had been placed in a culvert in the City Cemetery which overlooks Brandywell Stadium. The game was in serious danger of being called off. Supt. Frank Lagan – who had advised the Government not to bring the Paras to Derry on what became Bloody Sunday – was on duty. He knew the importance of the game to the city and the community. Frank approached directors of the club as well as members of the SDLP and responsible members of the community. He spelt out the situation. Things looked bleak. But at Frank's suggestion, a Derry City delegation called on Martin McGuinness at his home, which was a few hundreds of yards from the stadium.

McGuinness was a Derry City supporter and the commander of the IRA in Derry. A short time later, Martin McGuinness and others from the IRA came down to the stadium to deal with the bomb. They threw down a rope with a grappling hook on the end and hauled up the device. They defused the bomb and washed the explosives down a drain. As they were completing the operation, the British Army appeared on the scene. They recognised McGuinness and assumed that he was in the process of planting the bomb not defusing it and promptly arrested them.

They were all taken to Strand Road RUC station, but the club chairman arrived to plead their innocence. Frank Lagan must have been a very persuasive negotiator as well as a good chairman. McGuinness and his unlikely bomb-disposal team were all released without charge. The game went ahead. The atmosphere was fantastic. Eusebio received a standing ovation. Benfica won 2-1.

El Salvador invaded with a 12,000-strong army force. Above them, the limited might of their air force, eight Second World War mustangs, launched air raids on strategic Honduran targets. The Hondurans had a smaller but more capable army. The smaller of the two countries had developed a military posture built around their air force, the FAH. Its aim was to dominate the airspace above their own territory and around their borders. The Salvadorian assault secured some initial gains. But a desperate stand by Honduran troops and a successful counter-attack by the FAH against the invader's oil storage and supply facilities halted the advance.

As the fighting raged, another 75,000 peasants escaped in frightened desperation back across the border to the sanctuary of El Salvador. On 15 July, the Organisation of American Security demanded a ceasefire and threatened the invaders with punishing economic sanctions. The United Nations joined the call for a cessation of hostilities. But the El Salvadorian government dug their heels in as their troops dug in to the Honduran soil they had captured. A ceasefire was eventually agreed on 18 July and took hold two days later. But El Salvador refused to retreat from captured land. They held out for guarantees over the protection of the 200,000 of their citizens still living behind the Honduran defensive lines. It wasn't until the first week of August when Honduras finally provided credible assurances that the Salvadorians started to withdraw.

A 26-year-old journalist, Vincent Cable, travelled to the region and researched the opening hours in the conflict. As part of my research, I uncovered an article that he wrote a few days after the war for a Chatham House publication. Describing El Salvador's tactics, he wrote, 'They attempted to divide Honduras by advancing in two directions – northwards to the prosperous banana growing northern Syla Valley and eastwards along the Central America Highway to the Nicaraguan border and to Tegucigalpa, the capital of Honduras.' His was one of the most detailed analyses of the conflict. The young Vincent went on to become the better-known and more mature Vince, the future British Cabinet minister. Peculiarly for a man who claims to be one of the few people to have predicted the 2008 financial crash, he managed to get the playoff score wrong, claiming that El Salvador won 4-3.

By the time the ceasefire took hold, 2,000 were dead. Reflecting on the aftermath of the encounter, the newspaper *La Tribuna* wrote, 'Football is the most beautiful sport there is, but just for having such a large significance in the life of Salvadorians and Hondurans, was used by a few, to antagonise and sow hatred among many.' The awful truth is that by 1969 there was among both populations enough fertile land for those seeds of bitterness to flourish.

As for the region's economy, it suffered a worse fate than the Honduran football team as the Central American Common Market collapsed. The ceasefire didn't bring anything like a permanent end to frictions. In 1980, troubled flared up as desperate Salvadorians again came in search of land. They were fired upon by the Honduran authorities and as many as 500 were killed.

But by the 1980s both football teams seemed ahead of their governments in seeking to keep the conflicts of the past behind them. El Salvador qualified for the 1982 World Cup finals only thanks to the efforts of Honduras. The latter were already through but to qualify the Salvadorians needed Honduras to get at least a point against Mexico. The Hondurans played out of their skins to draw 0-0. And for the first time ever both neighbours headed off to the same World Cup.

On 20 July 1969, the original ceasefire came into effect. On the same day, Neil Armstrong was taking his 'one small step for man' onto the moon. The relationship between Honduras and El Salvador, which had exploded onto the world stage, disappeared again back into international obscurity. Tensions ebbed and flowed for more than two painful decades. It took so long to finally settle the border dispute that, by the time the two Presidents shook hands on the deal in 1992, Armstrong was nearly a pensioner and the International Space Station was well on the way to being built.

West Germany's Gerd Muller celebrates after scoring the winner against England at the 1970 Mexico World Cup. Peter Bonetti, the scapegoated goalie, can only look on.
© *Getty Images*

Chapter Seven

'Everything went downhill from that moment on': *England v West Germany, 1970*

'THEY THINK IT'S all over! It is now!' are the two most celebrated sentences ever uttered in the history of English football commentary. Those words, immortalised by Kenneth Wolstenholme, were, as every football fan knows, uttered as England's Geoff Hurst closed in on the German goal. The celebrated BBC commentator was of course referring to what he saw out of the corner of his eye; jubilant England fans clambering onto the Wembley turf, thinking the ref had blown for full-time. The fans were wrong about what they thought they had heard. But two seconds later, there was no doubt about what they were seeing. Hurst's left-foot screamer made it 4-2 to the new world champions.

Growing up in politics, it is part of the zeitgeist that Sir Geoff Hurst's Wembley hat-trick won the 1966 general election for Harold Wilson. For some Scots, it's the one good thing about that famous day. However, the truth robs those Scots of their relief but more importantly also invalidates a famous piece of political folklore.

Why such a myth ever existed is even more puzzling than why Azerbijanian linesman Tofik Bakhramov awarded Geoff Hurst his second goal in the first place. The election myth is exposed by the most basic fact check. Labour's Harold Wilson won the election in March 1966; England won the World Cup three months later. Wilson couldn't have won the election off the back of football-fuelled jingoism from a victory that hadn't yet happened, and that even the most optimistic of England fans in their heart of hearts never really expected to witness.

England's victory over Germany in extra time didn't win Wilson the 1966 election. But their extra-time defeat four years later to the same opponents is felt by many on the Labour side to have pushed the party towards its next defeat. As the 1970 teams kicked off in the Mexico quarter-final, Labour was 9 per cent ahead in the opinion polls. The reigning champions went into a 2-0 lead in a game played just five days before Britain chose its government. But Germany fought back to win 3-2 after extra time. England were out. So, later that week, was Prime Minister Harold Wilson. Former Labour minister and one of the party's sharpest ever thinkers Tony Crosland blamed the defeat on 'a mix of party complacency and the disgruntled *Match of the Day* millions'.

Complacency undoubtedly played its part. Politics seemed to take the Wolstenholme approach to the 1970 general election. The opinion polls, the pundits and the parties thought Labour were cruising to victory. But unfortunately for Harold Wilson, he didn't have a Geoff Hurst in his team to put it beyond doubt.

So what went so badly wrong so late in Wilson's campaign? This is the story of how a hat-trick of goalkeeping howlers in the Mexican sunshine 5,500 miles away from Downing Street, helped cause one of the biggest upsets in Britain's electoral history. It's the story of the unexpected humiliation of England's football team and the part their defeat played in the humbling of Britain's Prime Minister. After one of the research interviews, this chapter took an unexpected turn. It now includes the story of football and a second Prime Minister.

During my discussions with Tony Blair, he told me the incredible true story of how football smoothed his path to Downing Street; but more of that later.

In the build-up to the 1970 election, the signs had been ominous for Labour. For two years, the Tories were way ahead in the opinion polls. By September 1969, they were out of sight. Ted Heath's Tories had a seemingly unbeatable lead of anything between 17 per cent and 26 per cent over the Labour government. With that sort of gap, the election was shaping up to be a one-horse race. But, despite the party fast becoming a lost cause, Labour hadn't lost its will to win. They were determined not to lose by default. The party picked itself up after a morale-boosting annual conference by the Brighton seaside. On top of that, some good economic news bolstered public optimism and the UK's balance of payments.

The opinion polls over the Christmas of 1969 offered some seasonal cheer for Wilson; Labour had closed the gap, albeit to a still impregnable 10 per cent. The party's recovery faltered in the new year after they introduced plans to abolish hanging. Ted Heath also benefited from what must surely be one of the most peculiar boosts in any political opinion poll. He took time off to take part in the Sydney to Hobart yacht race. Nowadays, could you imagine the public outcry if the Leader of the Opposition disappeared to Australia for weeks on end just for a yacht race. Remember, this was the pre-internet, pre-email age and being out at sea meant being out of touch. But these were different times, and the public seemed relaxed that their potential next Prime Minister had travelled across the globe to indulge his hobby.

By the spring of 1970, unhappy Labour supporters were returning to the fold more quickly than they had originally abandoned the party. That year the pound was devalued. After Roy Jenkins' budget, Labour stormed into what a year before would have seemed an unthinkable, albeit narrow, lead. It was starting to look like that lone horse in the one-horse race of 1969 may be about to come second. The election rules meant that a newly emboldened Wilson had until the following year before he had to go to the country. But, carried away by his own confidence, Wilson began to tentatively circle dates in the Downing Street diary for a possible early election. A bit like Sir Alf Ramsey having to change his quarter-final tactics and call up Peter Bonetti, Wilson switched his game plan and went to the country a year sooner than he needed to. Ramsey's enforced switch and Wilson's change of heart helped cost both men their top prize.

If the 1970 election had taken place in America, Wilson would have easily beaten Heath to the presidency. He was the more popular of the two leaders. By then, elections here and across the world had started to be influenced by TV performances. Behind in the polls and in the personality stakes, the Tories still retained a big lead on the policy issues that mattered most to the British public: namely, immigration and crime. 'People wanted Wilson but not Labour, the Conservatives but not Heath' was how one prominent politician of the day put it. As the election kicked off on 18 May, it was hard to disagree.

Wilson's decision to call a snap election had the type of impact that a savvy football manager switching from 4-4-2 to 4-2-3-1, the hipster football formation du jour, could only dream of. His opponents were caught flat footed. It took the Tories much longer than it should have to adapt their game plan. But when they got back on their feet they had an unexpected election ally in the shape of public suspicion. Just why had Wilson called an early election? Why was he cutting and running? What bad news did he know about on the horizon that he wasn't telling them? Ted Heath exploited that sentiment and fired a three-pronged attack against Labour, saying that another Labour government would mean higher prices, more strikes and higher taxes.

But, in one sense, Heath now needed what he had never before been able to provide – an energetic campaign that stirred Britain from a sense that things appeared to be on the mend. Instead, Heath was a worthy but dull campaigner. One journalist wryly reflected, 'Covering Heath is like covering El Salvador in the World Cup.' For the avoidance of doubt and for those who know nothing of Heath and little of Salvadorian football, the comment wasn't intended as a compliment. At the time, the Central American footballing minnows were competing in their first ever World Cup competition. Or, more accurately, I should say they 'had competed'. Because, by the time the general election was in full swing, El Salvador were already on the plane home without a win, a draw or even a goal scored packed away in their luggage.

While it was Heath who was the sailor, it was Wilson who set a course for a calm and 'steady as she goes' kind of election. The media's attention on England's progress at the World Cup was totally overshadowing the election. The media's blanket coverage of the football seemed to suit Wilson's plans for a low-key contest. He had pinned his hopes on a grateful nation patting him on the back for the improving economy, and putting him back into Downing Street. He was determined to portray a calm, assured persona; the man who had navigated the country through the worst of a financial crisis. His 'safety first' campaign was built on the fact that the £800 million balance of payments deficit he inherited had been turned around and into a £606 million surplus.

In the final week of the campaign, almost all the political commentators and pundits were of one view. Perhaps more significantly, Ladbrokes had Labour as red hot favourites at 20–1 on. For those of you who don't bet, that's the opposite of 20–1. Remember this was the year before decimalisation and back then twelve pennies made a shilling and twenty shillings made up a pound. Two hundred and forty pennies made a pound. If, like me, you don't remember the pre-decimal age, I know this all sounds a bit like a monetary history lesson. But all that non-betting readers under the age of forty-five need to know is that punters would get just twelve old pence for every old pound they risked. As the bookies set the odds and Britain went to the polls, the debate wasn't who would win but how big Labour's margin of victory would be.

The day before England's defeat in Mexico, the opinion pollsters NOP recorded Labour's lead at an impregnable 12.4 per cent. Other polls had the Tories closer but uncomfortably behind Wilson. On the morning of England's defeat, Ronald Bust wrote in the *Sunday Times*: 'Short of a miraculous turnaround in public opinion Mr Wilson is headed straight back towards 10 Downing Street, probably with an increased majority.' The next morning, *The Guardian*'s Peter Jenkins opined, 'What will become of the Tories after a third success-ive poll defeat? Why is the Labour Party winning with such apparent ease?' And two days later, on the morning before the election, the front page of *The Times* predicted a 150-seat Labour majority. Even those who carried the Tory cause in their soul didn't believe it in their head; only one in seven Tory voters believed that their party would win.

As voting came to an end on 18 June, the returning officers sealed the ballot boxes in schools and community centres across the country. That lovely summer's night, as the ballot boxes were loaded onto trucks to be taken to be counted, Labour were still overwhelming favourites. But a different truth lurked on the more than twenty-eight million marked ballot papers. By 11 p.m., the first result was declared in Guildford and showed a 6 per cent swing; the two seats in Wolverhampton came next and each showed a 9 per cent swing – astonishingly it was to the Tories. The country went to bed. The counting continued throughout the night. By midday, the Prime Minister had conceded defeat in a Downing Street

TV broadcast. As Heath nudged into an outright but tight parliamentary majority, the Queen was being driven along the finishing straight at Royal Ascot preparing for a day at the races. But by 6.30 p.m. she was back at Buckingham Palace ready to fulfil her constitutional responsibility of accepting Wilson's resignation. Twenty minutes later, she invited Ted Heath to be her sixth Prime Minister.

England had prepared for the game with a settled team. But, unfortunately, Gordon Banks their first-choice goalie, had an unsettled stomach. Most international sides from that era would have been spooked by the loss of their top shot-stopper, it would have been match threatening. But England, unlike many others, had a stand-out stand-in, in the shape of Chelsea's brilliant Peter Bonetti.

Then Franz Beckenbauer burst into the penalty area and hit a half-decent shot towards the far corner of the goal. Bonetti dived towards it, but somehow grasped at nothing more than air. England and Everton defender Brian Labone can clearly be seen punching his own hands and staring furiously at poor Bonetti. But the damage was done. Uwe Seeler's looping header left Bonetti stranded for the equaliser, before Gerd Muller volleyed home an extra-time winner.

Writing in *The Observer* newspaper the following weekend, the erudite Hugh McIlvanney, one of the finest sports journalists of any generation, mourned:

England dominated the Germans, until the wide crack in Bonetti's nerve let them through. Sir Alf Ramsey's team are out because the best goalkeeper most people have ever seen turned sick, and one who is only slightly less gifted was overwhelmed by the suddenness of his promotion. In sport disaster often feeds upon itself but this was a sickeningly gluttonous example. As in all nightmares the central figures and events were at once familiar and unfamiliar. Bonetti was somehow not Bonetti.

One unnamed England player is quoted anonymously in the newspapers, and he appeared forgiving of his traumatised teammate.

> But you've got to feel sorry for Peter. Banksie seemed to have got over Montezuma's on the Saturday night and he was playing about with the ball on the Sunday morning. He was in the side and then keeled over at the team meeting and Peter was told he was in the team about half an hour before we left for the ground. No wonder he was a bunch of nerves. If he'd had a lot of the ball early on he might have sorted it out, but there was hardly anything to do before Beckenbauer stuck that one in. In that sort of situation goalkeepers have no chance to find their feet.

In a strange quirk of footballing fate, the goalkeeper who helped England win the Jules Rimet in 1966 no longer has a winner's medal. The keeper who helped lose it in 1970 now does. Peter Bonetti was in the squad for two consecutive World Cup finals. But that fateful quarter-final against West Germany was simultaneously his debut and his final World Cup appearance. Despite being part of the 1966 winning squad, he was denied a winner's medal. Back then, FIFA's rules awarded medals only to players who got on the pitch in the final. But, despite not receiving one at the time, today he has a winner's medal. When FIFA later granted retrospective winner's medals to squad members, his was presented by a friend of Harold Wilson, another Prime Minister, Gordon Brown.

The other Gordon in this medal story, Gordon Banks, is regarded by many as having made the best save in the sport's history. His save to claw out a header by Pelé, one of the three best players to ever pull on a pair of football boots, defies physics. But sidelined by sickness, Banks didn't attend the quarter-final. Instead, he stayed in his hotel room and watched on television. Many of the media reports suggest he didn't even see England go out. As his teammates seemed to be cruising at 2-0, he turned off the small television in his hotel room. Unlike Bonetti, Banks doesn't have a world champion's medal. In 2001, he sold his 1966 winner's medal at auction for almost £125,000.

What made the defeat so painful for England wasn't just how they lost, although from 2-0 up it felt inexplicable. The agony was aggravated by who they lost to. England versus Germany is a footballing clash with a century-long significance. The tone of the contest often tracked the highs and occasionally terrible lows in the relationship between the two countries. The 1966 match against West Germany was beyond doubt the most happy and glorious for England. The clash in 1938 against what was then still a united Germany is beyond doubt the most grotesque. The two teams clashed on 14 May of that pre-war year as political tensions gathered purpose and pace. In the late 1930s, German football was on a roll. An already formidable German squad was strengthened further by the occupation or Anschluss of Austria. Germany considered that Austria's players were now eligible to play for them. By contrast, England were in the doldrums. They had played throughout 1936 without a single win. Results only improved the following year because they took on the weaker Scandinavian teams. Germany came into the game off the back of a fourteen-match unbeaten run. Germany expected. An astonishing 400,000 people applied for the 110,000 tickets.

The match was much more than a sports contest. The UK ambassador to Berlin telegrammed his superiors at the Foreign and Commonwealth Office back in London to inform them, 'The Nazis are looking for victories to boost their regime. It's their way of claiming a super-race.' The England team were also determined to put their atrocious run behind them. 1938 was the type of high-profile match that, if it had gone wrong, would have piled pressure on a defeated England manager; if only they had one. Back then, every member of the England international board took it in turns to be in charge. Sounds like a strange system but it didn't seem to matter. England won 6-3.

Now, I know right now many readers will be saying, 'I didn't know that England had thumped Germany 6-3, why not?' Most people know little of the match but much more about English football's pre-match antics. The supine English football hierarchy were keen not to upset their hosts and the pre-war Hitler. They issued a directive to their players on what to do during the German national anthem. What followed was the most humiliating two minutes of collaborating officialdom in the history of any English sport. The weak, gutless appeasers at the English FA and Foreign Office instructed the England players to raise a straight right arm in a Nazi salute as they turned towards the directors. Hitler wasn't there to appreciate it personally. But the directors' box was packed full of the 'who's who' of senior Nazism; the characters who, within a year, were to become household names in Britain. Because there in the directors' box, smirking down at England's finest, were Goebbels, Goering and Hess. The game was meant to be a two-legged friendly, with the return match scheduled for Wembley in 1939. It was postponed. They didn't play against one other again until 1954.

The disbelief at England's 1970 reversal should also be viewed through the prism of the teams' previous head to heads. The visitors had never lost to pre-war Germany. In fact, England had never lost to any Germany, unified or divided, until 1968. While the country was split in two, they also dominated against West Germany, winning seven, losing one and drawing one. They never went up against the old Communist East Germany. As the teams gathered in Leon, Germany had only a single win against England to their name.

The collapse from a two-goal lead, the loss of a world crown and being overturned by West Germany all combined to make the result so calamitous. To this day, England's unusually accident-prone goalie Peter Bonetti remains a ready-made scapegoat. Harold Wilson's minister of sport, the former League referee Denis Howell, knew that he'd been watching much more than a painful footballing reversal. In his memoirs twenty years later, he wrote, 'The moment goalkeeper Bonetti made his third and final hash of it on the Sunday, everything simultaneously began to go wrong for Labour for the following Thursday.'

Five days later, the Tories won fourteen seats more than they needed to get over the finishing line and have a parliamentary majority. There were fourteen seats where the new Tory majority was less than 750 votes. After all of the 28 million ballot papers had been counted, just 8,000 voters in those fourteen seats across the country gave Heath the outright majority that he needed in Parliament. With such a tiny margin of victory even the smallest thing helped tip the balance. England's football defeat in the week of the election was anything but a small thing.

The temptation for the opinion pollsters who had confidently predicted the opposite result must have been to fret, 'How did the voters get it so badly wrong?' But the uncomfortable truth is that few pollsters picked up on the very late surge to the Tories. As the definitive election guide 'The Polls and the 1970 Election' edited by Richard Rose of Strathclyde University recorded, 'The sequence of events in the last four days before 18 June was almost wholly favourable to the Conservatives...'

In the lowest turnout since the Second World War, the winners benefited from a determination gap. Some Labour campaign workers and voters, thinking that the election was in the bag, appeared lulled into a complacent sense of certainty. By contrast, the Tories, in anticipation of certain defeat, were determined to go down fighting. The losers suffered from a 'stay at home rate' double that of the winners. One in ten identified Labour voters abstained, whereas just one in twenty committed Tories didn't bother to vote. The non-aligned voters sitting on the fence fell off their perch late and, when they did, they helped decide the election. The Tories had a commanding 10 per cent lead among these late deciders.

So why did Harold Wilson, the party leader most of the public had wanted to lead the country, get kicked out? What went wrong for him and what part did football play in the turnaround? Back in 1616, England's King James I was attributed with saying 'No news is good news.' This election became the exception to the King's rule. A strike by the print workers union SOGATT meant that there had been no newspapers for four days the week before the vote. For many voters, it was a sharp reminder of the 1970s Labour Party handling of industrial relations. And when the papers eventually reappeared on the newsstands the Monday of election week, Wilson probably wished his comrades in the print union had prolonged their dispute. They made ugly reading for the PM. Back then the only meaningful regular economic figures were the balance of trade figures; the difference between imports and exports – the numbers were seen as the single most important statement of the nation's economic virility.

Wilson had constructed his campaign around the theme of having engineered a trade surplus. But that last Monday morning before the election the latest figures were released. The UK's £31 million trade deficit screamed from the front pages on their first day back. The galling thing for Wilson wasn't just the timing of the figures, but the fact that they were later proved to be almost certainly wrong. And it didn't matter that the figures were contorted by the import of two jumbo-jets and a mix-up on the calculations. It created the impression that the recovery had stalled. The Tories and Heath had an open goal to shoot at; and they did.

In researching this chapter, I decided to track down eye-witnesses to England's defeat and participants in Ted Heath's victory. There were three obvious candidates to try to interview, from among the many MPs first elected in 1970. As I read through the archives, two Labour personalities and a 'big beast' from the opposite side of the political divide jumped out at me: Labour's John Prescott and Dennis Skinner and the Tories' Ken Clarke.

Ken, who later served as Chancellor of the Exchequer, told me how the trade figures furore felt at the time. 'In those days the thing we were all obsessed about was the balance of trade figures. Harold had a real bit of bad luck and the balance of trade figures were published that week, which blew the apparent Labour recovery out the water.' The unlucky Wilson, much like the scapegoated Bonetti, seemed ill prepared to defend against the attacks. It all put more wind in the part-time yachtsman's electoral sails. In his final election broadcast on the Monday night, Heath seemed reborn. Ken Clarke, now Tory Party elder statesman, tells me about how, as an eager young Tory candidate, he watched the broadcast. He remembers being both surprised and delighted.

> During the week the other thing that happened was that Ted [Heath] went on television to do his final party political broadcast. Once he became party leader, Ted on television or on a public platform was usually death. He couldn't campaign to save his life. But Ted laid on a terrific star performance.

By the election day, Wilson's personal lead over Heath had evaporated.

1970 was the first time eighteen-year-olds could vote; and yet Labour's appeal seemed to deliberately lack much sense of inspiration to excite young voters. It's hardly a surprise that only half of the eighteen-year-olds who had bothered to register to vote made the journey to the polls. In retrospect, the old adage 'if something sounds too good to be true then it probably is' applied to Labour's unprecedented poll surge. Labour's late poll lead proved too fragile. Heath's assault on Wilson's economics unsettled enough people who had only recently and loosely become re-attached to Labour. And in such a close election the mundane things can make a difference. In their post-mortem into the defeat, Labour discovered that the Conservatives had three times more professional agents, more helpers, more money and more billboards. They were better even at the basic tasks such as picking their supporters up by car and taking them to the polling stations to vote. Back in 1970, even that mattered when far few voters were car owners.

I decided to ask someone from 1970 who watched that election more closely than most seventeen-year-olds. Tony Blair was born in 1953 and narrowly missed out in the chance to vote in 1970. However, rather than pick through his teen-age political memories, I wanted to talk to him about how he saw the relationship between football and politics, from his later-life vantage point in Downing Street. I went to meet the former Prime Minister in his Grosvenor Square offices. As you might expect, it's a prestigious location along from the Italian and Canadian embassies. Perhaps I should declare an interest before you read my interview with Tony Blair. He gave me my first break in politics by appointing me as a government minister. It's not a universally popular thing to say in the party that we are both members of, but I've always got on well with him. His new office set-up seems busy but calm. While sitting for a couple of minutes in the waiting room, I was surprised to see that even a former Prime Minister collects pictures of himself with other famous people. In Blair's case, it's framed pictures with Obama, Mandela and a group photograph of those most involved in the Northern Ireland peace process. The only surprise was that, alongside the pictures of him with the 'A List' of the political world, there's one of him sitting next to Arnold Schwarzenegger, flanked by dozens of school children.

I don't have much time to puzzle over it before Tony creaks his neck round his office door. He welcomes me with one of his broad gap-in-his-tooth smiles. As we sit down to talk, I ask him about a mix of football and politics. He stares off into the middle distance and thinks back more than thirty years. On 11 May 1983, five friends who were all Labour Party members gathered around a television in the north-east of England, to watch Aberdeen in their first ever European final. The team from Scotland's North East were taking on the mighty Real Madrid. Those few hours in that living room helped change the UK pretty dramatically; and still do to this day. Alex Ferguson had guided the Scottish Cup holders and League runners-up into the final of the now defunct European Cup Winners Cup. As Aberdeen and their 14,000 fans celebrated in Sweden, something even more dramatic was beginning in the world of politics. That victory propelled the now Sir Alex onto the footballing world stage; it also helped launch the career of a little known 31-year-old lawyer and would-be politician by the name of Anthony Charles Lynton Blair.

'That was the night I first went to Sedgefield for the Labour Party nomination,' the now sixty-year-old former PM tells me. Sensibly, most readers won't have any insights into Labour's processes for picking an election candidate. More often than not, you need a strong group of local people talking to others and speaking up for you, if you're to have any chance of being selected. It's a tactic that seems to have evaded the young Blair. There's no polite way of saying it. He had become one of the party's most accomplished serial losers when it came to the business of Labour selections.

I tried for about twelve seats before Sedgefield all over the north-east. I lost out in many places because of my attitude on the Militant Tendency. Pre-1983, a lot of people didn't want them expelled. In those days in Sedgefield there was a majority of Labour Party people who were in favour of expelling Militant from the Labour Party.

Tony picks up the story of what happened on that 11 May evening, when he set out to recruit influential Sedgefield Labour members to his cause.

I met the critical people that night. I knocked on the door in Front Street South, which was the house that belonged to John Burton, who later became my election agent. And as he opened the door the Aberdeen match had literally just begun. I needed to see him but he basically said, 'Sit down and shut up.' Which I quickly realised was very important, because if I'd blabbered away throughout the game then it was obvious I wouldn't have been suitable.

Blair had arrived too late to see Aberdeen's Eric Black put his side into a fifth-minute lead from a corner. But he was able to join in the general sense of annoyance that they conceded their lead so quickly, just seven minutes later to a Juanito penalty.

The match went into extra time before Aberdeen's John Hewitt, a substitute for Black, the injured scorer of the first goal, netted the winner. It meant a late night for the five Sunderland fans and their Newcastle-supporting visitor. Despite having a crowded mind, Blair remembers it pretty clearly: 'It was a stellar achievement for Aberdeen even at the time, but today it would be impossible. I had a beer and made sure that most of the conversation was about football. We got on to politics after the game.' When the youthful Blair had walked into Burton's home, they had most of the ninety minutes plus extra time ahead of them. By contrast, Blair was really up against the electoral clock. 'The election was on 9 June. The selection of the Labour candidate didn't start until 18 April. I was chosen right at the last.' With the official deadline for candidates to be selected being 23 May, Blair was right up against the wire and he knew it.

> I was the last candidate of any of the parties, anywhere in the country to be selected. It had been a new seat created by the boundary changes. It was a packed thing with lots of candidates and I squeezed through. The reason I got through was partly because of that night watching the Aberdeen game.

It seems clear what would have happened if that night he hadn't hit it off with Burton and the others over a drink discussing football. There's no way he would have become the MP for Sedgefield. More than that, this was the final candidate selection open to him. Without the support of his newly discovered footballing friends, he wouldn't have become an MP at all in the 1983 election.

Even after he was elected Labour leader, following the untimely death of John Smith, Tony was aware of the cultural impact of football.

> It was incredibly important. If you literally know nothing about football, people think it's a bit weird. It's easy enough if you're genuinely interested, like I am as a Newcastle fan. I still follow it a lot. It was really important. Wherever I would go it was football that would help to get people talking.

Although his football diplomacy wasn't without the odd hiccup, as he makes clear.

> When you go to a school the easiest way to get the kids talking is to ask them about football. I remember when I first went to

a primary school in my constituency of Sedgefield and County Durham. It was right between Newcastle, Sunderland and Middlesbrough. I remember as the new MP going along and I was supposed to say something to the kids at their assembly and I actually made the mistake of asking, 'What football team do you support?' And of course there were three different factions and all hell broke loose. I remember the head teacher saying to me later, 'Don't ask them that again, we spent the rest of the day trying to get them back down again.'

Worse was to follow for Blair in the world of footballing faux-pas.

'I remember being up in Scotland just after I became Labour Party leader. I went up to do a big event in Glasgow. I was doing a photo-line' (a politician's version of the family line-up at a wedding reception as guests arrive). He starts to laugh to himself as he thinks about the details of the story he's about to share with me.

As people would come in, you would say to them, 'Are you Rangers or Celtic?' I remember shaking hands with lots of people. I wasn't always able to look at the person before I asked them, but I then said to the next person before looking properly, 'Are you Rangers or Celtic?' 'I'm the Cardinal,' came the response from the formidable Cardinal Winning, the then leader of Scotland's Catholic community, 'so probably Celtic!'

Despite Blair asking the Cardinal about his affections for Rangers (see chapter on Celtic and Rangers if you don't understand the cultural relevance), he is clear that football helped ease tensions and soothe egos in and around meetings on the world stage.

Sport and football in particular was a huge ice-breaker with other leaders in Europe, Brazil and Africa. The one thing that everyone is absolutely fascinated by is football. At European Councils, football was a big thing when the European Championships or World Cup would be going on and for example Gerhard Schröeder [the German Chancellor] was a really keen football fan. And then Lula [the Brazilian President], football was literally the first thing you got round to talking about. So for sure, it was a really good ice-breaker.

Blair, who once swapped the Cabinet table for a seat as a pundit on the BBC's *Football Focus*, tells me about how other world leaders would sometimes pop out for a football top-up during international meetings. 'I remember once actually at one of the European Councils during the World Cup in 2002 Aznar [the Spanish Prime Minister] was watching his side outside all the time.' Blair then smiled, I think mischievously, as he remembered, 'When the French won the World Cup in 1998, it was a huge thing for Jacques Chirac [the French President]. He was with the trophy everywhere.' But he also realised that there were occasional, albeit important, limits to the power of footballing small talk. The 2002 World Cup was a big deal and the best ever performance for American 'soccer'. They defeated Portugal and Mexico and drew with South Korea, before going out in the quarter-finals to Germany, the eventual losing finalists. But, in a sign that there were some recesses of the world that football hadn't yet conquered, Blair makes clear that America's 2002 progress wasn't the talk around the White House water cooler.

I remember during the 2002 World Cup, the European Council was going on and I also had a conversation with George Bush during the course of it. He had literally no interest in football at all; he had no knowledge of how the American team was doing at all. By contrast all the Europeans were obsessively watching their teams.

I was about to turn off my iPhone that was recording our interview and get up to leave, when I asked what I thought was one final innocent question. It led to an astonishing and frank reply. It must make Aberdeen's win over Real Madrid one of the most important football matches ever played or watched on television. 'What would have happened if you hadn't gone to John Burton's house that night and failed to have been selected as the Labour candidate in Sedgefield?' I asked. 'Well, I wouldn't have been Prime Minister.' There it was, one of the shortest answers I've ever heard from Tony Blair. 'You wouldn't have been Prime Minister!?' I repeated, just to make sure I had heard my former boss correctly.

> Yeah, because I wouldn't have got into Parliament until the next election in 1987. I wouldn't have been at the right stage of development. In those days the political development process was a little longer. To be absolutely blunt about it, Gordon [Brown] would have been, you know, so far ahead there wouldn't really have been any doubt about it. By the time John Smith died in 1994, I would only have been seven years in Parliament and at the time that just wasn't long enough.

So, while Tony without football may never have become an MP early enough to have ever become PM, the 1970 newspapers arrived back from strike just in time to help change the PM. The cluttered front pages of the post-strike newspapers had a second headline that competed with the balance of payments blow. The fallout from England's shock defeat in the World Cup quarter-finals screamed from the newsstands.

Even before a ball had been kicked or a vote cast, the speculation had started about the possible electoral impact of an England defeat. Philip Howard asked in an article, 'If England are knocked headlong out of the World Cup, will the electorate turn on the Prime Minister with all the sporting impartiality of a Mexican crowd?'

Throughout the election, football had been on the public's mind and in the Prime Minister's calculations. Interviewed by *The Times* in advance of the vote, he used football as a way to warn his supporters against complacency. 'You can have public opinion polls saying whether England is going to win against West Germany, but what matters is the number of balls you get in the back of the net.' Well, England got two balls in the back of the net and Wilson got 12,208,758 votes in the ballot box. His only problem was that Germany scored three and Heath got 13,145,123. Having already had some insight from Ken Clarke on the winning side of the 1970, I arranged to catch up with John Prescott and Dennis Skinner. We met in one of the few places in Parliament reserved for MPs – the Members' Tea Room. As I sat talking to them, it was clear that they knew one other so well that each almost finished the other's sentence for him. It was almost as though they were brothers or, dare I say, a married couple (an unlikely image, I know). But what I wasn't aware of is that they used to be Parliament's very own Odd Couple, the Jack Lemmon and Walter Matthau of British politics. For a long time as young MPs, they were unlikely house mates sharing a tiny London flat.

I was a couple of minutes late to meet them that morning. I was slower on my feet than usual because of yet another injury I got playing for the parliamentary football team, this time in an undeserved 2-2 draw. I asked if they had ever played for the team when they were first elected to Parliament. Both had novel answers. Prescott said that his biggest contribution to the team was being photographed by the *Telegraph* stuffing copies of the 200-page Hansard publication (the verbatim record of the previous day's parliamentary debates) down the front of his socks to act as shin-guards. Dennis's reply is characteristic. 'Never played 'cos there was Tories in the team, never did anything cross party, not even football. Don't like Tories. Never have, never will. Won't play football with them.'

John Prescott was Tony Blair's full-time Deputy Prime Minister and part-time human shield. He talks at such a speed about sport and politics that it's sometimes hard to keep up. He's now known as Baron Prescott of Kingston upon Hull in the County of East Yorkshire. But back in 1970 he was a 33-year-old fresh-faced former merchant seaman, about to be elected for the first time as an MP. He remembers the context of the campaign: 'Labour was always fighting the sense that we had a heart but no bloody head'; a contest he and Tony Blair fought again in the mid-90s. (Gratuitously, this author adds that, despite the lazy parody, Blair had a heart and Prescott a head.)

The former Deputy PM is first with his 1970 recollections; he has his own memories of the balance of payments moment. 'That balance of payments debate,' he says, 'the whole thing was jumbo-jets and diamonds.' But he also senses that football infected the public's mood about the government. For Prescott the defeat was more than just a footballing reversal. Occurring so soon before polling, he believes, 'It contributed to an essence of failure, let them go, this is the final straw, it did feed it.' The former Deputy Prime Minister recalls:

I remember, I was on a train during the England v West Germany match. I kept asking the guard for the score. No one had a bloody radio. He told us the score after we stopped at each station because he spoke to someone while we were stopped. While England were winning the whole train was rocking about the score.

Before I can find out where this seaman's train journey ended, his former flat mate jumped in. Dennis Skinner is universally known in the media and in the Palace of Westminster as the 'Beast of Bolsover'. The nickname describes the directness of his politics and the name of his constituency. Politicians aren't made like Dennis anymore. His bark has always been as bad as his bite. When we spoke, he had recently celebrated his eightieth birthday. He is a former miner and a brilliant orator with no sense of entitlement or luxury – he cuts his own hair with an old pair of scissors in his office in the Palace of Westminster. However, the man behind the reputation is warm, funny and clever with a vast passion for sport. Of all the characters I've met in British politics, his is the one unwritten autobiography I'd like to read or biography I'd love to write. The high point of his footballing career was playing, not surprisingly, on the left wing for Claycross and Deynsmore Miners Welfare. Those pit matches are the summit of the football career for a man who confesses that he was always a better cross-country runner than footballer.

Dennis is one of the few characters about whom I've always enjoyed the fact that, when he starts talking, it's sometimes hard to get him to stop. The footballing moment he talks about with most passion and a loud chuckle is from the 1960s. He was serving as the delegate to the Parkhouse Colliery on behalf of the then all-powerful National Union of Miners. One of his teammates, George Bradley, looked like he was about to be sent off. Dennis ran in from the wing to remind the referee about the union's rules on solidarity, which he declared trumped those of the FA's. He said to the ref, 'What the hell's going off? I tell you something,' he explained, loudly enough for everyone else at the colliery match to hear, 'where I come from, one off, all off!' The official was shaken and, like many people dealing with Dennis over the decades, he retreated. Bradley stayed on.

Thinking back to his time as a young candidate in 1970, he reflects, 'I felt that everything was going swimmingly ... and a week or ten days before we were calculating a reasonable majority but it didn't work out like that.'

Skinner took a break from campaigning to watch the England game in a friend's house in Sherbrooke. He is in no doubt even today that the five goals he saw on that small black and white telly in that pit village home influenced the course of the election:

> Things certainly faded away. We sat there and it looked like this was going to be another string to our bow, England were on the way and all the rest of it. And then suddenly Norman Hunter the Leeds half-back made a mistake and they came down the field. Bonetti's in the goal – didn't play well – and then the ball is in the bottom of the net.

So often when I talk to Dennis, I feel like he has two jobs. The first is as an MP; the second as a walking football results service. Whenever we go into a late vote in the House of Commons Division Lobby, Dennis always seems to know the score from that night's matches. What's more is that he has as strong a view about every match, no matter how obscure, as he has about the big political issues of the day. But thinking back forty-five years he reminisces unhappily:

> Everything went downhill from that moment on. On the streets the following day it was flat. A lot of miners watched the match. That was the big topic in the pits the following day. Remember they discussed a very limited number of topics in the pit. The pit was dangerous, it's hazardous, and it's like slavery so you talk about subjects that help you escape. It's football, it's cricket to a lesser extent, horse-racing...

Pausing, lost in his thoughts for a moment, he adds '...and sex. That's usually later on in the day as they're getting ready to go home. In between all that if I wanted to talk about politics I would have to pick my moment.'

After the third German goal went in, Dennis thinks back:

We all felt very sad. From then on you could smell it because my campaign is not in an office, it's on the street and in the pit villages with a loud speaker. We would travel around and meet hundreds of people on the street corners. Everything felt different. It faded away, there's no doubt in my opinion. We were sick as dogs.

At the age of seventy-three, Ken Clarke is the baby of my three 1970 MPs. Despite his relative youth (compared to Dennis and John at least), he's been around a long time. A bit like his suede loafer shoes, he defies appearances to boomerang back into fashion from time to time. Not for him the modern vices of Twitter or Facebook. He's not even caught up with the 1980s and the merits of the dictaphone. As I arrive in his office, he is in the middle of thinking out loud at his secretary across the room. She is working harder than any electronic gizmo, energetically scribbling his thoughts out in shorthand. After Ken greets me, I cheekily interrupt his rehearsal of a defence of the government's plans for the NHS. I speak over him to suggest a modest but mischievous one-word idea of how to improve his letter to a worried constituent. Where he has dictated, 'Our plans will improve healthcare for patients', I simply suggest adding an extra word before 'improve': 'not'. My mucking around forces both Ken and Charlotte to stop, stare and then continue. It's well known in Parliament that staff have an enormous influence on the diary of their employers. Fearing I might be about to get thrown out because of an 'urgent and unexpected' phone call, I decide to shut up.

Ken's office is directly above the Prime Minister's in the House of Commons; his office floor is the PM's office ceiling. He shares his room with his hobby and his habit. The first is collecting political poster cartoons and the second the accumulating of unwanted gifts received from overseas politicians. It feels like a cross between an expensive poster gallery and an antiquities shop, packed full of unsellable objects. As we settle down to talk, he sits below his favourite Churchill cartoon. I take a seat opposite him, between a sculpted Chinese lady in a fish-tank-sized glass case and a life-sized black marble tasteless, but possibly expensive sculpture of a horse's head.

As his secretary leaves us, I want to ask, 'How did you get that horse back from the Philippines?' But, instead, I am distracted by the realisation that, despite our being by ourselves, we aren't alone. Almost no one outside of Parliament knows this but the House of Commons is infested with moths; these tiny little creatures have the run of the place and devour everything they find. Parliament's moths have been here for years and have found their way to Ken's office. There are competing truths and myths about how they first got into this ancient building. My favoured explanation is the one that claims that they arrived inside a Persian rug imported from the Middle East by the prominent Tory MP Michael Gove. The fact that it's my preferred option doesn't make it true; certainly not true enough to send Michael the bill for my suit they chewed through when 'his' moths made their journey with me to my flat near Parliament. Anyway, there are thousands of the little buggers and hundreds of moth traps all over Parliament, which Ken's moth collection had so far skilfully avoided.

The MP for the East Midlands constituency of Rushcliffe is a keen Nottingham Forest fan from long before the time of Brian Clough's all-conquering double European Cup winners. He had a peculiar relationship with Cloughie, the Labour-supporting footballing eccentric. The Forest manager even helped lead demonstrations against government policy past Ken's Nottingham constituency office. Clarke tells me that, after one of the demos, he took Clough aside and told him, 'If you march past my office yet again I will get a counter-demo up outside the City ground because at the moment you've got to admit that our bloody team is doing worse than my bloody government!' And Ken claims, 'He never marched by again.'

But he does reveal that his manager did get in touch from time to time, looking for the support of his MP.

> He used to ring up when he wanted a work permit for one of his foreign players. He was trying to sign a Swedish left-sided midfielder. Brian had written into the government depart-ment. A Miss Smith on her first day in the job had sent him back the standard work permit response along the lines of, 'Dear Mr Clough. We are not satisfied that the post could not be filled by a local unemployed person.' Clough got on to me and said, 'Your Miss Smith is saying that I have to advertise in the local paper to see whether some unemployed person can play in my first team.'

Parliament's best-known jazz fan explains that his team's manager wasn't the only one to lobby him in that way: 'Ronnie Scott's jazz club used to do the same, calling me looking for a permit.'

History is a version of events recorded by the victor. Like everyone else, Ken Clarke knows there were bigger factors at play in 1970 than a single football match. But he accepts that there may have been those at the heart of the Labour govern-ment who believed that England's footballing failure was to blame. 'Harold took this kind of thing much more seriously. It wouldn't surprise me if, today, someone working with Harold were to tell me now that Harold insisted that this was part of his thinking. On this occasion I think he was deceiving himself.'

In 1970, the 29-year-old Clarke was already a seasoned campaigner. This was his third attempt to get into the Commons and for him it turned out to be third time lucky. Today's wily elder statesman takes a similar view to Dennis Skinner, acknowledging:

> Where football might have a relevance is I think that what matters an awful lot at a general election is a general sense of well-being; a feeling that at least the government is doing its job. Harold had had a terrible period in government. He hadn't shaken off the devaluation of the pound.

This sense of what Ken calls 'well-being' is what one exasperated Labour MP had in mind in 1970 when he was reported as mentioning 'the damned bug in Gordon Banks's tummy that punctured the mood of euphoria'.

Despite the double defeats, Sir Alf Ramsey kept his job as England manager and Harold Wilson stayed on as Labour leader. Many observers believe that, if Heath had lost, then the unnamed but powerful 'men in grey suits' would have tapped him on the shoulder and 'invited' him to stand down. The Tory Party is traditionally ruthless towards failure (and sometimes towards success) at the top of the party. Defeated in 1970, they would have immediately begun the search for a new leader. In truth, during the election campaign, some party grandees spent much of their time discussing who would succeed a soon to be defeated Heath.

But, by winning, Heath led the country and his party until 1974, when Wilson, the comeback kid, came back. A year later, when Heath finally did stand down, the party elected a relatively untested leader – a grocer's daughter by the name of Margaret Hilda Thatcher. It's intriguing to think 'What if?' the Tories had lost in 1970. They would have elected a new leader. It wouldn't have been Mrs Thatcher.

Back then 'Mrs T' was little known and hardly featured in the top ten of Tory politicians. She had spent much of the 1970 general election campaign touring the country speaking to unimpressive and often unimpressed gatherings. Most people believe that she was just too inexperienced to lead in 1970 – someone else would have taken over and become the potential future Prime Minister. Looking back, Willie Whitelaw would have been the bookies' favourite to defeat all-comers. His old-style moderate politics were a world away from the Thatcher revolution that a decade later Britain was to have unleashed upon it. 'What if?' indeed. Take a bow the statisticians who couldn't add up the balance of payments figures alongside the brilliant but flawed Peter Bonetti.

Pat Nevin is a marked man at Selhurst Park in 1984 as the vast Chelsea
support looks on in the background. After scoring the winning goal his
post-match press conference captured the headlines.
© *Press Association*

Chapter Eight

There's Only One Pat Nevin: *Crystal Palace v Chelsea, 1984*

AN END-OF-SEASON ENCOUNTER between Crystal Palace and Chelsea from 1984 hardly sounds like the stuff of footballing history. It sounds more like a game that all involved in, on and off the pitch, would struggle to remember beyond the fast-approaching close season.

But this meeting of these near neighbours at opposite ends of the league proved to be one of the most important matches ever played in Britain. So incendiary was the reaction of many in the crowd to the simple footballing act of a substitution. And so brave was one man's response. It changed football and ended the country's tolerance of mass-scale recreational racism. The game helped to kick off a campaign that British football is still struggling to win.

For both teams that April afternoon at Selhurst Park, there was more than just two points at stake. Chelsea arrived as title-chasers in the old Second Division, desperate for promotion and the chance to play the First Division 'Big Boys'. For Palace, their goal was an escape from an unwanted flirtation with the Third Division. The visitors arrived days after being dislodged from top spot by Sheffield Wednesday. They had their noses just in front of fellow chasers Newcastle and Man City. Palace were fresh from the humiliation of a 3-0 defeat away to Derby, one of only four teams struggling below them in the league.

It was make or break for Palace or more accurately make or broke. Under real financial pressure, they hiked up their turnstile prices to £9 a head and cancelled all concessionary prices. And yet thousands still came. An astonishing 15,000 Chelsea fans made the short journey across London. This, in the days when travelling away from home was a minority sport associated with a hooligan hard core. Chelsea's mass pilgrimage to Croydon meant it was by some distance the home team's biggest crowd of the season.

For Palace, it must have felt like an away game at home with their fans outnumbered three to one. It might have unsettled their players but it didn't perturb the Palace hierarchy. With a season's best bumper crowd and inflated prices, it guaranteed a life-saving pay day with record gate receipts of over £70,000. If the Palace boardroom were pleased, the tax man was delighted. The following Monday morning, Palace agreed to send Her Majesty's Revenue and Customs a cheque courtesy of the Chelsea fans for £40,000 to settle some of their unpaid tax bills.

The match itself was a game of few chances but enormous incident. As the clock ticked down towards ninety minutes, there were many among the heaving mass of away supporters whose behaviour shamed their club. For years to come, their actions that day meant that Chelsea paid a far heavier price than Palace paid the tax man. On the pitch, Palace manager Alan Mullery picked a different team for a different purpose to the eleven who had just capitulated to Derby. They welcomed Chelsea determined not to lose. Mullery described his new picks as 'battlers'. Out went Tony Evans, Jerry Murphy and Stan Cummins. In came the youngsters Gary Stebbing, Phil Barber and John Lacy. And battle is what these three and every one of their teammates did.

So physical were the Palace players, that in his post-match interview the Chelsea manager, John Neal, complained they were 'not willing to take any prisoners' and had an 'uncompromising' attitude in their tackling. He was far from happy and didn't hide it when he opined, 'I saw a lot of things in the match that I abhor.' The typically robust Chelsea chairman Ken Bates branded Palace 'kickers' not 'battlers'.

The first-half shots on target statistic tells its own story. A single Pat Nevin cross-cum-shot well saved by George Wood was the only time either goal or goalie saw the ball in anger. But it was anything but dull. It was the type of game we are no longer allowed to see. It was an old-fashioned blood and guts physical encounter. If it was played today, it would end up as eight players versus ten and see demands for a 'something must be done' type of FA inquiry. But this was the 1980s when football was still a contact sport, free from fourth officials and all-angle slow-mo analysis of every decision. The ref kept his red card a secret and only shared the yellow when he had run out of other options. Gary Stebbing was eventually booked for a foul on John Bumstead, as was Gary Locke for a wild tackle on Nigel Spackman.

Both sets of forwards struggled, albeit for totally different reasons. For Palace, it was hard for them to break their season-long habit. Their partnership of Andy McCulloch and Phil Barber had huffed and puffed in a team that had scored just once in their previous 500 minutes of football. Chelsea, on the other hand, had the best from north and south of the border in England's Kerry Dixon and Scotland's David Speedie. They had bamboozled all-comers all season and already shared thirty-nine goals. But even they couldn't navigate a way through, around or over Mullery's surprise decision to play Billy Gilbert as a sweeper mopping up behind the central defensive pairing of Jim Cannon and John Lacy. The latter, often the lazy focus for Palace boo-boys, was immense.

Chelsea looked like they might never score. Palace seemed like they might never create a chance to score. In their desperation to avoid a draw and close the gap on Sheffield Wednesday, Chelsea made a late substitution. It helped change the game and with it footballing history. They risked all and threw on a winger. Paul Canoville ran onto a raucous, poisonous and racist reception. But the game still seemed to be petering towards a point apiece until Palace cleared their lines and battered the ball out of play. Chelsea's Colin Lee picked it up and stole a full twenty yards in taking a foul throw-in. For once, Speedie got clear of his marker and knocked the ball on to Canoville. He back headed it into Pat Nevin's path and he volleyed home from close in. The ball hadn't touched the ground once it had illegally left Lee's hands. It was the eighty-third minute. Palace couldn't and didn't respond. At the final whistle, Chelsea fans poured onto the pitch to celebrate what they hoped was now almost certain promotion.

But Nevin was furious: not about the Palace kicking or the Chelsea invasion but about the racism that greeted Canoville's arrival. The post-match shower did nothing to wash away his emotions. As he dried himself, he spoke to no one as his anger grew. When the media arrived for the big interview with the smallest of goal scorers, he decided there and then to do something about it. The journalists probably expected the standard platitudinous responses to their tired formulaic questions. But he refused to talk about the game or glory in his goal. He simply announced, 'I'm disgusted by the fans. How dare they boo any Chelsea player and to do it because he is black is sickening.' What angered Nevin more than anything else that fateful day was the source of the racist taunts – it came from hundreds if not thousands of his and Canoville's own fans.

He was the first prominent white player to speak out. His words were broadcast to the world. By being the first, he exposed a silence about the sports' self-enforced denial over the racism corroding its heart and rationalised in its head;

tolerated on the pitch and celebrated on the terraces; accepted in the boardroom and in far too many changing rooms.

Perhaps we shouldn't be surprised by Canoville's experience. Britain was a different country then. There was a popular tolerance of racism. The non-racist comedians of the time were labelled 'alternative'. Enoch Powell was still front-page news. White South African runner Zola Budd was in England running under a convenient flag to get around the world's sporting boycott of apartheid. It was a country ill at ease with itself just a year into Margaret Thatcher's second term. As is often the case, our national sport reflected a national character.

Tolerance of public racism within football was widespread. The legendary George Best often captured the mood of Britain as it was – the good, the bad and the self-indulgent. He once boasted, 'I spent a lot of money on booze, birds and fast cars. The rest I squandered.' That was his way of life. It also perhaps helps explain his untimely death.

From the moment he made his debut at Old Trafford, this teenage sensation electrified crowds across the globe. He reflected a nation in touch with its occasionally hedonistic and overwhelmingly optimistic '60s self. Best was the celebrated poster boy of a colourful era and in at the very start in the game's journey towards decadence. He was the first to be described as 'The Fifth Beatle' and rivalled the Fab Four for the attentions of both the media and young women.

But, when asked in later life about the transfer of Andy Cole from Newcastle to Manchester United, his answer jarred with his image and made many shudder. The Northern Irishman proclaimed, '£7 million is a lot to pay for a nigger.' And, while no one really believes that Best was a racist, his racist response was an uncomfortable echo of the settled attitude of far too many in the sport. Canoville had endured the friendly fire of his own fans' racial hatred from his very first moments as a

Chelsea player. He made his Chelsea debut against the same team at the same ground where Nevin spoke out. It was two years earlier and, from that point onwards, almost everyone had looked the other way.

Like most young boys, Canoville had dreamt of making his footballing debut and scoring a hat-trick for his boyhood heroes against their biggest rivals, cheered on by delirious fans chanting his name. For a tiny number of the tiny number who turn pro, they live that dream. Like Best, the teenage Alan Shearer and Wayne Rooney's first games were unforgettable because both scored three times. Jimmy Greaves lived the dream not once but five times, scoring in five different debuts; four for separate clubs and on his England debut.

Others probably wish that they could wake from their real-life nightmare debuts. Everton fans will remember Glen Keeley back in 1982. He was sent off for bringing down Kenny Dalglish in a 5-0 humiliation and never played for the 'People's Club' again. Jonathon Woodgate's debut for Real Madrid was marred by a unique double. He saw red but only after scoring a brilliant own goal, worthy of any goal of the season award. Future fame has never been a guarantor of a successful debut. Perhaps the greatest player ever to pull on a pair of boots fared only marginally better than Woodgate. After lashing out in a meaningless friendly away to Hungary, the soon to be magical Lionel Messi was Argentina's sixty-fifth-minute debutant substitute who became a sixty-seventh-minute dismissee.

Perhaps the strangest debut sounds like the opening line of a bad joke. It took place on England's south coast and involved a Scotsman, a Yorkshire man and an Ivorian. Graeme Souness was the manager and Lawrie McMenemy was his and probably the country's first Director of Football. Back in the 1980s, two men had competed for the title of England's Mr Football; Ron Atkinson and Lawrie McMenemy. One has since ruined his reputation and Lawrie hasn't. He won the FA Cup with Southampton and at one point was in the *Guinness Book of Records* as the highest-paid manager in the country. He took Matt Le Tissier and Alan Shearer to Southampton and made Gary Bennett Sunderland's first black captain. I have known Lawrie for almost fifteen years; he is a giant of a man with a heart as big as the Tyne. Today he is the chairman of the UK Special Olympics Committee.

He told me how, in 1996, he tried to do what so many players have attempted over the years – deliberately take a swipe at Graeme Souness. The strange thing about his kick was that it was under the Southampton boardroom table, out of sight of everyone else. But, like so many of the others who tried, he missed. Souness's misdemeanour was that he wanted to sign a new player he hadn't seen on the strength of a phone call. The caller claimed to be the legendary World Player of the Year George Weah. The signing target was his cousin Ali Dia. Two days later, he was in the squad and on the bench against Leeds.

Matt Le Tissier, whom he came on for as a sub, remembers him 'running about like Bambi on ice'. He was so painfully laughably woeful and was substituted. Of course, George Weah hadn't made the call and the subbed sub wasn't his cousin. In a world of often hurtful football chants, the Saints fans' witty ditty of 'Ali Dia; He's a Liar' is perhaps the nearest any fans have come to a truism masquerading as a terracing insult. Lawrie tells me about the next and last time he met Dia. The Monday morning after that Saturday afternoon, Dia knocked on Lawrie's door asking about his contract. Plain-speaking McMenemy said, 'There's the door, now bugger off. Tell you what, you can keep the kit. And don't think about complaining 'cos it's even got your name on it.'

For all the hit and miss and occasionally comical debuts over the decades, one category of player has had to live through something much more sinister. For more than a century in Britain, black footballers' debuts were accompanied by racism.

In a crowded contest with a dreadfully long list of entries, Paul Canoville's treatment is perhaps the most shameful. Canoville singled out for a simple reason and it wasn't just because he was black. It was because he was daring to go where no black player had ever gone before in the entire history of Association Football – the home dressing room at Chelsea's Stamford Bridge. Second Division Chelsea were a different creature back then. This was life pre-football superpower whose only successes were a single First Division championship in the 1950s and two cup wins the following decade.

The events that day are painfully captured in Canoville's autobiography, *Black and Blue*, one of the most unsettling sports books ever written. So horrendous were his experiences that, when we meet thirty years and one month after his hate-filled debut, he arrived with a documentary-making camera crew in tow. In his book, he recounts his first game for Chelsea: 'It was supposed to be the fulfilment of my life's ambition ... It should have been one of the greatest days of my life, not a nightmare that came back again and again. But this wasn't the Hollywood version. This was the snarling, nasty, '80s-Britain version.'

Canoville, who was once confronted by men in Ku Klux Klan hoods at a reserve game at Millwall, relived his debut as we talked. He explained how nothing could have prepared him for what happened. As he sat on the subs bench, he seemed to be captured by an almost child-like exuberance. 'I can do something here, let me get on,' he screamed to himself in his own mind. 'Am I going to get on here? 'Cos I fancy this, I fancy this.' Then he got the shout saying, 'Paul, get on!'

I started to hear this abuse and the fans are really close. I'm getting myself ready and not turning round. I didn't want to

214

stop concentrating on getting ready. As I'm stretching and running, I hear loud individual voices through the noise: 'Sit down, you black cunt!' 'You fucking wog – fuck off!' Over and over again, lots of different people. I hardly dared look round.

But here, at the very moment that footballing history was being made, Canoville looked over his shoulder. When he did, he wished he hadn't. 'They were all wearing blue shirts and scarves – Chelsea fans, my side's fans, faces screwed up with pure hatred and anger, all directed at me.'

In thinking how to write about these events, I had decided to always refer to the 'N-word'. But, as I interviewed former players and others, many were more direct. For me it's distressing to write a word that I have never said, and for many it will be uncomfortable to read, but I decided to accurately record what people told me. Paul Canoville continues with the story of his dreadful debut:

Then it came. Chanting, not just by one or two people, but what sounded like scores of people, a huge mob: 'We don't want the nigger! We don't want the nigger! La la la laaa, la la la laaa!' Again and again. So loud, my God. This ain't the way it's supposed to be. A banana landed near me as I walked back, head bowed, to take off my training top.

Years later, Barcelona's Dani Alves had a banana thrown at him at a match away to Villarreal. In a rebuke to the racist, he picked it up, peeled it and ate it. But what Canoville faced was on a vastly different scale and he thinks back: 'I felt physically sick. I was absolutely terrified. It was so loud, so clear, so near, the hatred, they didn't want me here.' At that moment, the feeling became mutual. 'I didn't feel like getting on, I didn't want to get on. It didn't make sense getting on anyway.' But he did, for three very long minutes.

When I got the ball I had no thought what to do with it. It was as much as I could do to run about, leave alone have any effect on the game. When I got the ball, then boy, that's when bananas were thrown on the pitch and the abuse was so much and that was just for my first touch. If I remember I just gave the ball back to the player. I was really shocked, I was shocked, shocked. Thankfully, the ordeal was soon over and I dashed off to the dressing room, those cruel voices chasing after me down the players' tunnel. It seemed like the longest torture of my entire life. I still can't remember how I got home. I was in that changing room for a long time with my head in my hands. None of the other players spoke to me. Nobody said a word, not even the next day. I didn't say anything as I didn't want to look weak; I just got on with it. I really don't know why the white players didn't speak out.

That was the experience of the first black man to ever play in Chelsea's first team. 'I made history and the fans made my life hell,' he told me. Canoville turned out for Chelsea in just two more games that year. The racism continued in every game the following season and into the next.

Shock at Canoville's revelations is natural; surprise shouldn't be. Racism was never a stranger to British football. It was a century-long relationship going back to 1890 and the first black professional, Arthur Wharton. But contrary to many historical accounts Wharton wasn't Britain's first ever black player. That honour goes to amateur Andrew Watson who in 1881 turned out for what was then possibly the biggest club in world football, Glasgow's Queen's Park. So magnificent was he that he was capped by Scotland. There are no records of his being singled out for racism. But as any lawyer might tell you the absence of evidence of racism is not the same thing as evidence of absence of it. Intriguingly, even if he was the victim of unrecorded racism, he was also enormously appreciated.

Not only did he captain his country but he was also invited to join Corinthians – the nineteenth-century footballing forerunner of basketball's Harlem Globetrotters – an elite, select team of invited stars of the day. So significant a character was he that he is listed in some of the studies of the hundred most influential black Britons.

But without doubt the most inspiring story of any black footballer in Britain or possibly any footballer of any background is of Walter Daniel John Tull. He had grown up in an orphanage in London's East End and went on to play for Spurs and Northampton in the first decade of the twentieth century. So appalling were the scenes of racism at one Spurs game away at Bristol that unusually for the time it was recorded by the media. The incensed reporter at the *Football Star* newspaper wrote, 'Let me tell those Bristol hooligans that Tull is so clean in mind and method as to be a model for all white men who play football ... In point of ability, if not actual achievement, Tull was the best forward on the field.'

Despite the abuse by his countrymen, he volunteered to serve in the Football Battalion of the Middlesex Regiment in the Great War. He overcame the absence of parents and the abundance of racism to become a British Army officer. No big deal, some might think, but this was 1914; a time when the Military Manual banned 'any negro or person of colour' from being commissioned as an officer. This Rangers-bound striker survived the Battle of the Somme and was mentioned in Dispatches. But in the last months of the war he was killed aged just twenty-nine. In a final rebuke to the Bristol racists, his fellow soldiers, almost all of whom were white, risked death to rescue his body from the battlefield. One of those who struggled through enemy fire was the then Leicester City keeper Tom Billingham. But they failed. To this day, Tull's body has never been recovered. His is one of the 35,000 names engraved on the Arras Memorial.

But progress for black football was slow. While white soldiers followed him on the battlefield, very few black players followed in Tull's footsteps onto the football field. There was only a smattering of black pros in Britain prior to the Second World War. In 1938, Northampton Town signed John Parris who went on to play for Wales. Celtic signed Abdul Salim from Calcutta who played barefoot but left because he was homesick and sick of the weather. Derby, Cambridge and QPR all imported Egyptian players in the inter-war years.

The three decades after the war saw a steady increase in the numbers of black footballers. The sport was becoming more popular in Europe's former colonies and with the children of new immigrants. Among the most prominent were Charlie Williams at Doncaster Rovers and the prolific Jamaican Lloyd Delapenha at Middlesbrough. Watford were probably the most persistent pursuers of African talent.

But the highest-profile import was surely Albert Johanneson who turned out for Leeds. He had fled 1960s apartheid South Africa only to be taunted by British football's racists whose insults were usually trivialised by footballing authorities. He made history as the first ever black player in an FA Cup final, losing to Liverpool. But for all his success the story of his death should unsettle every genuine fan. In a sorry tale of demise and isolation, he died in 1995; a poverty-stricken, lonely death in a high-rise block of flats in the city that he had long thrilled. The precise date of his passing is unknown because his body lay undiscovered for several neglected days.

Even in the 1970s, there were still only a few top black players in the English league. Stoke's Garth Crooks, Bob Hazell and George Berry at Wolves, Luther Blissett at Watford and Viv Anderson at Forest. West Brom stood out from the crowd where Cyrille Regis, Laurie Cunningham and Brendan Batson became known as 'The Three Degrees' after the prominent African-American act of the time. On some Saturdays in the '70s, West Brom fielded more black players than most of the rest of the league put together.

Some of those who did make it were nearly broken by the response to their success. Shrewsbury's Michael Brown is one such example. During one match at Leeds in the '80s, the stadium rocked to the sound of a sickening fans favourite of the time, which went 'Fucking Nigger, where's the Fucking Nigger? There's the Fucking Nigger. We're going to shoot the Fucking Nigger!' Brown was in no doubt who it was aimed at. For there on the pitch in front of the mob there was only one black player – him. Barely out of school, he was just sixteen years of age. Huge numbers were involved with hundreds screaming as each stand took it in turn, while the others applauded until it reached the Elland Road kop. During the half-time team talk, Brown struggled to hold back his tears as the experienced Shrewsbury players pretended not to have noticed. No one was punished.

So, while football racism was nothing new and goes back to at least the second ever black player on our shores, by the 1980s it was ubiquitous. Some of it was a reflection of the moment. Many of those who chucked the abuse and some of those on the receiving end just put it down to 'banter'. One such example in the mid-1980s involved Newcastle striker Tony Cunningham and the nickname he was given by his manager Jackie Charlton. His gaffer often forgot the names of his own team. Instead, he simply said what he saw when talking to and about his players. So most were 'big man' or 'wee man'. But Cunningham was 'Blackie Milburn' in a racially overtoned homage to Newcastle's most celebrated player Jackie Milburn. No one seemed to take offence.

But it's difficult now to grasp just how much that racism was expected by some and accepted by many. For a lot of black players, it wasn't new. It was the extension of what they had grown up with. As one of 'The Three Degrees', Brendan Batson told me, 'Players were born black; from an early age they experienced racism, what changed was the volume.'

Football was a reflection of what was happening in the country. It often emphasised the worst of Britain. It wasn't alone and even today some sports seem unbalanced. Still today, there are very few black top-class jockeys, swimmers, show-jumpers and the next time the tennis or golf is on the telly take a glimpse at Wimbledon centre-court crowds or British Open golf galleries. They still don't look much like modern Britain.

But all of that is a molehill compared to the mountain of football racism. And it hasn't just menaced professionals. Some young players were typecast from an early age by school teachers. Others have told me that they were victims of overheard whispering campaigns boasting that they would 'never make it' as a footballer. The parents of many brilliant black boys, including Canoville's mum, urged them to avoid football as a profession. It's sobering to think about those dejected young men of the 1970s who are now approaching pension age as time-served plumbers, pipefitters or joiners who maybe, just maybe, could have been football internationals and household names.

Those whose passion for football survived early prejudice went on to play at amateur level where for some the racism went up a notch. Brendan Batson confided to me that he was only sent off three times in his entire pro career; twice for retaliating to racial abuse from the same opponent. He also talked to me about his time as an amateur. As a pro, he was angered by the hundreds of people screaming at him from the distant terracing. But as a young amateur playing in London's Regent's Park, he was genuinely shaken by the 'terrible abuse' of the up-close and personal one-on-one hatred of the bigots on the near-deserted touchline.

Most players coped with instead of confronting their tormentors. One exception to this rule was Everton's Dixie Dean. In the 1930s, he was racially abused but instead of just rolling with it he responded in a way that Eric Cantona would later emulate. He walked over to the perpetrator and punched him. Even more exceptionally, the police officer who was called to intervene admonished Dean and informed the abuser that he 'got what he deserved'.

Dean was unusual but each player had their way of dealing with it. Batson wasn't alone in receiving hate mail but he didn't burn, bin or report it. Instead, he pinned it up on the wall in the home dressing room next to the manager's tactics board. He used it to inspire himself and mock his uninvited racist pen-pals.

Of course, the abuse at some grounds was more hostile than others. Ex-pros say that among the worst culprits were Leeds, Newcastle, Birmingham and Chelsea. More than one former player I spoke to reserved particular criticism for West Ham as 'horrendous'. And it wasn't just opportunistic, 'join in the fun' fruit-throwing racism. Often it was orchestrated and more sinister. In the late 1970s, in a world before text and Twitter, the National Front would still manage to be at grounds to 'greet' team coaches carrying black players. This was entirely in keeping with a nauseating tradition going back at least fifty years. The contamination of football by Fascists had been going on intermittently way back to the days of Oswald Mosley's Hitler-loving British Union of Fascists in the 1930s.

Batson remembers one such terrifying incident with total clarity as if it had just happened the morning we spoke. The former Baggies defender thinks back, 'It seems unbelievable now but I remember distinctly getting off the coach at Chelsea and they were handing out leaflets and spitting abuse at us.' In the 1980s, the NF's youth newspaper *Bulldog* ran a regular

221

column, 'On the Football Front', which exhorted fans to 'join the fight for race and nation' and published their own league table of racist fans. At some notoriously unwelcoming football venues of the time, such as Upton Park, the National Front publicly sold unofficial club memorabilia with 'NF' slogans emblazoned alongside the team's logo.

Again, rather than demanding action from ambivalent football authorities, the players responded in the only effective way they knew how – on the football pitch. Some compiled a table of clubs with the most racist fans with top spots in this unspoken mini-league going to teams with a National Front following. For many, winning against this half-dozen or so clubs guaranteed that the post-match celebrations were all the sweeter. They knew that the screaming bigots who met them as they got off their team bus would now be crying into their pints, puzzled by just how they had lost to a 'racially impure' team.

Racism infected so much of the sport. Think of the goal celebrations of the top players today. Many will acknowledge their family before being mobbed by their teammates. Others kiss their taped-over wedding ring, while some blow kisses to girlfriends sitting behind the directors' box. I have always found all of this a bit over the top, although I guess it's pretty harmless. But for some black players none of this was possible. Not because they didn't score goals or because they didn't have loved ones but because many of their loved ones just weren't able to watch them scoring their goals. Family and friends would go along to one match and never go back. They simply couldn't put up with the aggravation from the terraces and the expectation that they like everyone else should say and do nothing about it.

England B international centre-back Paul Elliot shared with me how during matches he sometimes had more important things on his mind than putting in his tackles.

Psychologically during some games I was concerned about my family members in the stand because of the tension and because of the hostility particularly when playing in the north of England. You had areas like Leeds, Newcastle and Burnley; they were very, very intimidating environments. It was really difficult.

And it wasn't just inside the grounds that there were fears for friends and family. Despite the abuse at the game, many black supporters still thought the safest place was in the stadium. Their thinking was it provided respite from the dangers of the journey to and from the match. One former pro told me he knew supporters who arrived deliberately late and left early to avoid a chance meeting and possible incidents with opposing or even their own team's supporters.

Few if any black players seemed immune from racism. Viv Anderson has aged well; like all of us, he has a little less hair but is still instantly recognisable. He is celebrated as being the first black England international. When I catch up with him, he tells me about another first that very few football fans remember. He was on Manchester United's books as a youngster, went to Nottingham Forest and returned to Old Trafford to become the very first of Alex Ferguson's Manchester United signings.

He achieved so much, including winning the European Cup with Forest, but will always be remembered for one match in 1978. Ron Greenwood picked him to play against the now non-existent Czechoslovakia and so he became the first ever black England cap. It's impossible to overstate the significance of the event. He received telegrams from around the world and from the powerful and countless celebrities including Elton John and Queen (of Her Majesty's variety not the Freddie Mercury version).

But Viv so nearly wasn't the first black England player. He certainly wasn't the first to be told that he was playing for

England – not by a long way – by almost five decades in fact. That honour goes to striker Jack Leslie. He averaged almost thirty goals a season for Plymouth over an astonishing four-teen years from 1921. After another fine run of form, he was informed by his proud club manager, a Scot, Bob Jack, that he had been selected to play for England. His goals kept on coming but the cap never did. Leslie went to his grave convinced that it was his colour that led to his cap being cancelled. It raises the intriguing question of whether the England selectors only discovered that the Pilgrims' goal machine was black after they had decided to pick him.

Whatever the truth of Leslie's non-cap, Viv Anderson tells me that he escaped the worst of the racism because he was unlike many other black players in one important regard. He explains that he confounded some of the racist stereotypes. I don't want to be rude but I have to admit to him that I have no idea what he is on about. He replies without any sense of self-regard or boast: 'I was different to others because my job was to kick people. It wasn't like the forwards who couldn't play 'cause of bad weather and had to wear gloves. I didn't like long-sleeve shirts.' He tells me that Brian Clough gave him a precise role in the team. 'Cloughie told me that he paid me to stop the ball going into my net and stop the other player playing – end of story. So, my job was to kick the winger and, if he came back again, I'd kick him again.'

But, despite escaping some of the worst of the abuse, he wasn't inoculated against it. He recounts one of his first games as a sub with a mixture of horror and humour when he was 'Canovilled', albeit by the opposition's fans. Life on the subs bench is frustrating for most players, but for many black players it was uncomfortable. Some could be forgiven for thinking that it was better not to be in the squad at all and sit in the relative tranquillity of the only occasionally racist stands rather than take their chances on the bench. Sometimes the abuse during their warm-up at the side of the pitch meant that black subs wanted to get onto the pitch but not leave the dugout. They were desperate to set aside their professional routine and avoid any warm-up before going on. If they had to, they would sprint to the sanctuary of the corner of the ground housing their own fans. But for some like West Ham's Clyde Best or Portsmouth's Noel Blake not even that guaranteed an escape. It just meant doing their limbering up jeered on by their own team's racists.

Anderson takes up the story of when Forest were away to Carlisle and he was sent out to warm up by Brian Clough. He was greeted by a shower of fruit falling all around him; he turned round and headed straight back to the dugout. 'I thought I told you to warm up,' shouted Cloughie. 'I have done, Boss, but they're throwing bananas and pears at me,' Anderson complained. Clough, one of the first to sign up to football's anti-racism campaigns, shot back, 'Well, get your arse out there and fetch me two pears and a banana.' Anderson knew then and tells me now that even today he appreciates that this was Clough's way of toughening him up. He warned him, 'You can't let small-minded people like that disrupt you 'cause I'll pick someone else and you won't make a career.' Anderson didn't and because of that he did – thanks at least in part to Brian Clough's unorthodox man management.

Anderson made thirty-eight appearances for his country. Competition on the pitch from the likes of Phil Neale and Mick Mills rather than racism off of it limited his England career. He could never have foreseen that only twenty-four years after he became the first black player Darius Vassell created a different England record. The Villa striker came on as a sub for Michael Owen in Japan's Shizuoka Stadium against Brazil. It meant that for the first time in England's history there were six black men, the majority of the team, in their nation's white shirts. This was true for one minute and one minute only. After a few seconds, Sven-Goran Eriksson's desperate search for an equaliser saw Teddy Sheringham replace Ashley Cole. But history had been made.

Paul Canoville never played international football but the man who came to his rescue did. Pat Nevin was an unknown teenager who had recently arrived in an unnoticed £95,000 transfer from Clyde. Canoville and Nevin hit it off straight away. Canoville told me that he marvelled at Nevin's football skills.

> Pat was unbelievable, this little wee guy that nobody had heard of. He was like an icon to me. God, if I had his skills or if he had my speed. Wow! He was OK Pat, we exchanged music, he introduced me to the tunes of Cat Stevens. I really did respect Pat.

All of this despite Nevin not yet being a career footballer. He had just finished his second year as a student at Strathclyde University. While his friends went off on their long summer break, Nevin headed to London on a two-year footballing sabbatical. I have known Pat for many years and we have played together in charity football matches; including anti-racism games. Like Canoville, I am always amazed by how the ball sticks to his feet. I don't think I have ever won the ball from him fairly. He is also a ubiquitous type of character. Suitably, when we meet up to talk about his memories of that game, he suggested we have lunch in Glasgow's fashionable West End. Most cities have these types of restaurants; where everyone speaks in polite whispers, where there is too much cutlery on the table, small portions and big prices, and when you leave you feel like popping into the chippy round the corner to fill up. But it seemed like the entirely natural location to interview this soccer sophisticate.

We chatted about the arts, politics and football. When we got round to his time at Chelsea, I was hoping that he would be open. But I was stunned by some of the things he told me.

But perhaps football shouldn't have been surprised about Nevin's actions. He had form not just in a footballing sense on the pitch but also off it for standing up for his beliefs. In an earlier game away at Cardiff, he heard racist chants from the Chelsea end. Instead of ignoring it, he stopped the ball under his foot and halted the game. He even remonstrated with the fans at one point and kicked the ball out of play in a vain attempt to embarrass them into shutting up. These earlier protests appear to have been missed by the media.

Of that late afternoon at Selhurst, he reflects:

> I was getting more and more sick of the racism. A couple of times before that I had heard racist comments from our own fans. I wasn't looking for a moment to make a statement but when it happened at the Crystal Palace game I hadn't been in the team that long. For some reason the fans had really took to me, which doesn't make sense 'cos I was known as a Leftie and so clearly they weren't all right-wing hoodlums. It was just a minority. But that night at Crystal Palace I felt it beforehand. There were racist chants going round. I was disgusted by the racist abuse. I quickly realised, Oh God, it's my own fans. When I saw that I was furious. I played the rest of the game and didn't talk to anyone else in the team about how angry I was.

Canoville knew nothing of his friend's actions until the next day. But he told me:

> When he scored that winning goal he had the chance to big himself up on TV and say, yeah, great goal, great game or whatever. No, that's not what he said. I think that's where he gained a lot of respect. He spoke out. I owe him a lot.

The shock waves of that shameful day at Selhurst Park were felt way beyond the Chelsea chairman's office. The reaction to

Pat was immediate and over the top. 'I didn't rush out and buy the papers but I knew there was a furore 'cos the manager and chairman called me in the next day. Manager John Neal was really good about it and wanted to make sure that I knew what I was doing.' He was also 'invited' to meet with the Chelsea chairman Ken Bates. As he headed for his office, he wasn't sure what his chairman would say or how he would respond. Pat had met Bates as part of his contract negotiations but they weren't close and it was unusual for him to be summoned. But during their meeting the lack of regular contact was more than made up for by the bluntness of the conversation.

Bates message was direct: 'You can't do this. It's not your place to do this.' The five foot two teenager stood up for himself and many others and announced, 'I can bloody say what I like!'

Nevin, by now warming to his cause, took the view that, while his chairman had the authority to threaten him, he probably didn't have the power. It was a brave guarantee-free gamble. He simply faced Bates down and said, 'Do you want to sack me, yeah, sack me?' Nevin recollects: 'He thought it was an act but he quickly realised it wasn't.' But Bates couldn't move against Nevin. He was popular with the fans and on the way to being voted Player of the Year. He was on buttons of a wage. His income didn't even cover his rent. It was only his win bonuses that meant he was earning more as a Chelsea first-team player than he was getting as a second-year student.

Nevin was relaxed about any Bates disciplinary action. He only had a year left on his contract and two years left in his university studies. He was already planning to head back home. 'He couldn't really annoy me 'cos if I walked out he would have lost his asset. This asset was telling him he was going to walk away. I was happier in Glasgow, I was happier as a student. So all the things came together. I had nothing to lose.'

And, if any proof was needed about the effects of Nevin's intervention, it came sooner than anyone could have hoped: at Chelsea's next home game. Nevin reveals that the response was not entirely spontaneous and was at least in part orchestrated – by him.

The fans always sing your name one after the other. You know how popular you are by who gets sung first. When we ran out for the next home game, I made sure that Paul Canoville, myself and Kerry Dixon and the better-known players all ran out together. They sang Paul's name first and that was it. I thought, Yes!

Even now as we chat over lunch nearly a quarter of a century later, the other well-heeled diners turn round as he excitedly proclaims the 'Yes!' as he shares the moment with the neighbouring tables.

Lawrie McMenemy, who was guiding The Saints to a record-breaking second in the old First Division that season, is full of admiration for the man half his size and these days a quarter of this Geordie's weight.

Too many people in the game foolishly shrugged their shoulders and didn't take it seriously. When I heard it, I would get out of the dugout and tell them to shut up. The amazing thing is that Pat was a kid, a strong-minded kid who could put words together. A stand had to be made as things were getting out of hand. You had to admire him 'cos not many people would do that.

And he is clear about how big an impact the little man's actions had.

What Pat did was an extreme measure. It made the majority of fans realise how wrong it was and I think it encouraged other people on the terraces to turn round and tell people to shut their mouths. He was taking a chance that the fellas having a go at the black lad wouldn't turn on him. What he was really saying is I don't care if you turn on me. You've got to admire him. Not many would do that and take the chance. Some would have supported the black lad in private in the changing room or training ground but he did it publicly. Pat helped change things and deserves huge credit.

But Nevin didn't really feel that he was ever in any danger. Instead, he still feels proud of the fans' response.

It had the reaction that I suspected all along. Chelsea fans weren't racist thugs but the silent majority were cowed by these idiots. But if you had a player on the pitch saying we weren't accepting it, then quite soon afterwards when the thugs started off their singing they started getting shouted down and that never happened before.

So, despite the reputation of some, Nevin is proud of the many. 'It was easy for me. I was on the pitch. I wasn't going to get hit but the decent fans were now standing up to them.'

So what was the impact on Chelsea, perhaps the most notorious club at the time? Who better to ask than one who followed in Canoville's footsteps and then went a giant leap further: Paul Elliot. While one Paul was the first black player to pull on the Chelsea strip, the other Paul was the first to try on the captain's armband. His is a story of a club and a game in transformation. He first came across Chelsea fans years before the Canoville–Nevin moment and it made him fear their reaction when he was thinking about signing for the club:

I recall as a young sixteen-year-old black boy playing against Chelsea and I remember some horrific abuse I received from

Chelsea supporters. But when I came back as Chelsea captain I thought, Wow! Look at this club as it is now. For me, it was a powerful defining moment in the face of a hundred years of history.

Elliot is in no doubt about the enormous importance of 'that match at Palace' in helping change his new club.

> Because of Pat's standing, he was a very kind and humble man. He has a mild-mannered temperament so if someone like Pat Nevin speaks up people always listen. It's an intrinsic part of Pat's demeanour. He is a bright, intelligent and thoughtful man. I think it was a very human thing.

The sad part of Elliot's admiration for Nevin is that he wasn't the only intelligent player but he was the first and for far too long the only one to speak up. A lot of savvy players and good men said nothing. The hardest question for many of them to answer, even today, is why did they let their teammates suffer throughout their silence?

Another conundrum from this period still persists. Why is it that no player who was targeted by their fellow pros is to this day willing to name the racists in their ranks? There seems to be a footballing *omertà* or an unwritten code of silence in a peculiar type of closed shop. Few will even name names privately and none will do so publicly. They grant their former tormenters an anonymity that their racism doesn't deserve. When I talked to Paul Elliot about it, he revealed that some ex-players have now apologised to him 'but fifteen years too late'.

Anyone who reads Canoville's book will be surprised by its emotional honesty. It is raw when he writes about his own weaknesses. But in one sense he is no different from the others. Because even in the book he pulled his most important punch.

That much became clear during our discussions. I was astonished by what he told me. The unwritten episode was as sickening as any in his book; probably more so when he explains that it involved a very well-known high-profile teammate. It's the true story of why he left Chelsea; and it had nothing to do with a loss of form, injury or any other run-of-the-mill reason. It is one of the most distasteful tales of how any footballer has ever left any club.

The incredible and violent events took place in the most unlikely of venues at a Chelsea pre-season training camp in the resort of Aberystwyth. After a night out, some of the players broke the strict curfew. They returned later than they should have after having drunk more than was sensible. The club management were waiting up for the players and gave them a real telling-off. One of those late back turned on Canoville.

He takes up the story that has been left out of his book.

Certain boys came back after the curfew. Some came back laced, drunk. We was laughing, 'You've just been told off, ha ha.' A certain player didn't like it and he basically racially abused me, he called me a 'black nigger'. I said, 'Sleep that off, I know you're drunk, sleep it off.' And he sneered back, 'Nah, come here, you black cunt.' I looked at some of the other players. What upset me, right, was that the two other first-team players had not stopped him and he said it a third time and I thought enough is enough.

Some of the other apprentices implored Canoville not to respond. But he thought: 'I'm not taking that shit, and I went straight in his face. "Say it again." And he did. So I knocked him out.' Canoville went to bed.

'I got up first thing next morning and thought, He's a team mate and he'll sleep it off, he'll realise what he's done. So I went down to the canteen on the last morning of the camp.'

The drunk from a few hours earlier came in just a minute later. One of the younger players queuing for breakfast with Canoville leaned over and whispered, 'Canners, you're not going to believe this but he's looking vexed up and he's got a golf club.' Astonished, he kept his back to the fast-approaching teammate and, with his pulse and mind racing, told the youngster, 'Just tell me when he's there, just tell me when he's there, just tell me when he's there.'

'Canners, he's here!'

'As I turned round, he's lifted the club up and I've had to block with the tray.' At that very moment, other players rushed in to prevent the two men who had played, laughed and celebrated together on the pitch from setting upon one another with a tray and a golf club in that bewildered Welsh canteen.

Chelsea acted and did so immediately in a way that still hurts Canoville.

After I calmed down, I was driven home by the club and England physio Norman Meadows while that teammate travelled in the coach with all the other team. I thought they're keeping us separated, that's cool. The next morning I got a call telling me not to report to the training ground and not to report to Chelsea. It was just left at that, I heard nothing.

The golf-club-swinging footballer with the hangover went unpunished. Canoville never played or even trained for Chelsea again. He told me that he only finally knew he was leaving Stamford Bridge when other clubs started to get in touch trying to sign him.

There's one more thing that came out in my conversation with 'Canners' – the other player's name. In what seemed like finally the relief at telling the full story he said much more than he had planned. He let slip the name of the footballer-cum-golfing assailant. He didn't even realise he had done it until I told him at the end of our interview that he had let it slip. His response was surprising. He wasn't annoyed with himself. He simply asked me in a matter-of-fact way not to quote that part of our interview. But in truth the identity of the player wasn't a surprise to me. Pat Nevin had named the same player weeks earlier during our lunch.

Nevin also shared with me an unsettling account of how Chelsea had supported their black players. It is an incredible insight not motivated by racism or confronting it but an exercise in conditioning the racists' target. In training, the Chelsea coaches called their young black players by two names – the one that appeared on the back of their shirt and the 'N-word'. What sounds like a racist boot camp had an entirely different purpose. Nevin takes up the story:

> I talked to one of the guys involved in it. He never struck me as racist but still I told him not to do it. And his reply really surprised me. 'We're doing them a favour. They're going to have to cope. They're going to get this from opposition fans and players. We're going to have to make it mean nothing to them so we're going to blast it at them. No use wrapping them in cotton wool. If we put them out in the first team and they walk about with tears in their eyes in their first game, that's no good to them.'

Nevin's dramatic intervention started something irreversible. The campaign continued to gather momentum. Herman Ouseley and the Commission for Racial Equality along with the Players Union set up anti-racism campaigns. New laws, action by the authorities and clubs, all-seater stadia, societal attitudes, police crackdowns, the commercialisation of the game have all helped. The work of the Football Supporters Association and the emergence of anti-racist fanzines also gave decent fans a rallying point. The influx of overseas players with up to a quarter of all the players in the English game being black meant that every team relied on its diversity to win. The emergence of the ecstasy-fuelled rave scene as an alternative focus for the football hooligans' energy also dissipated hooligans' interest and influence. About the same time, I'm told, the game also became respectable conversation in polite dinner-party company.

But despite progress at home many other European countries appear to be trapped in the Britain of the '80s. The most flamboyantly colourful footballing league in the world, Spain's La Liga is one that seems to see football in black and white. Things got so bad in one game away to Real Zaragoza that the great Samuel Eto'o started walking off in protest as the din of monkey noises poured down from the stands. He was only stopped by his teammates and coach Frank Rijkaard. But the former World Player of the Year refused to be silenced: 'We can't wait until some crazy fan jumps from his seat and kills a black player before measures are taken.'

Viv Anderson told me he shared Eto'o's anger: 'The FIFA fines are bordering on the ridiculous for racial abuse. If the fines were more stringent, the powers that be would wheedle it out.'

The continued ambivalence of international footballing authorities was shown again in 1994 when England were due to play Germany on 20 April – Hitler's birthday. German authorities planned the game for Nuremberg of all places, the city of the Fuhrer's infamous rally. After widespread protests, they switched the venue to the Olympic Stadium. When I speak to Nick Lowles from anti-fascist magazine *Searchlight*, he reveals that he called the FA's press office at the controversy's high point to voice his concerns about the likelihood of racist violence. The ever-helpful press office replied, only half in jest, 'Should I cancel a game in future because it's going to be on my birthday?' The game never took place.

Racism in British football may never be totally extinguished, but because of Nevin and the campaigns that followed it will never again be celebrated. But there are now age-old and some new issues in our game that just won't retreat on their own. Problems remain, including the lack of black managers and Asian players; homophobia persists and gay footballers appear to have a 'don't ask, don't tell' approach. It wasn't until late 2013 that Leeds United became the first team in Britain to sign up to the Stonewall iconic campaign 'Some People Are Gay, Get Over It' in their match-day programme. Islamophobia is filling the space vacated by the anti-Irish 'No Surrender' tendency on the fringes of the support of the English national team and among some clubs. Today, partly driven by the welcome progress in the Irish Peace Process and the continuing aftermath of 9/11, Islam has replaced Republicanism in the hierarchy of the racists' hatred.

But anti-Semitism is the hatred that has outlived all others and has inexplicably survived the Holocaust. It is also too common a cause in football stadia. Britain may have invented modern football but it didn't invent this, the world's oldest hatred. Tragically, football has offered it a home. Much of the anti-Semitism is aimed at Spurs. Until the mid-1980s, they were sometimes subjected to: 'The Yids are on their way to Auschwitz, Hitler is going to gas them again, no one can stop them.' Or 'Put a Jew, Jew, Jew, in the oven, gas mark two.'

The background to this of course is that Tottenham were thought of as a Jewish club and so they got all the anti-Semitic stuff hurled at them. Their fans decided they were going to ironically embrace a classic anti-Semitic insult and labelled themselves the 'Yidos' or 'Yid Army'. Peculiarly, one common chant from the White Hart Lane stands in recent years aimed at their own striker, who has publicly spoken about his Christianity, goes along the lines of 'Jermaine Defoe he's a Yido.'

Chelsea fan, comedian and author David Baddiel is perhaps the most outspoken critic of both the original hateful insults and the Spurs fans' response to them. When we meet up to talk about it, he arrives unexpectedly early after cycling through the darkness of a wintry London rush hour. We start by discussing the campaign video he has made with 'Kick It Out'. Its aim is to persuade all fans to renounce phrases like 'Yido'. He tells me that he and his older ('and much harder') brother had confronted the anti-Semitism of those they sat among at The Bridge. But he's also scathing of Spurs fans, especially non-Jews who scream 'Yido!' about themselves.

> It's not in their right as a non-Jewish football fan to say to me as a Jew that you are allowed to say the word Yid. I hate the banning of words. But why is it that the Y-word is allowable? Is anti-Semitism a second-class racism? Tottenham are not a Jewish club. Let's say there are 5 per cent Jews at White Hart Lane at any one time; that would be a fuck of a lot of Jews because there are 0.02 per cent of Jews in Britain and it's on a Saturday (or Shabbat, the Jewish Sabbath) so some won't go. Five per cent would be a really high estimate but even that means 95 per cent of people supporting Tottenham are not Jewish and they are using a race-hate word.

And it's not just the arithmetic of it all that frustrates him, it's the stupidity. 'They are not allowed to reclaim a race-hate word. It just doesn't make any intellectual, moral or logical sense.'

However, the most targeted club isn't Spurs but Ajax, whose supporters are even more likely to describe themselves as 'Yids'. This club, in the city of Anne Frank, is the focus of football's Jew haters from across the entire continent. In a match against Utrecht, their fans struck up what may be the sickest chant in the entire history of the sport when in rehearsed unison they sang, 'Hamas, Hamas, Jews to the Gas!' And it isn't even confined to the supporters. In 2011, Den Haag midfielder Lex Immers was caught on video singing, 'We're going to Chase the Jews' at a post-match party to celebrate beating Ajax. Things have become so bad that the Ajax club president has implored their own most vociferous fans to put away for good their Israeli flags and stop singing the Hebrew folk song 'Hava Nagila'. The club have also decided to remove the Star of David from the VIP entrance to the Amsterdam Arena and no longer sell Israeli memorabilia.

So, while Spurs occasionally and Ajax regularly are the target of hate chants, who exactly are the worst anti-Semites in world football? Well, that prize must go to Slovakia's Slovan Bratislava. In recent years, some of their fans have displayed banners in the stadium to mark the anniversary of the birth of Adolf Hitler. They also adorn shirts with the innocent enough appearing squad number eighty-eight on it. What most fans don't realise is that this is another sick salute to their Nazi hero. The number eight celebrates the eighth letter of the alphabet twice over as a tribute to Heil Hitler.

While progress has been made against racism, all of these hatreds need to be challenged. But how? The clue to the answer may come from the most unlikely of sources – in the guise of the Chelsea of old. Back then, the idiocy of the songs of Chelsea's racist minority shamed a sport. The celebratory chants of the sensible majority of 'There's only one Pat Nevin' idolised an exceptional player and a brilliantly brave teenager. But that song also proves a contemporary dilemma. Today's campaigns need a new champion. In the face of football's residual hatreds, it's time for someone else to take a stand. It's time for a second Pat Nevin.

Liverpool's Mark Wright and Nottingham Forest's Teddy Sheringham in an aerial duel during the first game ever broadcast on Sky Sports.
© *Press Association*

Chapter Nine

The Saving of Rupert Murdoch:
Nottingham Forest v Liverpool, 1992

When we did a launch party we did it out at Osterley. We didn't even have a pavement. I had to lay down planks of wood for people so they didn't have to walk through the mud. I actually had to put a mobile control studio at the back of the real one because the real studio wasn't ready and we couldn't control things properly. Nobody from the British establishment came to the launch.

AS UNLIKELY AS it sounds, that's the true story of Day One at Sky TV, as told to me by the then Sky chairman Andrew Neil.

The venture was expected to fail. So how did an organisation without a pavement or even a proper TV studio go on to become the dominant British football broadcaster? How did they manage not just to report the news but also to make the news by using their global reach to impact upon world events? No matter what your views are about Rupert Murdoch, it's beyond doubt that Sky transformed football. But football turned Sky the brand into what it is today. It now has a global calling card in the corridors of power. Football gave the broadcaster a reach that no other sports and news outlet could compete with.

It all started at 4 p.m. on 16 August 1992. That's when

241

Liverpool visited the city ground to take on Nottingham Forest in the first Premier League game ever broadcast on Sky. It was a clash of two of the great characters of the game, Brian Clough and Graeme Souness. A Forest team that included Roy Keane, Nigel Clough, Stuart Pearce and Teddy Sheringham dominated the visitors. First-choice keeper Bruce Grobbelaar was away on international duty with Zimbabwe and was replaced by his understudy, the future England internationalist David James. The debutant made a string of saves from Clough and Keane.

As the teams came out of the tunnel, the Sky commentator Martin Tyler proudly announced, 'Good afternoon, everyone. A new league, alterations and amendments to the very laws of the game, even a different button to push on your television set.' David James thinks back to his first team appearance:

> My debut for Liverpool, against Nottingham Forest, was Sky's first live Premier League game. That day I was nervous enough just making my debut, never mind the lads saying don't have a beast because you'll spend the rest of the week watching reruns of your mistakes on the telly.

In the twenty-ninth minute, Scott Gemmill gathered the ball and swept it out to Teddy Sheringham at the corner of the box. Referee Mike Reed waved away the offside claims of the three-man Liverpool defence. Ignoring the unmarked manager's son in the box, Sheringham struck a lovely right-foot shot high beyond James's left hand. James acknowledges that, after making 'a triple save right at the start of the game', as Sheringham shot, 'I pushed off with my right foot instead of my left foot...'

Liverpool joined Manchester United and Arsenal as the fancied teams to lose their opening weekend fixture. The majority in the 20,000-strong crowd in the City Ground went home happy with a deserved 1-0 win. James, who was one of Liverpool's best performers that day, concludes, 'It was TV history but I didn't think about that at the time. Sky still seemed like the unknown and no one could say if it was really going to take off.' But it did. And, as we all know, football would never be the same again.

Andrew Neil today enjoys his status as something of a broadcasting institution. An eventful career has seen him launch a satellite TV network, edit national newspapers and anchor BBC political programmes. Like most people in politics, I've crossed swords with him on air. His combative style means that I haven't always got the better of him. But, like some adversaries, once the camera has stopped recording, he can be entertaining company. I was pleased it was that version of Andrew Neil who turned up when we reversed roles and I interviewed him.

We launched four channels in 1989. We turned Sky into Sky One that was the entertainment channel. Sky News was invented from scratch, Sky Movies was the latest movies and all we had for a fourth channel was a deal with Eurosport which was a conglomeration of public service broadcasters and they had certain sports broadcasting rights. We didn't have the money to set up our own sports channel. We had spent so much money on the movies like £600 million in 1989 and Sky News cost a tonne of money too and we had to buy in some new programming for Sky One, which until then kind of did endless repeats of *Lost in Space*! You know that was all it did and then we got Sky One and I brought *The Simpsons* over as well as *Married with Children*. So we always knew we needed a sports channel but we didn't have the money to do so. Murdoch had the view, he's really not interested in sport, but he saw the business opportunity. You know Murdoch doesn't follow cricket, he doesn't follow football, he only goes to the SuperBowl in America.

Neil confirms that sport wasn't the company's Plan A.

> The business model to begin with, what we thought would drive the sale of the dishes, was the chance to watch the movies that only came out in the cinema six months before uncut and with no commercials. Because in the early days that was the driver of HBO in America. Remember at that time you had to wait three years to see a cinema movie on terrestrial television. So that was the original business model but sport was always at the back of our minds and the Eurosport was really just there to keep us ticking over, it was pretty mundane stuff.

The launch cost £100 million and carried the boastful slogan of 'New World of Freedom'. It hardly felt like a new world. They got underway with an interview with the no longer box-office Dolly Parton. Eurosport was worse; they began with tennis. Even though this is a book about football that isn't meant to be a kick at tennis. This wasn't tennis à la Wimbledon or the French Open but a Davis Cup rubber between Italy and Sweden. Next on the schedules was bobsleighing, a sport of skill and genuine bravery (and with *Cool Runnings* the subject of a passable movie), but it was hardly the broadcasting freedom that paying customers had been promised. And things were to get even worse later on in that disastrous first week; subscribers had to endure a Baltic Cup hand-ball competition.

It's hardly surprising that the launch was a flop. Some shops only had a single dish in stock, which they put on display, leaving them with none to sell. By June, Sky was losing Murdoch £2 million a week. A mini-respite came not from bobsleigh but from the cricket Down Under. Sky managed to add 26,000 new subscribers from the 1992 Ashes, meaning that they were now in one in eight homes.

By 1990, both of the UK's two satellite companies, Sky and British Satellite Broadcasting, were floundering. Out of necessity, they merged to form British Sky Broadcasting. But Rupert Murdoch was still losing a fortune. David Conn, the *Guardian* journalist, describes how 'In February 1991 Murdoch's company came within minutes of being put into receivership, before 146 banks finally agreed a tough £4.2 billion refinancing package.'

The lesson the company took from the Ashes was that it was compulsory to give sports fans what they want and they'd be willing to stick a satellite dish outside their bedroom window to get it. From now on, that meant keeping away from the Baltic Cup hand-ball. They needed to urgently get the sports people liked onto the screens, before the company was dragged under.

Andrew Neil takes up the story of how Sky and football became synonymous.

I remember Murdoch saying to me that there are really only three sports that matter in Britain and its football, football and football. He knew that and he knew that's where the money was. He also had this view, he looked at the way that American television covered American football with incredible camera angles and great razzmatazz and he wanted to do that in Britain rather than the BBC pedestrian way of covering football. And he thought they could do a wonderful job and he brought over this guy from Australia who had revolutionised cricket coverage in Australia. And suddenly they packed in a lot more cameras than the BBC would use. And he always thought if you could give it proper coverage, if you gave it proper money, you could take it away from being a kind of slum sport and make it much more an all-seater game where women turn up as well; and that was the dream. Add on to that that, on our first idea of movies, the widespread use of DVDs and other ways of seeing movies was beginning to catch up. Movies stopped being such a significant dish-driver. The Premier League would become the dish-driver. You add all that together and you found the money to do Sky Sports. So Eurosport was canned as far as Sky was concerned and Sky Sports was launched entirely on the back of the Premier League. That was all the time I was there. After I left they began to up the ante. The government introduced all manner of new rules like it had to be all-seater stadia after Hillsborough. So the clubs needed the money and decided to put their rights out to contract.

In 1992, BSB offered £191.5 million. Simon Banks, the author of *Going Down: How the Game Went from Boom to Bust*, wrote: 'Few now doubt that had Sky not won the bidding war, it would have failed to establish itself as the dominant pay-TV platform.' He is in no doubt why Sky were so determined to win the auction: 'When the bidding for the Premier League rights was opened, it really was a matter of life and death for Rupert Murdoch's nascent platform.'

BSkyB defeated a peculiar offer from the Swiss Bank Corporation for a joint venture with the Premier League underwritten by the bank. BBC didn't try for the live rights. But ITV got involved with a £165 million bid for five years of thirty live games a season. The BBC was reduced to joining forces with BSkyB to see off their old foe. In their joint proposal, Sky offered £191.5 million and the BBC topped it up with a £22.5 million highlights tender.

The 1992 deal contractually obligated Sky and the BBC to bid again for the next round in 1996.

Four years later, they seemed delighted that it did. Sky bid an incredible £670 million for the live rights to sixty matches over each of the subsequent four years. The BBC tripled their highlights tender to £73 million, defeating ITV's £66.5 million offer. The combined value of the bid was now £743 million. The results were immediate. Within the first year, losses of

£47 million morphed into profits of £62 million, £170 million in 1994, £237 million in 1995 and £315 million in 1996. Sam Chisholm, the former BSkyB Chief Executive who took over when the company was losing £10 million per week, said that football had been the 'turning point' for Sky. He claimed that Murdoch, would have bid double to get his hands on football. Almost overnight, Sky also transformed football clubs' finances. In the 1991–92 Premier League season, the clubs' combined incomes totalled £162 million. In the next season, which was the first of the Sky contract, clubs' finances rocketed to £201 million.

But there was a potential killer blow against Sky when the Office of Fair Trading launched its investigation into uncompetitive practices. The complaint was that only those who subscribed to satellite could watch. But Mr Justice Ferris controversially adjudged that, while the contracts were restrictive, there were benefits to football because money flowed into the clubs and the sport.

What surprises Andrew Neil is that a pay-per-view contract was awarded in the first place.

> The regulatory thing that surprised even the Americans was that the British government allowed the national sport to go onto pay TV. No one had ever done that before. In America the NFL is on the networks CBS or ABC and so on. If you tried to do that in America, there would be an outcry. The NFL is still a Sunday-afternoon event on a BBC- or ITV-type channel. They never thought Murdoch would get away with that.

Sixty-seven Labour MPs thought he shouldn't and tried to stop him by signing a motion in Parliament condemning the ending of free-to-air football. When I spoke to Professor Ralf Negrine from Sheffield Hallam University, he shared the sentiment that Sky

...helped bring English football and cricket to a global audience and in the process these sports have made Sky stronger. But in the same way that Sky may have changed the nature of the game, it's not left the sport intact. It's no longer a community sport, it's much bigger, it's much more exciting. The way that sport has been developed under the wing of Sky has created it like a commodity like a bar of soap, you sell it as an exciting commodity.

Warming to his theme, Professor Negrine tells me:

What it's done in some ways is it's excluded the majority from having access to it on their television sets. It's improved the game possibly, saved it possibly with all the money; changed it possibly but then excluded it from the majority of the public ... but in a way if you make a deal with the devil you will sell your soul to it.

To this day, I have managed to avoid Sky's embrace.

Andrew Neil speculates at a wider motive behind the government's agreeing to the switch to Murdoch and away from terrestrial TV.

It may have been because the Tories are friendly to him or whatever because it never became an issue that they allowed the national sport to go onto a pay for channel. Now you just accept it, don't you? Murdoch saw it as an opportunity to bring American standards of stadia to Britain, to change the whole nature of people who went, to jazz up the coverage, have almost American-style presenters and he saw they could make a tonne of money out of that and in the process change the game forever. I never saw it and he didn't see it either. We knew this was going to make a huge difference, I don't think we ever thought that the English Premier League would become the world leader. I don't think we ever thought that.

But by the time of the third contract in 2000, Sky had six million paying customers and were able to shatter the £1 billion barrier. But even though Sky had survived the OFT inquiry, the advance of football TV wasn't without major setbacks. In 2000, NTL pulled out of its £328 million deal to show forty-four British matches each year for three years. Add to that the collapse of ITV Digital and the demise of Setanta, and it's clear that this was still a risky business model at these inflated prices.

All of this is light years away from the original competitions in the British media. Those who lived through the birth of ITV as a rival to the BBC thought they were experiencing a revolution. Some welcomed it more than others. At the time of ITV's birth in 1955, it all felt pretty dramatic. Lord Reith, the first chairman of the BBC, had argued in a passionate speech in the House of Lords, 'And somebody introduced smallpox, bubonic plague and the Black Death. Somebody is minded now to introduce sponsored broadcasting into this country ... Need we be ashamed of moral values, or of intellectual and ethical objectives? It is these that are here and now at stake?' But in hindsight, compared to the energy of subsequent events, it was more of a glacial speeded evolution. Since its creation in 1922, the BBC enjoyed a three-decade-long broadcasting monopoly. The newly launched commercial rival struggled against the most experienced TV network on the planet; they had no reputation to trade on and limited resources to invest in sport.

Perhaps we shouldn't have been surprised that ITV could only take unsteady baby steps to start with. It's hard to believe, but the BBC had itself gone through the growing pains against a bigger and more established rival. Long before television, BBC or otherwise, BBC radio was confronted by the powerful instinct of self-preservation from the totally dominant newspaper industry. Since the nineteenth century, sport has been an important driving force for the newspaper and magazine industry. Among the first titles to be launched after the 1855 abolition of newspaper stamp duty were national sporting titles. By the end of Queen Victoria's reign, newspapers knew that spending money on sports coverage was a great way to grow circulation. That was the logic that guided newspapers' first large expenditure on the newly introduced telegraph technology. They wanted to break the news about England's cricketing fortunes in Australia the morning after a Test Match rather than waiting for the results to arrive weeks later by ship.

In the 1930s, the newspaper owners tried to persuade the government to ban radio from broadcasting any sporting results. They were terrified that their sales would be decimated. Until now, there had only been two ways to find out how a favourite football, rugby or cricket team had got on: attend the game or buy a newspaper. Most people relied on the print media as their first and only source of results. The proprietors insisted on a 24-hour broadcast news black-out. As incredible as it may seem, they were insisting that the BBC would withhold their results service until after their readers had had the chance to see the match reports in the newspapers the following day. It's the type of wartime news management that became necessary within a decade; but to their credit the government faced down the commercial interests of the print media. The BBC had won the day.

Radio and newspapers quickly found ways to co-operate to bring sport to life. Most people had never been to or even seen a football stadium nor a horse-racing track. In a pre-television age, they had no picture in their minds or sense of perspective. The early stuffy, emotion-free formality of the first BBC radio broadcasts were pretty one dimensional and added little colour. It must have sounded like the Radio Four shipping forecast on a particularly mild summer's day. The BBC and newspapers worked together on the creation of sports graphics. They would be printed in the morning newspapers. The new coded graphics would at least give listeners a sense of the layout of the course or contest. For the earliest football commentaries, a map of the pitch, divided into squares, was published in the *Radio Times*. In what felt like the cutting edge of modernity, families would huddle round as dad clutched the newspaper or *Radio Times* at the table. They would then track the ball as the radio commentator announced who was in possession and which squares the ball was travelling between. Many sports fans believe this to be the origin of the now widely used phrase 'Back to Square One.'

But, with further technical advances and following the 1925 Crawford Report, the BBC was able to carry its first outside broadcasts and commentaries. But conscious of the newspapers' concerns, the BBC tried to meet them halfway. They self-regulated by suggesting just four initial broadcasts. The historian Asa Briggs captured the restrictive nature of the BBC's ambitions when outlining their wish-list:

> a running story on the first half of an England versus Scotland rugby match, a coded narrative of the Boat Race (the key to the code as well as the plan of the course having been published exclusively in the early papers that day), a coded narrative of the Cup Final and broadcasting of various sound impressions of Derby Day.

The BBC eventually took their new technology to the Grand National, the boat race, university sport contests, Wimbledon, amateur golf and rugby union in that first year.

Sport and broadcasting were disrupted by the war. But, when normal service returned in 1946, BBC Radio faced a new and formidable foe that would eventually overpower it. And it didn't come from another company or a freshly reinvigorated newspaper industry. Instead, it came from within its own organisation – BBC TV. But it was a slow start for television as Gordon Ross makes clear in *Television Jubilee*, his book to mark twenty-five years of BBC TV:

Television was at first very much the poor relation. The coronation in 1937, the victory parade in 1946, and the 1948 Olympics were major outside broadcast events that did a lot to publicise the medium (of television) and probably boosted set sales, but it was the 1953 coronation that marked the significant breakthrough.

The viewing figures prove Ross's point. In 1937, Sunderland beat Preston North End 3-1 in the first live televised FA Cup final. So sparse was the television population that barely 10,000 watched at home. Trevor Francis was the first £1 million player but in 1950 the first million-viewer game was Arsenal beating Liverpool 2-0. And by Queen Elizabeth's coronation year, ten million watched Blackpool beat Bolton 4-3 at Wembley.

For most people in the 1950s, watching TV and watching the BBC felt like the same thing; until 1955, it was the only thing. But even after ITV's birth, the BBC dominated everything in the way that, four decades later, Sky Sports seemed to monopolise British football coverage. In 1950, there were 340,000 TV sets in Britain; just one in fifty families had a television. Within four years there was almost ten times that number. Within five years of ITV launching, 82 per cent of the population had access to a television. Those with a television were mesmerised. In the face of their first rival, the BBC remained confident of its 'BBC for Sport' catchphrase.

Looking back at the BBC's coverage, perhaps they should have lengthened their slogan to force it to tell a truth. It's hard not to think that 'Sport for BBC Senior Executives' would have been a better description. The company appears to have covered those sports that their executive elite had played at their private schools and ancient universities. Reading back through the lists of those first few years' coverage, it looks like the management had opted to stick with the games they had played, knew and loved. Hence the Oxford v Cambridge Boat

Race was considered part of the core business. By contrast, greyhound racing, a genuinely mass participation sport of the 1950s with 200,000 people a week going along to one of the more than 200 dog-tracks, was shunned.

The head-to-head between the two terrestrial channels was as much competition as anyone really ever expected. The BBC's *Grandstand* and ITV's *World of Sport* were four-and-a-half-hour marathons, by far the longest programmes on the box. Confronted by the more nimble ITV, the BBC sometimes behaved like the worst of the old nationalised monoliths. Having fought the newspapers in the 1930s for the right to announce the football results, they were about to surrender it. This time it wasn't the newspapers who wanted to cut the BBC off, but the BBC itself. The *Children's Hour* programme was due to run until 5.45 p.m. and, for it to be an hour, *Grandstand* was cut before the football results were in. Paul Fox, who was planning *Grandstand* in 1958, argued:

> Quite frankly, unless we can give the results as they come in and stay on air until five o'clock to present them in tabulated form, the programme is not worth doing at all. I see this as a sports news programme and I do not see how we can go off air at the very moment the news of the day is happening.

Despite Fox's protestations, the BBC hierarchy forced *Grandstand* to end by 4.45 p.m. Bizarrely, the BBC gifted to ITV the monopoly that all those years earlier the corporation had seized from the newspapers. After months of plummeting audiences, *Grandstand* was allowed to devour a quarter of the *Children's Hour*.

ITV also proved to be the better innovators. BBC's *Grandstand* was like a conveyer belt – if you were willing to wait, you would eventually see what you were looking for. ITV introduced five discrete sections. The ITV company

London Weekend Television invested £60,000 on their first ever slow-motion sports replay machines. To maintain their momentum, they hired in the opinions of the former Fulham footballer Jimmy Hill, who became the first recognised football analyst.

By the late 1950s, the decades-long templates for football programming was established – Saturday-afternoon coverage, Saturday-night highlights and the midweek magazine programme. *Sports Special* was the first Saturday-night football programme. The publicity for the launch programme almost marvelled at its own ambition by boasting it would broadcast: 'Up-to-the-minute coverage of the best in today's sport. Aeroplanes, a helicopter and a fleet of cars and motorcycles are standing by to rush personalities to the studios.' But contractually it was limited to a miserly fifteen minutes of football coverage per show. Budget controls meant that none of the planes, helicopter or cars was asked to get Scottish football to the London studio; and the north of England footage didn't always arrive in time to be shown.

All of this was light years away from everything that had gone before. In 1960, ITV offered just £15,000 a year for ten years for live coverage. Clubs were worried about the impact of live football on attendances. The bigger sides wanted the biggest slice of what, at the time, was considered a broadcasting cake. The clubs couldn't agree on what, in hindsight, looks like a dispute over who got to peck at the biggest crumbs.

In 1964, the BBC offered £3,000 for the right to show highlights on a Saturday night; the money was to be split between all ninety-two English league clubs. The offer was accepted and *Match of the Day* was born. But there was one strict condition inserted into the contract at the clubs' insistence. The broadcaster had to keep it a secret which of the games they were to feature. That way, the clubs would share out the £3,000 and the paying punters wouldn't be put off from turning up. Over ten million viewers tuned in. The following year, the clubs got to share twenty times more but it was still a paltry £60,000. In 1983, the BBC and ITV agreed to pay £4.6 million for ten BBC Friday-night games and ITV showing ten Sunday-afternoon matches. Each club got £28,261. On 2 October of that year, Spurs beat Nottingham Forest 2-1 in the first game under the new improved contract.

By the 1970s, BBC Sport had started to lose out to ITV. Hard to believe now, but ITV's advantage was driven by their Saturday-afternoon *World of Sport* focus on wrestling. This wasn't the glory or glamour of today's WWE, but the amateur efforts of the near-comic-book characters from my childhood including 'Big Daddy' and 'Giant Haystacks'. Despite its ham-fisted dreadfulness, it somehow captured the mood of the moment and the affections of the five million viewers. Not even the massive influx of new money from the more expensive colour TV licences could halt the BBC's slide.

As well as giving very large sums of money to the game itself, Sky have also invested in technology and production standards of broadcast television football. And, if you look at the way Sky cover matches, it has changed the nature of sports coverage on the BBC. There are very few people, either in the BBC or ITV, who don't acknowledge that they learned a lot from how Sky did sport. Sky recognised that the new possibilities of subscription TV meant they had unlimited time when compared with the terrestrial broadcasters who were fixed to their tight schedules. In those days, they had only a limited number of channels.

Tim Luckhurst, the Professor of Journalism at the University of Kent and former journalist, explains:

What is astonishing and perhaps one of the things that differentiates Sky from News Corporation's newspaper titles in this country was the extent that they were prepared to spend on it in order to do it. They could have simply taken the view 'We don't have to do this particularly well' because the fact that we do it all is a huge advantage over the BBC, which of course doesn't have enough air-time to do it properly and could alienate part of its audience if it dedicated an entirety of BBC2 or BBC1 to football coverage.

Today it's not yet clear how Sky will respond to the twin threats of the drama and movies offered by Netflix and BT Sport's football ambitions.

Andrew Neil, a self-confessed football agnostic, adds,

Sky Sports hasn't only transformed the way that football is funded and covered. It has also impacted upon the way we see our news. BSkyB now has a market capital of about £14 billion and throws off almost £1 billion in free cash every year. I mean, it's a huge cash generator and the sport in general and football in particular is such a big part of it. We never thought we were building a global brand. That wasn't the aim at all. Sky News is now seen in seventy countries and they haven't globalised it yet. There was talk about producing a Sky News global but Murdoch's view was: fuck this, there isn't enough money in Sky News. It's in seventy countries. It's pretty much everywhere you want it. I don't know if it makes any money but it's created a brand.

For a long while, other than the Americans and CNN, it was the BBC and Sky News. So, if you wanted to see what was happening, you had to go to an American or British channel. It was a kind of soft power and the British Foreign Office understood that as well. And everybody else has watched that and, starting with the French, they said we have got to do that and it has to be in English and hence the French, German, Chinese, Japanese and Iranians all have English-language stations.

John Ryley, the head of Sky News, boasted probably with a degree of accuracy that it wasn't just on what we call the 'Arab Street' that Sky News reached near omnipotence: 'We are the first port of call for opinion formers, attached by civil servants in Whitehall, diplomats in the US State Department in Washington's Foggy Bottom, and by party officials in Beijing's Zhongnanha.'

In some ways, the inspiration for this chapter proves Ryley's point. I decided to write about how Sky had changed football, which in turn transformed Sky, after a meeting in the most unusual of places with the most unlikely of people – the President of Azerbaijan. We were in his cavernous office in Baku, the capital of the oil- and gas-rich central Asian republic. As I took a seat across from Ilham Aliyev, I had no idea what to expect. *The Economist* magazine had labelled this man's government as an authoritarian regime. His country was on a one-way journey down the democracy league table.

Back then, I was the UK Foreign and Commonwealth Office minister responsible for relations with central Asia. As part of my visit preparations, I had been warned that meetings with Aliyev could often be cold and abrupt. Many international visitors found it hard to even get into his office for a meeting in the first place. But I found it harder to get out. Our scheduled thirty-minute meeting overran then overran again. One of his sheepish assistants knocked gently on the office door in the corner of the room. My presidential host waved him away. I could almost feel the British ambassador pacing outside in the waiting room. She had prepared me on every detail of UK-Azeri foreign and energy policy. It turned out she would have been better simply giving me the football cuttings from that morning's British newspapers. Because, as our discussions went on way beyond the agreed moment of interruption, we were only just warming up.

We hadn't got round to talking about Nagorno-Karabakh, which in Foreign Office speak was a continuing 'frozen conflict'. Nor had we discussed whether the Nabucco pipeline, which was to take Azeri gas to Europe, would be routed through Russia, a potentially strategic problem for Europe if Moscow's mood ever led them to turn the switch to the off position. Instead, the one topic he was determined to debate was British football. Aliyev was fascinated by it. He appeared to know more about it than any President should have had time to. I had always known how the world tuned in to our football. I did it myself as a teenager, listening to the BBC World Service in South Africa. But sitting there, in that President's office, discussing the previous weekend's Premiership goal scorers was the moment when I finally realised that the English Premiership, courtesy of satellite sports broadcasting, was now much more than just a game. It had become a worldwide language all of its own. Like nothing else on our islands, it's a globally connected junction box of soft power and a currency in international relations. It entertains, fascinates and influences residents in the overcrowded slums of Nairobi, Manila and Soweto as well as the Presidents and Prime Ministers who govern over them.

Tim Luckhurst is also clear that it's the sports that helped and help make the news happen. 'I'm quite certain that Sky News is subsidised, I know it is subsidised, clearly it is subsidised by the profitable parts of BSkyB and the profitable parts of BSkyB certainly include football.'

In the interests of total transparency, Luckhurst happily tells me that Sky News pays for a single scholarship for a student at the University of Kent. But, much more interestingly, he talks about the impact of football on the politics of his travels.

When I covered the Romanian revolution in 1989 for the BBC *Today* programme, I crossed the border from what was then the Serbian part of Yugoslavia into Romania on Christmas Eve 1989 to cover the fall of Ceausescu. Among the first things I was asked by young Romanians who had never been outside their country before was about English First Division football scores. It's not wrong to think that Sky has spread it more widely as satellite broadcasting has made it more accessible but people used to listen to the football scores on the BBC World Service or on creaky long wave radio in parts of Eastern Europe behind the Iron Curtain in the 1950s. If you read Denis Healey on his trips to Germany in the 1930s, he talks about discussing football in youth hostels while the Hitler Youth were marching around outside. When I was nineteen, I rode my motorbike over the border from what was then Yugoslavia into Greece. We stopped and some guy saw our UK number plates and he wanted to talk to us about something. The first thing he said was: 'You English? You support Nottingham Forest?'

As a die-hard Partick Thistle fan who went to every match home and away when he lived in Scotland, Luckhurst jibed back, 'Oh, never heard of them! Did Forest beat Liverpool?'

There is a modern phenomenon of crowds acting up when the camera crews of live satellite news broadcasters appear. As the second jet crashed into the Twin Towers, Stuart Ramsay, chief correspondent for Sky News, decided to head to Pakistan and was there within twenty-four hours. He immediately travelled to the fundamentalist stronghold of Peshawar. Ramsay tells the story of being at a rally where indignant locals burned the obligatory American flags, promising jihad and death to Christians.

> Towards the end of the rally I saw a young masked man with eyes burning seemingly with hatred running towards me … I didn't want the crowd to turn on me … He approached quickly mouthing muffled words through his scarf as he tried to pull it down. I braced as he stood in front of me, finally releasing his mask, I was pretty scared. He smiled and in a

broad Yorkshire accent said, 'Bloody Sky News, great, me mum loves you and she'll see this – fantastic. I'm on a gap year from Bradford Uni. Nice to meet you.' And he turned and started shouting, 'God is great.'

When the satellite truck turns up, demonstrations are sometimes infused with a new energy, anger or volume. It's why, at the height of the uprising, the soon to be ex-Egyptian government accused global broadcasters of fuelling protests. But the impact of Sky, the BBC News channel and others can also influence the perceptions at the heart of the most powerful of governments. The tentacles of even the best resourced intelligence services can't be in all places at all times. Satellite TV crews will often have the best eyes on the ground. Sky News special correspondent Alex Crawford and her camera crew were first into the heart of Tripoli after the fall of Libyan tyrant Muammar Gaddafi. On that dramatic day in August 2011, she stood alongside the rebel fighters pounding against and then taking over Gaddafi's headquarters. After reporting the events, she said, 'Everyone was watching our pictures as the incredulity spread around the world ... first reaction from the US State Department, Downing Street, the UN ... it went on. We realised our pictures were having an impact but never anticipated the scale of it.'

Less dramatically, I remember visiting the military headquarters of one of the UK's closest NATO allies. We went deep underground inside an impenetrable mountain designed to withstand a Soviet nuclear attack. Here I was in the nerve centre of their emergency military response. Yet, even here, they told me that, when they had suffered one terrible attack, their intelligence services couldn't get to the scene quickly enough. Instead, they watched the unfolding tragedy via satellite TV on the bank of huge screens designed to monitor troop or fighter aircraft movements.

At the start of the Iraq War, Sky correspondent David Bowden commentated over live pictures throughout the American assault on the town of Umm Qasr, almost as though it were a football match. His coverage was broadcast live around the world, complete with 'pitch-side' interviews with the US commander on the developing battle.

Last word to Andrew Neil, who laughs, 'I loved it. I loved it. I loved doing something everyone said would fail!'

He's not alone: ten million Sky Sports subscribers agree.

The Hillsborough disaster remains the worst in British sporting history. As the news sank in, Liverpool's Anfield pitch disappeared under a carpet of floral tributes.
© *Mirrorpix*

Chapter Ten

'Justice for the 96!':
Liverpool v Nottingham Forest, 1989

'GOOD AFTERNOON. WELCOME back ... As you look around Hillsborough you will appreciate why it has been regarded for so long as the perfect venue for all kinds of important matches.' Those were the unfortunate words of welcome from the Sheffield Wednesday chairman in the match programme for the FA Cup semi-final.

Within minutes of reading those words, ninety-six Liverpool fans lay dead or unattended dying. Almost immediately a lie was concocted and repeated by police, politicians and the media in a sickening effort to blame the dead for their own death. The world was told that drunk Liverpool fans had broken in to the stadium, causing the crush that killed their own. The supporters robbed the dying while the police bravely fought to save them. But the world was lied to. This is the story of an event that is simultaneously Britain's biggest footballing disaster and one of the worst abuses of power in modern British history. This is the story of how a proud but temporarily weakened city took on the British establishment and won. In doing so, they defeated the oldest rule in journalism: that the truth can never catch up with a lie.

It was a lovely sunny spring afternoon in Sheffield as both sets of supporters made their way by car, bus and train north from Nottingham and east from Liverpool towards South

Yorkshire. Both sets of fans travelled with a genuine sense of optimism that this would be their year. But for some there was also a distant nagging doubt about their own safety. Those who had made the journey before knew that the ninety-year-old stadium was far from the perfect venue. Major incidents had been narrowly avoided in 1981 and 1987. The two teams met at the same venue, at the same stage, in the same trophy the year before. And just like in 1981 and 1987, there had been a close escape at the Leppings Lane end of the stadium when Liverpool fans narrowly avoided a crush at the turnstiles.

This record of near misses makes the police and authorities planning for the 1989 semi all the more inexplicable. There appeared to be a lazy, bordering on callous, disregard for the safety of the fans. The mindset of the time seemed to be that football fans were hooligans and the few decent supporters among their number just had to put up with it.

Decisions taken in the days running up to the fixture added to the likelihood of disaster. In a highly unusual move, the experienced Chief Superintendent Chris Mole was substituted just three weeks before the game. The calamitous decision was taken to appoint Chief Superintendent David Duckenfield as the new supervising officer. He hadn't worked at the stadium for a decade and hadn't policed the previous incidents. No reason was given or has ever been uncovered as to why an officer so experienced in policing Hillsborough was replaced so close to such an enormous match. No matter why it happened, it is undoubted that the decision had an enormous impact on the biggest footballing tragedy in British history.

On top of the anxieties about changing the top cop, it was also decided to cut the number of police on duty. Despite the worries about safety from the previous year, there were to be eighty-eight fewer police officers than the year before. The decisions to appoint the wrong senior officer and dozens fewer police were compounded by the pre-match security briefing. These meetings are standard procedure before every big game. I've attended a few of them. They are intended to analyse all possible incidents and flash points. While the pre-Hillsborough meeting rightly focused on safety, it emphasised the threat of hooliganism above all else and omitted any mention whatsoever of the possibility of crushing. Worryingly neither the Ambulance nor Fire Service attended the planning meeting. The year before, there had been a minor pitch invasion. This time around, officers were placed on their guard not to allow anyone to encroach onto the pitch. The operational order was crystal clear: 'No one is to be allowed access to the track from the terraces without consent of a senior officer except to receive medical attention.' Younger fans will have no experience of how fans were treated in the 1980s. As strange as it might seem today, they were caged in behind high steel fences, which were designed to be hard to climb over. The officers were instructed that the gates in the perimeter fence were to remain locked at all times unless a coded signal was given over the public announcement system.

Of course, for this FA Cup semi, there was no home team. The police decided on the division of the stadium based on motorway access routes into Sheffield.

Liverpool were allocated to the Leppings Lane end and the North and West stands. Nottingham Forest had the rest of the stadium, meaning the smaller club had the majority of tickets. Having made the allocation, the police failed to deal with the consequence of it.

South Yorkshire Police Superintendent Marshall was on duty outside the Leppings Lane end of the stadium. From an early stage, the lack of proper planning was having an impact. Before previous big matches police cordons were set up to check tickets, direct the supporters and minimise dangerous bottlenecks from building up. Disgracefully no effective system of that sort was put in place. Fans were being left to their own devices. He believes that, with a little more than a quarter of an hour to go before kick-off, his police force had lost control outside the ground. In his mind he thought that perhaps as many as 8,000 Liverpool fans were now caught up in an enormous crush. Such was the backlog of fans trying to get in, there was a vain attempt to delay kick-off to enable fans to see the start. But by the time it was received the players were already on the pitch and raring to go.

On the other side of the turnstiles inside the ground, police seemed to be even more negligent. Many modern-day fans have little experience of the old terracing. Supporters entered through the turnstiles and then stood wherever they could. Understandably they congregated where they would get the best view or atmosphere and in many cases that meant directly behind the goal.

In Hillsborough, the Leppings Lane end was divided into pens. On any normal day, once you were in a pen, it was very difficult to get out. For this semi, the police opted for a system where the fans were expected to 'find their own level' free from police or stewards' guidance. It was a 'you're on your own' attitude and 'nothing to do with us' policing. Fans were left to decide when the central pen was full. In Hillsborough the path from the turnstiles to the central pens behind the goals was through a narrow tunnel. As more and more fans arrived and tried to take up a place behind the goal, they began to pile more and more pressure on top of the fans already squeezed into place.

Trevor Hicks was originally a Middlesbrough supporter but became a Liverpool fan through marriage to wife Jenni. By the time daughter Vicki was five and Sarah was nine, all four of the London-based family had Liverpool season tickets. They drove up to the games most weeks. As they got older, the girls loved having their own season tickets away from their parents in Anfield's Kop. The family had driven up on the motorway from London and had a packed lunch in the car. Many of the cars and buses on the M1 next to them were full of Forest fans travelling north. Trevor told me that he had been at Hillsborough the year before for the semi-final and that their tickets were checked and re-checked and there was much more effective crowd control. As they approached the Leppings Lane end, they almost swapped tickets with the girls. Jenni went to her seat. As Trevor, Vicki and Sarah approached the tunnel leading to the central pens, Trevor told me that he said to the girls, '"Hang on a minute. I'm just going to get a coffee." They smiled at me and shot off down the tunnel as if to say, "We've escaped from our dad!"' That was the last time he ever saw their smiling faces.

Trevor took up his place in pen two, away from the girls, and was forced to watch impotently as every parent's nightmare unfolded in full public view. 'I knew there was something going wrong just before the kick-off. I was in pen two where the police box is. I called over to a police officer, "Look, can't you see what's going on?" And he told me to "shut my fucking prattle"!' Hicks, dressed in jeans and a leather jacket snapped back, 'If I had my managing director's suit on, you wouldn't have said that to me.'

'We had arranged to meet the girls at a nearby sweetie shop if there were any mix-ups or problems.' That meeting never took place. 'The next time we saw our daughters was when we went to identify the girls' bodies in the gymnasium.'

When I arranged to interview Trevor, I had decided that I wasn't going to ask him anything at all about his family's loss; I was going to stick to talking about the campaign for justice and the impact it had on Liverpool. I thought that the last thing he needed all these years later was a politician asking him about his heartbreak. But his personal answers to my wider questions about the campaign were impossible to ignore. He asked that I tell his story of that day.

I always thought that I saw Victoria passed over the fence. I was told several times I was wrong. I was told that she had been passed from pen three to pen two on to the field. Even though I saw it with my own eyes, when you're told for twenty years you're wrong, you question your own memory.

It wasn't until twenty-five years later that he finally discovered the terrible truth. That slight figure he had seen in the near distance being lifted over the perimeter fence all those years ago was in fact his dying daughter Victoria.

Outside, Superintendent Marshall was becoming increasingly agitated. Concerned that there may be injury or death outside, Marshall radioed the police control room inside the stadium. Unaware of the pressure already building inside the central pens, he asked that the exit gates be opened to allow spectators an escape from the bottleneck and a quicker entry. In a catastrophic failure of communications, police inside had little idea of what was happening outside. Police outside had no sense of the impact their request to open the exit gate would have on the fans already inside. Chief Superintendent Duckenfield could see into the already crowded central pen from the control room. But despite the obvious dangers he ordered that Exit Gate C should be opened. He had failed to see the fatal impact his decision would have on those already in the packed pen. Worried fans relieved to be free from the crush outside flooded in. From Superintendent Marshall's vantage point, he could see that the congestion outside had been relieved. Those outside, now free from a potentially dangerous crush, could again queue safely. With the possible danger avoided, the exit gates were closed again.

The Liverpool fans who entered through Exit Gate C now edged down through the tunnel towards the central pens. But it was hard and slow going and such was the force of numbers going in that entrance there was no way to back up out of the tunnel. Ever more fans who were unaware of the deadly pressure building up in front of them tried to move the only way they could – forward. Police Constable Smith who was on duty nearby would later give evidence in which he said that by 2.45 p.m. the tunnel from Gate C and into the central pen was already three-quarters full of supporters. He told the inquiry that none of his fellow officers was deployed at the tunnel entrance to redirect the newly arriving fans towards less crowded parts of the terracing.

Once through the tunnel, the pen was a sloping rectangle of confined space. Those who had arrived early couldn't move backwards because of the sheer pressure of those squashing in behind them. They couldn't move sideways because of the lateral fences preventing them shifting left or right into the neighbouring under-crowded pens. And they couldn't escape forward over the perimeter fence. Those who desperately tried to climb to safety were pushed back into the pen by police at the side of the pitch. Denied the chance of life-saving escape back, forward, left or right, some went up. Near the back of the terracing terrified fans pleaded for help from above; a fortunate few were plucked to safety by their fellow fans in the stands above them.

Even before kick-off, fans of all ages were shouting to the police that they were under pressure from behind, many were already finding it hard to breathe. The police officers just yards away, fixated on a threat of hooliganism, ignored them or worse still told them to stop complaining and keep quiet. The desperate pleas for help by those losing consciousness turned into angry screams from others aimed at what seemed like disinterested police. The louder the innocent fans who still had breath to shout did so, the more the police felt they were dealing with an outbreak of hooliganism. So fixated were they with hooliganism that at 3.04 p.m. there were calls by the police for police dogs and dog handlers. Some help seemed to be at hand as South Yorkshire Ambulance Service staff approached and looked at the scene through the perimeter fence. But the crowd's anger grew into a fury as the ambulance staff retreated. They had come to the same view that this was a dangerous outbreak of violence among the Liverpool fans.

Unforgivably, despite all that they could see and hear through the fence, the scale of the catastrophe doesn't appear to have dawned on emergency services until a full fifteen minutes after the match stopped. In a further sign of the scale of police failure, it was left to a Superintendent Greenwood to run on to the pitch to ask the referee to call a halt to the game. Tellingly, he did so off his own back without any instruction at all from the police control room, which had already lost all control.

There are many beautifully written personal accounts of the tragedy. I am not a Liverpool fan and wasn't in Sheffield in 1989. More importantly, I didn't lose anyone that day. As a consequence, this chapter's story of Hillsborough doesn't attempt to be what it's not. I make no attempt to replicate the painful writings of the devastated families. Instead, this is the telling of the story from the perspective of a small and unusual band of supporters; those fans there that day and who were later elected to Parliament. They have used their voices to stand against authority and get justice for those fellow fans they saw die. Derek Twigg is a true red in his football and his politics. He's the type of thoroughly decent person you can find in most political parties; no one and I mean no one has a bad word to say about him, ever. In 1989, he travelled to Hillsborough with three mates. He can remember that 'It was a beautiful spring day driving across the Pennines. Who could have known about the horror of horrors that was about to happen?'

He has vivid memories of the day, much of which are included in the official statement he gave to the police. He told me:

I was at the match and the police had already lost control outside. It wasn't something that just happened. It had been going on for ten, fifteen, twenty minutes beforehand. I got caught up in the start of the crush. When I got inside what drew my attention was how full the two centre pens were and how empty the other two were so close to kick-off. It's impossible, it is impossible for the police not to have seen and known that control was lost outside the ground and about the overcrowding in the two pens. I could see it a hundred yards away at the end of the North stand.

Twigg watched in horror. 'I remember seeing a body, just arms flopping over the side of the advertising board that was being used as a stretcher. They had soiled themselves. It was then that I knew that people were dying.'

At 3.21 p.m., the transcript of the ambulance control room's radioed conversation with ambulance station officer Paul Eason shows that he contacted them from his ambulance to declare 'a major incident'. But in another dreadful failure a 'major incident' was never declared. If it had been, a rehearsed disaster deployment of police and medical assets would have kicked in automatically. Aspects of the South Yorkshire Metropolitan Ambulance Service major incident plan, such as notifying nearby hospitals and the deployment of an emergency response team, were never enacted. Instead, people lay dying while many of their fellow supporters and some police officers spontaneously tried their best. Of course, there are always going to be uncertain moments immediately after a tragedy but what happened on the Sheffield pitch was of an entirely different order. On top of the complete failure in policing, there was sheer incompetence within the leadership of the Ambulance Service. Doctor Glyn Phillips who was there as a supporter said:

The supporters were now impatient and angry at the slowness of the response to the emergencies. There appeared to be only one or two stretchers on the pitch and one ambulance was making its way around from the far corner ... I then tried to find somebody in charge to tell me who to report to. I asked several officers but none of them knew ... By this stage I realised that there was no organised response and I was angry ... I came to the view that somebody needed to take an overview of the situation and began to go around all the casualties to appraise them.

As chaos reigned on the pitch, the agreed police code word 'Catastrophe' that would have alerted all emergency services to the seriousness of the event was never broadcast.

When those police officers still outside the stadium were finally summoned to get inside, Superintendent Marshall followed in the footsteps of the fans that had been waved through the exit gate. He entered the tunnel connecting Exit Gate C to the central pen and, as he did so, he couldn't avoid the injured and desperate supporters now heading in the opposite direction.

Because of the chaos, Derek Twigg didn't leave the ground until nearer the time of the anticipated full-time whistle. Travelling back with his shaken friends who had been in the Leppings Lane end but had avoided the crush, they listened to the car radio. It's strange what your traumatised mind retains but Derek recalls, 'As we were getting closer to Liverpool we was listening to the local radio and, instead of playing pop music, they had melodic sad music as you would expect when a monarch or great statesman dies. Liverpool's mood had already changed. That's always stuck with me.'

As news broke of the disaster, worried families were desperate to hear from loved ones in Sheffield. While they waited and waited for a phone call that never came, many organised travel across the Pennines to Sheffield. Once there, many started to congregate outside the gymnasium, which was acting as a temporary mortuary. Arrangements to allow families to see the deceased weren't finalised until later in the evening. Distraught relatives needed somewhere to wait. The local vicar asked that the key to the boys' club next to the police station be found and the centre opened. But this well-intentioned suggestion added to the families' sense of frustration. It was worse for wear with too few chairs and only one phone line. The club was overwhelmed by families as yet not confirmed as bereaved and inundated by well-intentioned volunteers adding to the sense of confusion. Many of the families still hoped that their relative lay injured and unidentified in a Sheffield hospital or better still had unknowingly passed them on the other side of the road travelling in the other direction as they made the silent journey to Sheffield.

Relatives were allowed to enter the gym from 21.30 p.m. It was the moment that their lives would change forever. As relatives waited outside hoping to recognise none of the eighty-four bodies, their quiet apprehension was shattered by the sound of a family member catching a first glimpse of their loved one. Inside the gymnasium, there was a policy of one body, one cop. A police officer stood over each of the deceased. Mothers and fathers were told that the son or daughter they had brought into the world were now the official property of the coroner and shouldn't be touched. Heart-broken families were then escorted by the police officer who had been standing over their relative's body and joined by a detective in another part of the gymnasium. There they were asked for basic family details but were also confronted by questions about their deceased's drinking habits and how much they had been drinking before the game. By night's end twenty bodies remained unidentified. Jenni Hicks told the *Mirror* newspaper on the twentieth anniversary: 'My then husband Trevor and I were on our knees, utterly devastated. We'd lost our daughters, we hadn't had so much as a cup of tea for hours but we were told we had to make a statement to police.' Trevor told me about that terrible moment: 'I knew there was something strange going on because the police asked us several times about how much the girls had been drinking.'

The authorities invested heavily in twin arguments aimed at keeping the blame away from their door. Part of the police blame game was that drunken late arrivals had battered down an exit and staggered their way into the stadium causing the crush. The second part of the self-preservation plan was that there was nothing that could be done after 3.15 p.m. that could have saved any of the deceased.

Post-mortems took place over the following two days on the ninety-four fans who were by that time dead. There are still unanswered questions about the determination to rush the enormous post-mortem process in this way. Nor is it clear why a process usually reserved for fatal car crashes was then used on each of the deceased. Blood samples were taken from all the victims, regardless of age, to ascertain the blood alcohol levels. It's as if standing at a football match required the same degree of self-control as sitting behind the steering wheel. In the following days when the ninety-fifth victim, Lee Nicol, a fourteen-year-old boy, passed away and he too had a blood alcohol measure test taken. A further attempt was then quickly made to smear the names of the deceased. Every one of the dead with a blood alcohol level above zero had their names run through the Police National Computer system. There was no recognised official reason ever given to undertake what was possibly an illegal endeavour. Even all these years later, no one is able to say why they went in search of criminal convictions among the as yet unburied dead. But in a police force driven by one single objective of avoiding blame very little seemed off limits – except the truth.

The inquest process was used and, reading through it, I would suggest abused to link the drinking habits of the deceased with their own demise. Insultingly, all but two of the mini-inquests started with the announcement of each victim's blood alcohol levels. Dr Jonathon Nicholl, an epidemiologist, told the inquests that those who arrived latest were more likely to have a raised blood alcohol level. The morning after each inquest, much of the media dutifully reported the alcohol level of each victim as though it was a compelling fact. By itself, it seems like a peculiar thing for a free press to do. But they were informed not just by the coroner's behaviour but by their own editorial line immediately after the disaster. Remember, many of them bought and repeated the police lie of drunken Liverpool fans; much of the press then joined in the police demonisation of the dead. Those immediate mini-inquests became another chance for the media to serve as cheerleaders, parroting the favoured theme of South Yorkshire Police of drunken Liverpool fans. Peculiarly, sections of the media then made that connection between each of the dead fan's alcohol level with the legal drink-driving limit. For the record, only fifteen of the dead were above the drink-drive threshold. But it was an utterly pointless but malevolently intended reporting. None of the fifteen had driven to the game. None had planned to drive home.

While the police concocted a concerted lie, there was one group of people who couldn't speak but who revealed the truth. The independent panel report into Hillsborough contains an explosive Chapter 5 entitled 'The Medical Evidence: The Testimony of the Dead'.

An international expert on alcohol testing, Professor Jones reviewed the evidence and concluded: 'The insinuation that many of the victims were drunk at the time of the disaster and thus too impaired through drink to respond to a novel situation and that this played some role in their death is unjustified.' He found that sixty-eight of the ninety-five who died during or in the aftermath of the disaster had undetectable alcohol levels; twelve had alcohol levels consistent with 'minor social disinhibition', nine would have had impaired rapid response and just six showed signs of being intoxicated. All of which exposes the lie and humiliated the liars who told Prime Minister Mrs Thatcher the day after the disaster of 'a tanked-up mob'. The surprise to many people reading those findings is that so few fans of any club had drunk so little in advance of such a big Saturday-afternoon game in the spring sunshine.

Ninety of the deceased died because of two types of asphyxia. Seventy-three from traumatic asphyxia, which is the compression of the chest preventing breathing; a further seventeen died from crush asphyxia. The coroner argued that nothing could have been done after 3.15 p.m. that could have saved any of the dead. He explained: 'As a marker, I picked the arrival of the first ambulance on the pitch, which was timed at 3.15 p.m., because on the overwhelming pathological evidence available to me, by that time permanent irreversible damage would have already occurred.' While that appears to have been generally accepted at the time by many people, it's no longer a credible assertion.

The coroner's view was that, no matter what that single ambulance or any other medical professionals could have done, none of those who died could have been saved. Families were told to simply move on with their lives as the establishment closed ranks around a lie. But just like the parents of Stephen Lawrence, the victim of a racist murder, the families of the ninety-six continued their campaign with a pride that South Yorkshire Police had long ago lost.

Hillsborough is of course the worst but not the first disaster at a British football stadium. Uniquely, Rangers' Ibrox stadium has suffered two. Firstly, in 1902, when twenty-five people lost their lives during a Scotland v England international. And in 1971, sixty-six Rangers fans died at the end of an Old Firm derby. And like Hillsborough, the 1985 fire at Bradford's Valley Parade stadium was captured by the television cameras. The inferno destroyed the old wooden stand and fifty-six fans' lives within moments. But even some of those who should have known better thought it acceptable to stamp all over the families' emotions. The chair of the Bradford Inquiry, Sir Oliver Popplewell, complimented the Bradford families by criticising those still heartbroken by Hillsborough. He compared the two:

> The citizens of Bradford behaved with quiet dignity and great courage. They did not harbour conspiracy theories. They did not seek endless further inquiries. They buried their dead, comforted the bereaved and succoured the injured. They organised a sensible compensation scheme and moved on. Is there, perhaps, a lesson there for the Hillsborough campaigners?

Trevor Hicks has campaigned alongside so many others for justice for his daughters; firstly for sixteen years as the chair of the Hillsborough Family Support Group and more recently as the president of the organisation. When I ask him about the passage of time, he laments:

> Some days it seems like an eternity and others it seems like the blink of an eye. This was never about a pursuit of compensation. But if someone is basically telling porkies about you including police officers, then you have to do what you know is right. The authorities thought they could get away with it. But they didn't and they won't.

When I ask him what I think is a stupid question of whether he has ever thought of throwing in the towel, I am surprised by his admission. 'Many, many times,' he says.

But when you know you're right, it just gives you great strength. And perhaps if the terrible dirty tricks campaign hadn't been run we might just have gone away much sooner. But they tried to besmirch those who died including our two daughters. We weren't ever going to let that happen.

Trevor and every relative were treated in an intrusive manner by a hungry media. In the immediate aftermath of the tragedy, they had decided that someone had to take the blame. While supporters were still struggling to stay on their feet to avoid being crushed underfoot, Graham Kelly, the chief executive of the Football Association, and Graham Mackrell, the Sheffield Wednesday club secretary, joined Chief Superintendent Duckenfield in the police control room. Both visitors were told that 'a gate had been forced and there had been an inrush of Liverpool fans'. Pointing on a police monitor at Exit Gate C that he had ordered open, Duckenfield told English football's most senior official, 'That's the gate that's been forced: there's been an inrush.' In good faith, Kelly repeated Duckenfield's report. By 3.40 p.m., TV broadcasters including the BBC's Alan Green were speaking of unconfirmed reports that 'a door was broken down...'

They had a ready-made scapegoat in mind – the Liverpool fans including the dead. Much of the media were only too willing to champion the police version of events. A local Member of Parliament, Irvine Patnick, and the chairman of the South Yorkshire Police Federation, PC Paul Middup, went further still. They alleged that Liverpool fans had deliberately arrived late.

Over the next few days, the news media rounded on the fans and the one-sided news was broadcast around the world. The Monday after the deaths, on the very day when the Liverpool players returned to the city to visit the injured fans in hospital, the local *Sheffield Star* newspaper blamed a 'crazed surge' of visiting fans. The *Yorkshire Post* said 'thousands of latecomers tried to force their way into the ground' and caused a 'fatal crush'. Manchester's *Evening News* printed the report, saying that fans were 'foolishly late getting to the game and furious at the prospect of missing the start, kicked and hammered on the steel [exit] gates'. Many newspapers printed graphic pictures of terrified fans crushed against the fence, some of whom were only moments from death. The London *Evening Standard* joined in the assault. The paper's Peter McKay wrote, coarsely, that the 'catastrophe was caused first and foremost by violent enthusiasm for soccer, in this case the tribal passions of Liverpool supporters' who 'literally killed themselves and others to be at the game'. Even in Liverpool, some turned on their own. On the Tuesday, the *Liverpool Daily Post*'s John Williams described it as 'yobbism at its most base' and that 'Scouse killed Scouse for no better reason than twenty-two men were kicking a ball'. The same morning, *The Sun*'s editorial column gave a sneak preview of the shattering approach it was to take the following day: 'Is it fair to make the police the scapegoats for the Hillsborough disaster? It happened because thousands of fans, many without tickets, tried to get into the ground just before kick-off – either by forcing their way in or by blackmailing the police into opening the gates.'

On the Wednesday, *The Sun* newspaper published the second of the two headlines for which it will be forever infamous. The first was seven years earlier during the Falklands War when the paper marked the death of 323 Argentinean sailors with a celebratory 'Gotcha!' headline. Three days after Hillsborough, under the editorial guidance of Kelvin MacKenzie, the paper was at it again. MacKenzie is one of a kind. On Tuesday 18 April, the *Sheffield Star* ran a story claiming that Liverpool fans had 'attacked an ambulance man, threatened firemen and punched and urinated on policemen as they gave the kiss of life to stricken victims'. Quoted in the story were the pairing of local Tory MP Irvine Patnick and PC Middup from the Police

Federation. Patnick had told a local news agency, 'I spoke to many policemen in the makeshift mortuary afterwards. They told me they were hampered, harassed, punched, kicked and urinated on by Liverpool fans.'

As families grieved, MacKenzie debated with the only person in the office he thought worth listening to – himself. He hummed and hawed about which of two headlines to splash across his front page; either 'YOU SCUM' or 'THE TRUTH'. Many of the journalists were taken aback by how far MacKenzie was willing to go in his treatment of the dead. The next morning, *The Sun* went to town on the tale. Under a headline to rival 'Gotcha!', the paper screamed across its front page 'THE TRUTH'. Below it, MacKenzie regurgitated three lies: 'Some fans picked pockets of victims; some fans urinated on the brave cops; some fans beat up PC giving life kiss.'

There was an outcry from grieving families and from across Merseyside. Even the toothless Press Council condemned the story. The newspaper's managing editor, William Newman, replied to families' letters of complaints as they prepared to bury their dead. In his unsigned, impersonalised letter, he refused to apologise for the story. He brashly asserted: 'We cannot possibly apologise for facts and to do so would be an abdication of our responsibility to a wider public beyond the city of Liverpool. If the price of a free press is a boycott of our newspaper, then it is a price we will have to pay.'

And they did and still do. Copies of *The Sun* were bought so that they could be burned. But many others lay unsold. MacKenzie lost the paper 200,000 sales daily at a cost of £10 million that year. The last time I was at a Liverpool game, fans were handing out leaflets for a post-match 'Boycott *The Sun*' rally. Some newsagents were so angry they wanted to ban the paper in their shops. But the book *Stick It Up Your Punter* reveals the extent to which MacKenzie and his team would go. Those newsagents who refused to sell *The Sun* 'received visits from Sun reps enforcing their further obligation to display the Wapping product as prominently as its rivals'.

The Sun took four days to produce its 'The Truth' lie. Lord Taylor produced his preliminary report into the tragedy in four months and his final report in January 1990. Not only did they revolutionise football stadia across the land but their detailed analysis of the tragedy was profound. The interim Taylor Report found that 'the main reason for the disaster was the failure in police control' and that 'senior officers in command were defensive and evasive witnesses'. The report added, 'Neither their handling of problems on the day nor their account of it in evidence showed the qualities of leadership to be expected of their rank.' Chief Superintendent Duckenfield was singled out for well-deserved criticism, recording that his 'capacity to take decisions and give orders seemed to collapse' and he 'failed to give necessary consequential orders or exert any control when the disaster occurred'. In a stinging criticism from such an establishment figure as Lord Taylor, he announced that Duckenfield was 'untruthful' when he had claimed 'that there had been an inrush due to Liverpool fans forcing open a gate'. Lord Taylor's words leave much to the imagination. In short, the most senior officer at Hillsborough that day was a liar, pure and simple.

But the report didn't go far enough for the families and went too far for South Yorkshire Police. Even after the report's publication, the force and their allies in the media and Parliament mounted a fierce rearguard action, rejecting many of the findings. They refused to let the dead lie in peace or give the survivors the space to grieve with a truth. Superintendent Bettison even took his campaign to the House of Commons in an attempt to water down the Taylor Report's conclusions. He carried with him a video in which he narrated a film about Hillsborough from the perspective of his police force. To this day, it has never been broadcast in public.

In 1991, all of the fatalities were ruled to have occurred by accidental death. Two years later, the families failed in their application for a judicial review of the 'accidental death' judgment. But then, in late 1996, Granada Television broadcast Jimmy McGovern's *Hillsborough* docudrama. In it, he claimed that some of those who died were still alive at 3.30 p.m. McGovern's programme influenced the mood in the build-up to the 1997 general election. Not long after coming to power, the new Labour government asked Lord Justice Stuart-Smith to scrutinise any new evidence and to decide whether any such evidence justified a further inquiry. Having got their hopes up, the Stuart-Smith findings and process were to prove a real blow to the families. He decided to side with the coroner's conclusion that there was no new evidence worthy of overturning the verdict of accidental death. He also accepted that the deaths were caused by 'dangerous overcrowding' rather than 'because first aid or medical attention failed to resuscitate them'.

In August 1998, after the disappointment of the Stuart-Smith process, the Hillsborough Family Support Group brought manslaughter charges against Chief Superintendent Duckenfield and his Deputy Bernard Murray. After a six-week trial, the jury found Murray not guilty of manslaughter but couldn't come to a verdict on his boss. But still the campaigners refused to go away. In 2009, however, many feared that they might have reached the end of the road when Anne Williams, who had lost her son at Hillsborough, failed in her approach to the European Court of Human Rights.

It's no wonder that the families' avenues were being blocked. They were the focus of a police cover-up, which seems to have been underway before the ninety-fourth victim had taken their last breath. One of the most sinister aspects of the entire quarter of a century of inquiries is the systematic editing of police records and statements. So widespread was the effort that it was later described as 'an unprecedented process of review and alteration...'

On the day after the disaster, it was decided that police officers should set aside their professional training and ignore what they had been taught. Instead of making entries in their pocket books, they were instructed to simply write down their recollections. The police logic was that pocket notebooks would have to be made available to any inquiry, whereas a set of written recollections could be kept confidentially by South Yorkshire Police. What followed was a deliberate attempt to cleanse any police statements of any meaningful criticism of South Yorkshire Police. No fewer than 116 statements that were critical of the force were substantially altered. Forty-one of the alterations removed or reduced criticisms of their own senior officers. The Ambulance Service also got into the attempt at face-saving editing. In all, the statements of seventeen ambulance staff were altered.

PC Kenneth Frost's statement that 'I at no time heard any directions being given in terms of leadership' was removed. PC Maxwell Groome's record that 'the control room seemed to have been hit by some sort of paralysis' was deleted. Also expunged was PC Alan Wadsworth's record that 'there was no leadership at the Leppings Lane end following the disaster either in person or on the radio'.

Senior officers wanted to prove to the public that they had maintained as much order as possible. A note circulated to officers ordered them not to make any criticism of police. It added that there 'should be no mention of the word CHAOTIC or any of its derivatives which would give rise to the assumption that complete control had been lost at the ground...' Numerous police statements were edited to remove the word 'panic'. The most revealing deletion was to PC Anthony Lang's written evidence. Considering the assertion that the tragedy was caused by late-arriving, drunken fans, it's little wonder that South Yorkshire Police felt the need to delete Lang's explosive second sentence. He predicted from afar what his superiors couldn't work out from up close in the control room.

> From what I could see throughout the incident the problem seemed to stem from the large number of people attending outside the ground at the same time. But when the gate was opened I felt at the time that we had transferred the problem into the ground and we would need a lot more PCs to control it.

Despite all the efforts to secure the inquiries, reports and legal appeals, the campaign hadn't yet been able to prove their most important outstanding claim – that many of the relatives could have been saved after 3.15 p.m. But the breakthrough was about to come and, when it did, it would be a tale of two football-crazy cities. On 16 April 2009, the British Cabinet met in Scotland for the first time in eighty-eight years. Back in 1921, the government's most senior ministers travelled to Scotland because the Prime Minister Lloyd George was on holiday in the Scottish Highlands. It was decided that they would all have to go to him rather than have the PM head back to London. In 2009, I was the Secretary of State for Scotland and was looking forward to welcoming the first Cabinet meeting to Glasgow, my home city. The country was still in the tail end of the 2008 financial storm that had shaken the world's economies. But it was an item not on the agenda that day that was to have the most lasting impact.

The day before the Cabinet meeting, the Secretary of State for Culture, Media and Sport, Andy Burnham, was one of the main speakers at the Hillsborough twentieth-anniversary Anfield tribute. But behind the scenes there's a fascinating account of how one speech, and the human response to it, can force the most surprising of political changes.

I didn't mention it earlier but Trevor Hicks is a Yorkshireman and also a Freeman of the City of London. He happily tells me:

> I've always been an establishment man. I thought that the establishment was always right, that they could be relied upon to tell the truth. I now know only too well that that's not the case. There were a lot of people like me because there was quite a broad public opinion that the police must be right.

On the day of the twentieth-anniversary memorial service, the organisers were taken aback by the size of the crowd that turned up. Trevor Hicks is big enough to admit that he was against the idea of Andy speaking at the event, and volunteers the view that he now knows he was wrong:

> Only really since Andy Burnham spoke did the tide turn our way. We had a policy of not allowing politicians to speak at the anniversary services. It was always a Church service in a football ground. Anfield was our Church. We didn't have a very high opinion of politicians. But Andy gave a commitment to release the documents. Here we now had a minister for the first time, with the blessing of the Prime Minister that the government would now do what it should have done years ago.

In the moments before his speech, he stood below the Kop flanked by religious leaders.

After receiving the warmest welcome that any Evertonian has ever had from the home fans, he started to speak. Andy and I have been good friends for many years. He and Ed Balls are the main strikers in the MPs' football team. Like all of us, he has lost a bit of pace but he still has that poacher's instinct. In 2008, he was appointed to the right Cabinet job at the perfect time. He was promoted to Secretary of State for Culture, Media and Sport in the year that his home city of Liverpool was elevated to be the European Capital of Culture.

> I was invited and my first instinct was that no one will want a politician there. I agonised whether I should go. I sat up late with my brothers and discussed whether I should go or shouldn't go. In the end the family consensus was that 'you can't walk away from something like that'.

Andy had decided that there was little point in going to Anfield unless he was going to do something. Before the twentieth anniversary, Andy and fellow MP Maria Eagle both announced that they wanted full disclosure of the Hillsborough paperwork and records. Derek Twigg, who later acted as a crucial link between many of the families and Parliament, was worried. He knew so much of the anguish that the families had lived with. He had watched hours of gruesome police video footage of the aftermath of the disaster, none of which I need to write about here. But Derek told me that he was worried and thought, '"What's he done?" Because I didn't want to give people new false hope again. We'd already had the inquiries and I was concerned the demand for full disclosure of documents would go nowhere.' Andy remembers, 'That day I was heading towards Anfield in the government car; tense is not the word for it.' As he arrived, some supporters started asking him, 'What are you doing here?', not because he was an Everton fan but because he was a government minister.

> I arrived in the boardroom area and Dalglish and the rest of them were there. Some of them were asking me, 'Is this a good idea?' So this was just building and building. Then my brother texted me to say, 'Andy, don't want to worry you but I'm in the Anfield Road End as there are no seats anywhere

else in the ground.' I felt ill. So then I stand up. I look back on it now and I knew something was coming. I almost wanted it to come. It was almost a relief. That first call of 'Justice for the 96!'

Andy isn't the only Hillsborough campaigner in Parliament; Twigg, Steven Rotherham and Maria Eagle have been joined by a new generation including Alison McGovern, the MP for Wirral South. But Burnham's intervention was the decisive one. Today, sitting in his office chair, he leans back and whispers the shout to mimic that initial lone voice. 'I can still hear it now,' he reveals. 'It was one fella. Then a few more. Then a lot more. I've met him since. He's a lovely fella.' What is less well known, and what Andy, understandably, has forgotten, is that applause interrupted his speech more often than anger. In an emotional speech, he thanked other Everton fans who stood with their rivals in their darkest moments. His tribute to the Liverpool supporters who helped the dying drew thunderous applause. Andy's words and their response was a rebuke to the lie that fans had robbed from the dying and urinated on the police who were trying to save the living.

As I continue to interview Andy, he doesn't seem to remember the applause.

I was shaken, walking off in the most bruised state that you can imagine, and the phone rang. Speaking in a slightly gruff Fife accent, the voice at the other end said, 'Andy, wonderful thing you've just done. You should be very proud of yourself. You did what was right.'

It was the Prime Minister, Gordon Brown, displaying a human touch that so few people realise he often did well. Andy, slightly surprised, simply said, 'Gordon, I'd like to raise it at the Cabinet tomorrow in Glasgow.'

Despite the call from his boss, Andy wanted to 'crawl off home'. But he bumped into the Lord Mayor of Liverpool and future Labour MP Steven Rotherham. Stevie is a close friend of Andy Burnham's. I've got to know him as a centre-back who takes no prisoners and is probably the best player in the MPs' football team. He is certainly the best talker. Thinking back to those few moments after Andy came off the stage, he reminisces, 'When a shell-shocked Andy told me he was going home, I told him, "Like fuck you are!"' He emphasises to me, 'You can quote me on that, Jim. I told him, "You're coming with me to the Town Hall to meet the families who are getting the Freedom of the City of Liverpool."'

When he arrived, Andy was met by a rogues' gallery of Liverpool legends – Dalglish, Carragher, Hansen and Gerrard. One of them put a smile back on his face with the sarcastic welcome of 'You've not come all the way here to upset them again!'

After speaking to the families in private at the reception, he knew he had to act. The next morning, he headed on the train to Glasgow Central. 'My head was getting into a different zone. I thought, Right, I'm going for this. My football teammate and fellow Cabinet minister started his journey northwards. About the same time, I was spending the morning with Prime Minister Gordon Brown. We started in Edinburgh at a business breakfast hosted by the then Rangers chairman Sir David Murray. We then travelled to Glasgow along the M8 motorway, heading to a meeting with shipyard workers on the banks of the Clyde. Most of the hour's conversation was about Scottish football and British politics, the general election being only a year or so away.

The Cabinet agenda was dominated by the economy. It was unusual to add a new subject onto the meeting. But, towards the end of the deliberations in the Glasgow Exhibition and Conference Centre, Gordon invited Andy to speak. He made brief comments about the events at Anfield the day before. He talked about how we needed to go further in search of the truth of what had happened twenty years and one day before. The most senior politicians in the land listened to him insist, 'It's clear that there is a real sense of injustice and Maria Eagle and I have called for full disclosure. We need to act.' After a short discussion, Gordon Brown summed up. He was convinced and announced that was what we were going to do. It was the end of the discussion. The relieved Culture Secretary knew then: 'That was it. That was the moment that it all changed.' The sound of the Kop had been heard in Glasgow; the independent panel inquiry was now on. The truth would win.

The independent panel was chaired by the Right Reverend James Jones, the Bishop of Liverpool. The panel looked at the clear evidence from the post-mortem reports that twenty-eight of those who died did not have traumatic asphyxia with obstruction of the blood circulation, and that asphyxia may have taken significantly longer to be fatal. There was separate evidence that, in thirty-one cases, the heart and lungs had continued to function after the crush, and in sixteen of these this was for a prolonged period. This analysis and much else in the independent panel's hard-hitting forensic report proved that forty-one of the ninety-six could have survived if only the emergency services had acted and been led professionally.

Hillsborough transformed football. The national sport's fans could never again be treated as an underclass. The Taylor Report made sure that the decades-old sloping sets of steps where fans 'found their own level' were replaced by all-seater stadia. The sport would welcome more women and families, fewer hooligans and more middle-class fans, and in many ways some clubs would be less connected to the communities that had created and sustained them.

The disaster also brought wider changes. The law on the location of inquests was changed. There was also the landmark legal judgment on the treatment of people in a persistent vegetative state. Twenty-two-year-old Tony Bland was only being kept alive by artificial feeding through a tube. During the Hillsborough crush, the oxygen supply to his brain was cut, with catastrophic consequences. His doctors and his devoted parents concluded that his condition would never improve. But they were concerned that withdrawing his treatment might constitute a criminal offence. After weighing up all the legal and moral issues, the judge ruled that such an action would not be a crime. Almost four years after the tragedy, Tony became Hillsborough's ninety-sixth victim. Poignantly, at Anfield, before the next home game, the crowd held up a banner saying simply 'God Bless Tony Bland.'

According to Andy Burnham:

> Talking about football matches that changed the world, Hillsborough unlocked a lot. I'm working with the Ballymurphy families [the campaign to get to the bottom of what happened in West Belfast when eleven people, including a priest, were killed by the British Army]. There's the debate about the 'Shrewsbury 24' [the campaign to overturn the 1972 convictions of striking Shrewsbury building workers], and now Orgreave has come up [the allegations that South Yorkshire Police fabricated statements during the disturbances at the mine in 1984].

But events in Sheffield still influence Liverpool the club, and have changed perceptions of Liverpool the city. After hanging up his Mayor of Liverpool chains, Stevie Rotherham was soon elected to Parliament. The former bricky was one of the Liverpool supporters at Hillsborough. He has made his mark in the Commons. He sung with and helped organise 'The Justice Collective' to cover the legal costs of the Hillsborough families. He recruited people from the world of music to join him in singing 'He Ain't Heavy, He's My Brother'. In 2012, it made it all the way to be the UK Christmas number one. He's the only serving MP to ever have topped the charts at Christmas.

There's no way to hide Stevie's love of his city:

> Over the years, Liverpool has changed beyond recognition. The European Capital of Culture did great things to regenerate the city physically. But if you think about the Hillsborough Inquiry, it has had a massive impact on changing people's perceptions of the city. It was the first time in a long time that they started to give Scousers a fair crack at the whip. If you think about it, in the 1960s, Liverpool was the epicentre. It was the time of the Beatles, the Merseybeat explosion and the football clubs coming to the fore. Wherever you went, everyone loved Liverpool, everyone wanted a Scouser for a pet. But by the early 1980s our city looked very grey; the future and attitudes were bleak. At that time, Liverpool was a very different city. There were the riots in 1981. We had the Militant Council from 1983 to 1985, the Heysel tragedy in 1985 and, four years later, Hillsborough. It was easy for them to go, 'There you are, it's you whinging Scousers again.' Too many people were willing to buy into that. It was a real problem. But it wasn't whinging. It was people saying, 'You can take us on if you want to but we'll fight you all the way.' A 1983 report to the government talked about the 'managed decline' of Liverpool, as if just to give up on the city, mothball it, have it as a ghost town. But look at us now. We are now a proper twenty-first-century city and popular European destination.

Margaret Aspinall knows the many lows and occasional highs of the campaign. She lost her eighteen-year-old son James that day and has campaigned ever since for both truth and justice. She is now chair of the Hillsborough Family Support Group. After years of being shunned by elements of the British establishment, it really was something for her and the campaigners to be given the 2013 *Daily Mirror* Pride of Britain Award. As she went up to receive the award, she observed, 'It's been one hell of a journey. It's not been easy. Every step we took has been hard for the families. What the establishment forgot was that there were 24,000 witnesses that day. It's not been an easy ride.'

Speaking without notes in front of a hall full of guests and to a television audience not of thousands but of millions, she added:

Andy Burnham stood up in front of the Kop and the fans gave that message and he took it back to the government. It's great now that we have the truth out. We haven't got justice. We've a long way to go until we get justice. What we have is truth for our city, our fans and for the survivors and that I hope relieves the pain of them fans. Because what them fans have gone through for all them years getting mud slung at them, being accused of being drunk, being late, being ticketless.

Just before she received the award from Kenny Dalglish and a standing ovation from the audience, she declared:

I just hope that on 12 September last year, when Mr Cameron stood up and apologised to the nation for what went wrong and the lies and the deceit that went on ... I hope that it took some of the fans' pain away. That was their day. We've still got ours to come. We're still fighting for justice.

For the Honourable Member for Liverpool Walton, Stevie Rotherham:

It was the first big victory against the establishment; it was more than just against any one individual. It took on the police. It took on the government. It took on the judiciary and everything else. Because these people were told there was nothing more they could do and nowhere else to go. But they kept going. We always believed that the law and the establishment would always win. As The Clash would say, 'I fought the law and the law won.'

But on this occasion, mercifully, they haven't.

British and German soldiers meet in 'no man's land' on Christmas Day 1914. They seem relaxed and relieved as they pose for photographs. Within hours they were back at war.
© *Mirrorpix*

Chapter Eleven

The One That Didn't:
Germany v The British Empire, 1914

THE RULES WERE clear. No footballs were permitted at the Front. But for Rifleman Frank Edwards, captain of the London Irish Rifles football team, this was the one and only instruction from his military chain of command that he was willing to ignore.

He knew officers had been instructed to shoot on sight any footballs they discovered. But, in the build-up to the Battle of Loos in 1915, he squeezed the air out of a ball, pressed it as flat as he could, and concealed it in his British Army-issued kit bag. The night before the attack, as soldiers wrote rushed letters of goodbye that they hoped others wouldn't have to send posthumously on their behalf, Edwards spent the time blowing life back into the ball. For he had decided that, in the morning, as the battle kicked off, the boys were going to play 'the ultimate game' and kick the football over to the German lines. In 1914–18, the universal signal for soldiers to climb from their trenches sounded like an angry referee's repeated whistling. When the sound came, the ball was kicked and the men went over the top. With a shout of 'Play up, London Irish', the men climbed up and scampered after the ball towards a wall of German bullets.

Loos was a small mining village in northern France. The battle in its name was yet another one of the Great War's brave but bloody encounters. It was such a vast military effort, it was known as 'The Big Push'. Despite gaining some ground on the first day, it failed in its limited objective of taking the German second line between the anonymous Lens–Bethune Road to the Loos cemetery. A century later, the anniversary of this battle disaster on 'Loos Sunday' is one of only three commemorations that the London Irish maintain, perhaps predictably, alongside Saint Patrick's and Armistice Day. But, for a long time, it was a battle that daren't speak its name, and not just as a consequence of the terrible British losses but because of a new British tactic. It was the first time British forces had unleashed poison gas upon any enemy in battle.

At 5.50 a.m. on 25 September in the war's second year, the Allies turned the taps on 5,243 gas cylinders. The plan was to attack from behind their 50-foot-high drifting barrier of poison. But, unexpectedly, the wind changed direction, the gas was blown off course and it trapped their own Black Watch troops, readying to attack the Germans. The British fought ferociously through their own gas and towards the German lines, but after nineteen days there were 61,000 casualties including 7,766 dead. Many of the dead lay unburied in no man's land for up to three months. But, bizarrely, it wasn't human horror but a horsing mishap that captured the news headlines back home. At the same time, King George V travelled to France and was injured after being thrown from his horse; painful for the King, but convenient for the military's media managers.

Rifleman Edwards's ball, like the King's pride, lay punctured in France. As he desperately tried to reach the dying troops, stretcher bearer Patrick MacGill found what he described as 'a limp lump of pliable leather' snared on the wire of the second trench line. Years later, MacGill spoke about how significant the ball had been as a motivator in that first wave of attack: 'It had played a very important part in a psychological way as it probably helped keep the fellas moving forward.'

Explaining how the ball escaped the battlefield barbed wire, MacGill said, 'Someone picked it up after the battle. It got hidden again among the kit.' The 'limp lump' remained in hiding for eight years. It didn't make another appearance until a commemorative dinner in London's Manchester Hotel where it arrived presented on a chef's silver platter marked 'Loos 1915'. The press release for this 1923 get-together reminded the diners of the story of the ball. The media were told: 'When the Rifles went over the top, they kicked this sphere ahead of them; kicked it so that the Germans could realise what they thought of bullets.'

More than ninety years after that dinner, I decided to try to track down one of the most famous balls in the sport's history. It was a surprisingly short search. I found it in the tiny London Irish Rifles museum in London's Flodden Road. It had lain in a tea chest for decades, a hibernation that had taken its toll. In more recent times, careful attempts had been made to extend its life. When I got to the 20-foot-square museum, I was welcomed by the aptly named former Rifles soldier Alex Shooter. He now acts as the curator of this proud treasure trove of a military museum. 'It's something that we as a regiment are very, very fortunate to have and to crow about, and all the young new recruits are told about it. It's part of our history and esprit de corps.'

In all of the black-and-white photographs of the Loos football pinned onto the crowded walls of the Regimental Museum, everyone coming into contact with the ball is wearing spotless white gloves. As I scanned the room for the curator's gloves, Shooter simply picked up the ball and handed it to me. I stared at him. He looked at me. If my expression properly exposed my thinking, my panic-stricken face would have read, 'Why have you just handed me one of the most famous and definitely most fragile footballs in the world? What am I meant to do with it? Please take it back!' I assume Shooter must have been a better shot than interpreter of facial expressions. He looked at me, then turned around and left. I was alone with the ball. All I could do was hold onto it firmly enough that I wouldn't drop it and gently enough that I wouldn't damage it. The leather was wafer-thin, soft and felt almost powdery to touch. I was worried that it was ageing before my eyes. I had no idea what to do with it. The devil on one shoulder was urging me to play secret keepie-uppies with it. The little angel on the other shoulder urged me to cherish the moment and put it back in its museum case. Thankfully, that persuasive angel won.

Loos was neither the first nor the last time football would be centre stage in the conflict. A young Winston Churchill wrote to his wife Clementine in 23 November 1914: 'What would happen, I wonder, if the armies suddenly and simultaneously went on strike and said some other method must be found of settling the dispute!' One month and two days later, that is what almost happened but didn't. This chapter is the story of the most famous football match ever played. It was the game that terrified the generals, mesmerised fighting men and stunned a disbelieving world.

A British Artillery officer, John Wedderburn-Maxwell, knew at the time that he was involved in 'probably the most extraordinary event of the whole war – a soldiers' truce...'

In his meticulously researched book about the ceasefire, *Silent Night*, Stanley Weintraub wrote: 'The event appears in retrospect somehow unreal, incredible in its intensity and extent, seemingly impossible to have happened without consequences for the outcome of the war. Like a dream, when it was over, men wondered at it, then went on with the grim business at hand ... that business was killing.'

The bloodiest battles of that brutal war still lay ahead.

This chapter's aim is to explore what happened when, on its first Christmas, the war paused. To understand that, it's inevitable to offer the quickest possible analysis of how it started. It's often said that the build-up to a war has its own momentum. It reaches a point when it's easier to fight than to find a way to avoid it. The events of Christmas Eve 1914 proved that, on a very rare occasion, peace can spontaneously create its own unstoppable force. I have stood on the spot in Sarajevo's Franz-Joseph Street where the first domino fell in the world's tumble towards the 'Great War'. On 28 June 1914, the street-corner killing of the heir to the Austro-Hungarian Empire and his pregnant wife precipitated a conflict that travelled to every corner of the globe.

The events of the next few weeks are, as we all know, complicated and the subject of a multitude of excellent books. So here, in one short paragraph, is a summary of what others have rightly taken a thousand pages to describe. My apologies to all war historians for this briefest synopsis of the collapse into cataclysm.

In response to the assassination, the Austrians issued an ultimatum, which the Serbs partly rejected, and, on 28 July, Austria declared war on Serbia. Russia had pledged to back Serbia, so, on 1 August, Germany declared war on Russia. Germany demanded that France give guarantees that they would stay out of the conflict, which Paris refused, and thus, on 3 August, Germany forced them into the conflict by declaring war. The next day, Germany invaded Belgium and Britain declared war on Germany. Later, Turkey joined the war on Germany's side and Italy joined to support the Allies. It became a conflict that engulfed the planet and its economies as European empire powers went toe-to-toe and enlisted support, men and materials from their colonies.

The First World War is the second bloodiest military campaign in human history, exceeded only by the Taiping Rebellion, in which up to thirty million died in a conflict stretching across fourteen years. But, on the eve of 1914, Britain acted as though she were about to be embroiled in a war of the previous century. I've often thought the Israelis fought the first day of the Yom Kippur War as though it were the seventh day of the Six Day War. Similarly, no one was set for the challenges of the Western Front. As if to prove their lack of preparedness, on the third day of the conflict, each officer was instructed to sharpen his sword – a weapon that served no military benefit but whose reflection actually self-identified the men in the middle distance as British officers. They were then picked off by disbelieving German snipers. The French approach was even more preposterous. Their attire was as ludicrous as it was dangerous, kitted out as walking bull's-eyes in their red kepis and trousers.

In 1914, Britain was still predominantly a naval power. As the war got underway, the British Army had just 100,000 troops ready to confront the strongest and best-trained army on the planet. In an unprecedented military expansion, an SOS was sent to British troops throughout the world. In a vast effort to plug the gaps in the line until new recruits could take the field, Britain brought in the India Corps, the Royal Navy Division and overseas garrisons from throughout the Empire. Within eighteen months, the British Army had grown to more than two million men.

The trench network came about after each side continually tried to outflank the other in an attempt to go around their enemy to the north. The flanking continued until they could flank no further and both sides collided with the sea. It led to a stalemate along a 500-mile line from the Belgian coast to Switzerland. The Germans had been able to pick their ground . after their retreat from the Marne River. The Allies were lower and more waterlogged. Here, both dug and died.

Trench life was like nothing ever before experienced by humans, either at peace or at war. The German artist Otto

Dix described it as 'lice, rats, barbed wire, fleas, shells, bombs, underground caves, corpses, blood, liquor, mice, cats, artillery, filth, bullets, mortars, fire, steel...' Occasionally, the mud was so deep that artillery became imprisoned by it, unable to fire. In some trenches and bomb craters, the freezing mud sapped the spirit and drowned the bodies of the exhausted troops weighed down by their kit. Occasionally today, we hear the heartbreaking story of a have-a-go hero dying while trying to save a friend or the family dog from drowning at the sea front. On the Western Front, men sometimes risked all to save their fellow soldier. But too often the flooded craters became the unmarked graves of rescuers who quickly became victims.

It may seem counterintuitive but German and British troops had more in common than their trench predicament. While they made different journeys, they travelled with a shared sense of their own patriotism, fear and faith. Both believed they had the cause of civilisation at their backs. All were subjects as well as soldiers, one side of an emperor, the other of a king, each of whom ruled from the vantage point of a shared family tree. Both rulers were grandsons of Queen Victoria. For most of the war, the troops on both sides served a German-sounding monarch. The British were not fighting for the House of Windsor, so revered by many today. Indeed, renaming the royal family after a Berkshire town was the 1917 way of escaping rampant anti-German sentiment. The King that the British troops asked their God to save in the national anthem of Christmas 1914 was a monarch from the Germanic-sounding Saxe-Coburg and Gotha family. They switched this to Windsor as, after all, it did sound a good deal less like the people Britain was fighting.

Both sets of troops had preconceptions about their opponents. Prussians were the dominant force in a German state that back then was still only forty-four years old. Allied troops knew that, if they were facing off against Prussians, they were normally in for a fight. The Germans also had their own hierarchy of who they hoped not to be lined up opposite in the trenches. They considered the Scots to be brave and gave the Glasgow Highlanders the nickname 'Ladies from Hell', on account of their kilts. They considered the Canadians and Australians, there in small numbers in 1914, to be fierce, but were often dismissive of Indian and other Commonwealth troops for getting involved in what some believed to be a 'white man's war'. However, they feared the Gurkha soldiers, with their famed fighting techniques, more than any other soldiers in the Empire.

Many of the troops and some of the politicians expected it to last just four months. No one thought it would last four Christmases. But, as winter deepened, there was some casual talk about a possible Christmas ceasefire. British officers urged vigilance against this, a supposed German ploy targeted at getting them to lower their guard. Pope Benedict XV prayed for, and urged, a Christmas truce. There was even a dead-end resolution tabled in the US Senate calling for a temporary seasonal cessation.

There had been limited ceasefires in the earlier months of the war and firing was very occasionally suspended for mealtimes. These were negotiated by clandestine shouts across no man's land, out of officers' earshot. Most were arranged in English. Very few British troops spoke German – they didn't need to. Tens of thousands of Germans spoke the language they had brought home with them from their pre-war lives in Britain or America.

Both sides started receiving gifts from home as the first, and what many expected to be last, conflict Christmas approached. The better-provisioned Germans were sent cigars. Brits got a Princess Mary's box with cigarettes, tobacco and a card from the King telling them, 'May God protect you and bring you home safe.' The *Daily Mail* newspaper sent more than two million plum puddings. On Christmas Eve, the Royal Flying Corp dropped plum pudding on the German lines and the Germans returned fire with rum.

The truce started to take hold at about 11 p.m. on Christmas Eve. It had been a cold, crisp, dry day, free from the torrential rain that had flooded the ground under the men's feet throughout December. The opposing trenches were often no more than the length of a football pitch apart, and sometimes barely the width of a regulation field away from one another. As midnight approached, many Germans set huge fires across their lines and lit candles on their Tannenbaums, or Christmas trees. Normally, the slightest flickered light would invite the professional snipers to do their worst, but something special was happening that night. The Queens's Westminster Rifles sent out Rifleman A. J. Philip to meet some Germans in the middle, after they had shouted, 'You no shoot, we no shoot.' On much of the Western Front that first Christmas Day, the only shooting was at makeshift goals and, as the world later discovered, from one or two concealed cameras.

The debate about who started the truce is something that will remain forever unresolved. What is clear is that it wasn't orchestrated. It was down to fits and spurts of spontaneous acts of human restraint and respect. It seems likely that most local ceasefires were probably initiated by the Germans. They were far from happy but were generally less miserable than the weary British. The better-supplied Germans had the upper hand as they had already pulverised the Russians in the East. In the West, they had dug in on the higher ground. The Allies were lower and waterlogged, a predicament they occupied for the next three years. Many believe that, on 24 December 1914, the Germans were in the ascendency. They, more than the British, could afford a halt.

At La Chapelle d'Armentieres, the German Lieutenant Niemann recorded:

Then at darkness we marched forward to the trenches like Father Christmas with parcels hanging from us. All was quiet. No shooting. Little snow. We placed a tiny Christmas tree on our dugout. Then we began to sing our old Christmas songs: 'Stille Nacht, heilege Nacht' and 'O du frohliche'.

In the British trenches, the men applauded. Among their number was Private Albert Moren, who, speaking many years later, said, 'I shall never forget it. It was one of the highlights of my life.' The Queen's Regiment applauded the Kaiser's troops. They demanded an encore as if at the theatre in London's West End, and in return the delighted German singers sang 'O Tannenbaum'.

Private Frank Sumpter of the London Rifle Brigade appeared liberated by the experience.

The devastated landscape looked terrible in its true colours – clay and mud and broken brick – but when it was covered in snow it was beautiful. Then we heard the Germans singing 'Silent Night, Holy Night', and they put up a notice saying 'Merry Christmas', so we put one up too. While they were singing, our boys said, 'Let's join in,' so we joined in and when we started singing, they stopped. And when we stopped they started again. One German took the chance and jumped up on top of the trench and shouted out, 'Happy Christmas, Tommy!' So of course our boys said, 'If he can do it, we can do it,' and we all jumped up. A sergeant major shouted, 'Get down' and we said, 'Shut up, Sergeant, it's Christmas time!' And we all went forward to the barbed wire.

The main clash across no man's land that Christmas Eve was the collision of competing songs. But even this conflict ran out of energy. Anyone who has read the soldiers' war letters or listened to the Imperial War Museum's audio archives would probably come to the same conclusion as I did: it's just as well the conflict wasn't decided by each side's singing prowess. If this had been the case, according to most contemporary accounts, the outcome of the war would have been very different, as the Allies proved themselves to be the better listeners. On parts of the Front, the Germans sang medleys. Their repertoire included 'Good King Wenceslas', 'Deutschland Über Alles' and 'Wacht am Rhein'. Incredibly, it also included 'God Save the King', which they seem to have sung without any sense of ill-feeling whatsoever.

As the night turned into early morning, many troops on both sides tried to sing as one. For some in the trenches, it was their first ever experience of Christmas. While the war was a conflict in Europe, it wasn't just for Europe; it reflected the continent's colonial history. Algerians fought alongside the French and the Indians next to the British. Christmas didn't mean much to these Muslim and Hindu troops, but for them it was undoubtedly as welcome as it was unexpected.

Men from four continents including north Africans, south Africans, Britons, Saxons, Prussians, Indians, Canadians, French and many, many more joined forces in song; some even belted out 'Auld Lang Syne'. The beautiful hymns and surreal folk songs filled the unhearing ears of the rotting corpses still scattered across no man's land. It sounds too surreal to be true but one impromptu concert was joined by a French concert opera singer, a German violinist playing Handel's 'Largo', and a French harmonica player playing 'Stille Nacht'. Lieutenant Sir Edward Hulse of the Scots Guards wrote home about the truce, saying, 'It was absolutely astounding, and if I had seen it on a cinematograph film I should have sworn that it was faked!' In the French section, the truce was initially less enthusiastic, but eventually peace broke out along the line and even included the French Foreign Legion. At one point near Aisne, a French musician serving as a captain organised his men into a ramshackle orchestra and invited the Germans over to join them.

The end of the war for most of a day was advertised on message boards, and not of the type we have become used to in today's social media. They were what the name suggests: boards held above the head over the parapet, with basic instructions scrawled on them that wrote the script for the unfolding day. First they declared 'Merry Christmas', then 'No Shoot'.

Lieutenant Kurt Zehmisch of the 134th Saxons wrote in his diary after attending Christmas Eve mass, 'I have ordered my troops that, if at all avoidable, no shot shall be fired from our side either today on Christmas Eve or on the two pursuant Christmas holidays.' Throughout the war, soldiers were desperate to force themselves to get to sleep every night amid the din of conflict. But, like many young children the world over, on Christmas Eve, the troops fought exhaustion in the hope of witnessing something special. Lieutenant Zehmisch wrote in his diary, 'I stayed awake the entire night. And it was a wonderful night.'

The footballing truce is the most written-about football event in history. We all feel that we know something about it, but, to discover the truth, the best place to start is London's Imperial War Museum. With the passing of Harry Patch in 2009, there aren't any living witnesses to the conflict. But in the Imperial War Museum they have created the next best thing: a beautiful archive of letters and audio recordings. The museum has painstakingly compiled interviews with the men who fought in the trenches, the nearest future generations will ever get to meeting them.

As I walked into the building, I was met by Terry Chapman, a flamboyant intellectual decorated in a red bow tie. After just ten minutes of chatting, it was clear that he has a memory as big as the museum, of which he is the senior historian. Such is the depth of his insight he is called upon for his advice on documentaries and research projects the world over, and is bombarded with enquiries from across the globe. He tells me that, not long before my visit, he had received a genuine request from a British broadsheet newspaper asking if he could help them with a story they were researching on whether it was really true that Adolf Hitler was an Everton supporter.

As a confirmed football agnostic, Terry was also the unlikeliest of military advisers in the making of the iconic 1980s movie *Escape to Victory*. It fell to Chapman to advise the film's director, John Houston, on how he could credibly lever in an improbable appearance by Pelé as the real-life Corporal Luis Fernandez, alongside Bobby Moore and Ossie Ardiles. I don't think its Chapman's fault that the rest of the team includes an improbable appearance by Sylvester Stallone and a rag-bag of what seemed like the entire Ipswich Town squad.

This encyclopaedic historian leads me to the most lasting tangible proof of the no man's land football. There, in a glass display case buried away in the building's basement, is a 20-centimetre traditional German beer tankard. Made in 1908, this ceramic bierstein is an unusual choice for a museum exhibit. But its importance doesn't come from its manufacture or its inscription. Instead, I am told, this most simple of exhibits is the footballing trophy presented to Private Bill Tucker of the Army Ordnance Corps by the losing German Army team on Christmas Day 1914. Tucker is thought to have been the captain of the British team, or so the story goes.

The bierstein isn't the only footballing reminiscence in the museum. Two floors above the tiny trophy is a larger-than-life reminder of football's importance in the conflict. During the war, the British society artist John Singer Sargent was commissioned to travel to Le Bac-du-Sud at the Front and capture images symbolising Anglo-American ties. What now hangs as a centrepiece at the Imperial War Museum is

Gassed, completed in 1919. It has nothing at all to do with UK–US relations. Instead, it records the relationship between the horror of war and the drama of football. It depicts small groups of British troops walking tentatively in columns, with the hand of each man on the shoulder of the soldier in front of him. Each is blindfolded, all are blinded by gas. They can't see in front of them, but can no doubt hear the scene behind them: it's a competitive game of football. Whether this Sargent masterpiece was an actual event or the artist merging two iconic scenes he witnessed will never be known. Whatever the truth, today *Gassed* remains, for many, the most important single piece of art from the Great War.

Slowly on Christmas morning, one by one, and then gradually by the hundreds and thousands, men lifted their heads, and then their entire bodies, above the parapet. In many instances, they left their guns where they had been standing. When a rogue shot did ring out, there seemed to be a silent agreement that a single volley would go unanswered. There also appeared to be a shared list of dos and don'ts between these fleeting acquaintances, including no repairing of barbed-wire defences or reconnoitring of their foe's trenches.

Before anyone could get down to the business of playing football, there was gruesome work to be done in no man's land. Bodies had lain unrecovered for months. All sides wanted to offer whatever was left of their comrades a Christian burial. Even in this horrible process of body retrieval, footballing imagery abounded. Captain Giles Lauder of the Scots Guards recorded how the Germans returned British bodies to the 'halfway line'.

In some places, Britons buried Germans, Germans buried British and, in certain sections, it was a joint effort. West of Lille, a British Army chaplain and the German Oberstleutnant conducted a joint Christmas-morning service. Teenage Lieutenant Arthur Pelham-Burn wrote home that the mass burial was 'awful, too awful to describe so I won't describe it'. But in a joint service where the troops lined up opposite one another, the 23rd Psalm, 'The Lord is my Shepherd', was offered and quickly translated into German: 'Der Herr ist mein Hirte...' Pelham-Burn told his family, 'It was an extraordinary and wonderful sight.' In a further footballing metaphor, Captain Loeder wrote in the Battalion diary, 'Both sides have played the game.'

Most officers looked the other way and some even had a hand in brokering the haunting silence that Christmas morning. The officers and the men knew that to be caught conniving with the enemy was a court martial offence. To avoid punishment, officers later lied and told their superiors that they had only tolerated the truce so that they could get a close-up of enemy positions. Many got away with that fiction; it wasn't as if the top brass had any view of what was happening. As the troops came together, their most senior officers could hardly have been further from them in every sense. At St Omer, General Haig and others sipped champagne at impeccably attired tables. In the Grand Hotel in the Belgian town of Spa, Kaiser Wilhelm was joined by those, and only those, whom he considered suitable to dine in his company. Not for them the lice and mud or even, come to think of it, a ceasefire.

Many officers at the Front didn't need much encouragement to look the other way. They had their own personal reasons for self-preservation, which helped them to appreciate the one-day respite. Six weeks was the average survival time of a junior officer in the British Army on the Western Front. The truce added an additional and welcome forty-third day to their life expectancy. Despite modern-day perceptions, the truth is that being a British Army officer was more dangerous than being an ordinary soldier. By the conflict's end, 12 per cent of soldiers were dead, as were 17 per cent of officers. Old Etonians suffered even worse, with a 20 per cent attrition rate.

Christmas lunch for the British was a tin of the infamous Machonochie's stew, stuffed with meat, potatoes and other vegetables. A lucky few cooked one of the rare farm animals that still meandered across the cratered fields. Both sides were unprepared for their unexpected visitors from across the trenches. They had no presents to give one another. Instead, they swapped whatever they had to hand. British soldiers got their first taste of sauerkraut and exchanged belts, buckles and helmets with their drier, and generally better-equipped, opponents. A real delight for the Brits was that the Germans seemed to have an endless supply of beer, which they had looted from Belgian and French cafes. All along the Front, men met, shook hands, swapped rations and talked. So what did these warriors talk about? Family and football, of course. Many Germans who had lived in Britain loved British football. They talked about players, scores and stadia. The British came across German supporters of most major British clubs, especially the London teams. Many of these pre-war German civilians turned 1914 soldiers had lived in the capital and adopted a team as their own.

But, for many, talking about the game just wasn't enough. It may come as a surprise but, despite the decades of reporting of a Christmas truce football match, there wasn't one single game of football that day. In fact, there appear to have been many, not just one. In some parts of no man's land, it took on the appearance of a Saturday morning in one of those great British public parks, where dozens of matches take place on multiple pitches. Hogo Klemm of the 133rd Saxons recalled, 'Everywhere you looked, the occupants of the trenches stood about talking to each other and even playing football.' Writing more than twenty years after the war, Johannes Niemann joked, 'At this soccer match our privates soon discovered that the Scots wore no underpants under their kilts so that their behinds became clearly visible any time their skirts moved in the wind.' Sergeant Bob Lovell of the London Rifles, who also played football that day, said, 'I could hardly credit what I have seen and done. It has indeed been a wonderful day.'

A major in the Medical Corps wrote to the *London Times* to tell the world about an unlikely football game. His letter was published on New Year's Day 1915 and told the world that, after singing 'God Save the King', the Germans agreed to a football contest. He informed the paper's uncertain readers that they 'actually had a football match with the Saxons, who beat them 3-2!' There is little doubt that this game took place. The official history of the 133rd Saxon Regiment also records that:

> Tommy und Fritz first chasing down hares fleeing from under the cabbages, and then kicking about a football furnished by a Scot. This developed into a regulation football match with caps casually laid as goals. The frozen ground was no great matter. Then we organised each side into teams, lining up in motley rows, the football in the centre. Das Spiel endete 3-2 fur Fritz.

The official history of the Lancashire Fusiliers has an entry detailing a game against the Germans. They had no ball, and no doubt scuffed their army-issued boots by kicking a tin can for a ball. Like the Saxon Regiment's match, this game also appears to have ended in what seems like an all-too-familiar score-line of 3-2, this time for the Germans. In the 1950s, Private Ernie Williams recounted details of a game:

> The ball appeared from somewhere, I don't know where, but it came from their side ... They made up some goals ... it was just a general kick about. I should think that were about a couple of hundred taking part. I had a go at the ball. I was pretty good then, at nineteen. Everybody seemed to be enjoying themselves.

There was no ill will between us ... There was no referee, and no score, no tally at all. It was simply a melee ... The boots we wore were a menace – those great big boots we had on – and in those days the balls were made of leather and they soon got very soggy.

The boots and the ball weren't the only impediment. The bodies of their comrades may have been buried but the barbed wire trapped any wayward pass or player out on the wings.

There are very few accounts of trophies being presented to the winning teams beyond the poignancy of the Tucker's bier-stein. Almost a year after my final visit to the museum, I had one final round of pre-publication fact checking to undertake, and it looked like all was not what it seemed with this special little trophy. The meticulous historian Terry Chapman told me that, since my visit, the museum's researchers

undertook enquiries into its authenticity, and found that in December 1914 the German Army unit depicted on the bierstein was serving on a completely different part of the Western Front to that of the British Expeditionary Force. Furthermore, a search through the Medal Rolls online at the National Archives, Kew, would suggest that Private Bill Tucker was not serving on the Western Front in December 1914.

So, while neither piece of evidence is conclusive, it would suggest that this little antique is not, and has never been, a football trophy on Christmas Day 1914 or any day in its 106-year life.

A further truth is that, while the truce was widespread, it would be wrong to believe that it, or the football, was universal. Those who had seen friends killed in the final pre-Christmas hours were in no mood for brotherly love.

Captain Billy Congreve of the 3rd Division Grenadier Guards wrote in his diary, 'We have issued strict orders to the men, not on any account to allow a truce, as we have heard they will try to. The Germans did try. They came over toward us singing. So we opened fire on them, which is the only sort of truce they deserve.'

Some French units on the Alsace Front launched an unfestive but unsuccessful assault against the distracted Germans who were sitting down to eat their Christmas lunch.

Occasional artillery shells exploded on or near the sites of the temporary peace – mostly longer-range munitions called in by both sides' superiors. It was a failed attempt to force the troops back into their trenches and to resume the violence. Some truces extended into Boxing Day. In a few instances, hostilities didn't resume until the first few hours of 1915. When the onslaught got going again, it was often with an old-fashioned sporting sense of fairness. Recommencement times were agreed during meetings in no man's land between almost apologetic officers. Some historical accounts claim that elements of the Saxon Corps downed tools and only when they were told to shoot at the enemy or be shot at by their superiors did they reluctantly take up their arms.

Percy Jones of the Queen's Westminsters wrote in his diary, 'We had a great day with our enemies and parted with much hand-shaking and mutual goodwill.' A German soldier shook hands with Rifleman George Eade of the 3rd London Rifles and said, 'Today we have peace. Tomorrow you fight for your country, I fight for mine.' And finished with a peculiarly chivalrous 'good luck'.

Many factors contributed to the conclusion of the truce, which prevented it from morphing into the mass disobedience that Churchill had feared. As troops who had no experience of the truce rotated into the trenches for their stint, they did so expecting to fight. Visiting generals on both sides demanded a return to hostilities. German commanders declared '*Die Schützengraben Freundschaft*' meaning 'Friendship between the trenches forbidden'. Gradually, things got back to the accepted madness of normality. Only a residual reticence, borne of a newly discovered respect for their opponents, hindered an immediate return to the industrial-scale slaughter. But German brutality against Belgium, British desire for revenge in France, the 1915 killing of nurse Edith Cavell and the sinking of the *Lusitania* and other passenger ships all fostered a sense that the 'ghastly Hun' had to be dealt with. It also soured any hopes of any future meaningful soldiers' truce.

At the resumption of hostilities, Sergeant George Ashurst of the 2nd Battalion Lancashire Fusiliers was angrier with his generals than he was with the Germans:

> The generals behind ... gave orders for a battery of guns behind us to open up fire and a machine gun to open out, and officers to fire their revolvers at the Jerries. That started the war again. We were cursing the Generals to hell. You want to get up here in this mud. Never mind you giving orders in your big chateaux and driving about in your big cars. We hated the sight of the bloody generals, we always did. We didn't hate them so much before this, but we never liked them after that.

The historian Nick Lloyd, based at the Joint Services Command and Staff College in Shrivenham, is a recognised authority on the First World War. When we discussed the context and consequence of the truce, he told me:

> It's the final moment of the old world, the Edwardian world, where there is a recognised set of rules; an almost gentlemanly approach to things. It's very difficult to hate someone who suffers alongside you. It is the last of the old way of doing business. Then you get Verdun and the Somme, which is the

dehumanising intensification of the war. The Christmas truce
is the last of the old world where the individual still matters.

Eight million more lost their lives after the truce, including
many of those footballing warriors. Some were killed within
just yards of where they had played their final game.

Accounts of the war, the temporary peace and the outbreak
of football aren't just the thing of thoughtful history books.
This was from an era of the long-ago-forgotten habit that led
men like Captain Billy Congreve, Sergeant George Ashurst and
Hugo Klemm to faithfully keep diaries and regularly write to
loved ones. We tend to think that the embedding of journalists
within active military units is a construct of recent conflicts
in Iraq and Afghanistan, but in 1914 there were legions of
volunteer warrior-journalists. In fact, there were citizen journalists in every unit, each recording their fears and thoughts.
Many events of the war were committed to scrap pieces of
paper and mud-caked notebooks. It wasn't just close family
members who were the recipients of these intensely personal
dispatches. Some soldiers sent letters to their home town's
newspaper. In 1914, many of these letters went uncensored by
the authorities. The local and regional papers proudly treated
the occasionally indiscreet correspondence as important
reports from the Front, by one of their own.

But, for their own reasons, newspaper editors chose to self-
censor and they didn't carry any news of the Christmas truce or
festive football. It's not clear whether this was out of disbelief
or a sense of misplaced duty. But none of that mattered after
one newspaper across the Atlantic revealed the truth of what
had happened. When the *New York Times* broke the story to
the world on their front page, it became impossible to conceal
the facts. Then, almost two weeks after the truce, on 8 January
1915, the *Daily Mirror* printed what, up until that point, was
probably the most astounding photograph ever published in

any British newspaper. It was a grainy black-and-white image of two dozen British and German troops. They were contentedly standing next to one another and staring straight into the camera. They seem unworried by the dangers of the war and untroubled by the consequences of being caught on camera. It's not clear from the picture if there's a football at their feet, but it wouldn't be hard to imagine that this group picture was a post-match photo of two teams of eleven, plus a substitute.

However, it would be hard to believe that the Britons in the team photo could be anything other than football fans, rather than players, because at that time too few of the nation's professional players had signed up, and the country was starting to notice.

As Britain failed to get its own way in the war that winter, football faced a moral dilemma. Play on and keep the nation's spirits up during a conflict that was expected by many to be over before the football season, or cease playing and get fully behind the war effort? In many people's minds, football failed the test, at least initially.

A minority of footballers and some clubs answered the call of war immediately. The Corinthians, who heard news of the outbreak while on tour in Brazil, returned and most enlisted. The English FA sent all of their clubs details on how to encourage players and supporters to volunteer. The day after the circular, Sunderland visited Aston Villa and recruitment officers went into overdrive. Patriotic spirits were bolstered by a band playing the French and Russian national anthems; both countries were aligned with Britain. Brighton quickly became the first club to organise military training on their ground. The English club with the biggest war commitment was Croydon Common, with thirteen of their players swapping their football boots for army boots. They were the only First Division club not to be resurrected after the war. And it wasn't just professional players who volunteered. Many amateur clubs did their bit. Sixteen of the Dulwich Wood FC squad enlisted. In London, almost 9,000 amateur players joined the war effort in the first four months. But recruitment among full-time players started at a trickle.

The War Office moved to commandeer stadia, taking Everton's Goodison Park as a drilling ground and Man City's then stadium, Hyde Road, as a 300-horse stable. Despite this, the sport found itself at the centre of an unwanted but probably warranted public and media backlash. Moral angst swept the nation. Huge crowds of fit young men were turning up every week to watch other fit young men play football. The followers of other sports and many army officers demanded that the football leagues should suspended until the end of hostilities. Such was the anger about football's perceived ambivalence that some newspapers decided to ban reporting the sport. Plans were also discussed at a senior level on how to prevent anyone under the age of forty even being allowed inside a football stadium on match days.

In a speech made just a month into the war, the author Arthur Conan Doyle considered

> ... there was a time for all things in the world. There was a time for games, there was a time for business, and there was time for domestic life. There was a time for everything, but there is only time for one thing now, and that thing is war. If the cricketer had a straight eye let him look along the barrel of a rifle. If a footballer had strength of limb let them serve and march in the field of battle.

The backlash against football quickly spread beyond the public and into the top of the military. In the first few weeks of the war, Field Marshal Lord Roberts of Kandahar told a new battalion of Fusilier volunteers:

> I respect and honour you more than I can say. My feeling towards you is one of intense admiration. For how very different

is your action to that of the men who can still go on with their cricket and football, as if the very existence of our nation were not at stake.

But with impeccable timing, and as if to prove Lord Roberts right, just two days after his outburst the English Football League Management Committee met. They decided that 'the great winter game should pursue its usual course'.

Football's failure to fulfil what many considered to be its patriotic responsibility started to become part of the zeitgeist of popular culture. *Punch* magazine reflected a growing view in the country when it published a cartoon entitled 'The Greater Game'. It showed Mr Punch informing a fit and healthy-looking footballer, in front of a packed stadium, 'No doubt you can make money in this field, my friend, but there's only one field today where you can get honour.'

Attitudes on the Front were also infected, but soldiers' opinions were divided. Many would rather have had some of those still cheering on the terraces standing beside them in the trenches. But, for others, the constant banter about the latest football results was becoming a crucial distraction from the lice and one of the few sanity-saving connections to home.

Even the British Prime Minister Herbert Asquith, who lost a son in the war, was dragged into football's war controversy after a *London Times* story of 26 November 1914. The newspaper claimed that just one fan had volunteered at the most recent Arsenal game. By contrast, the English Rugby Union told the paper that they encouraged every rugby player to sign up: 'The Rugby Union are glad to know that a large number of their players have already volunteered for service. They express a hope that all rugby players will join some force in their own town or county.'

Football's controversy couldn't have come at a more torrid time in the British war effort. The unexpected and high-profile war reversals helped turbo-charge the anti-football sentiment. That same month, British forces had come close to collapse at Ypres and only the actions of the Worcestershire Regiment in counter-attacking saved the day and the line. Asquith's response when questioned in the House of Commons was that at least footballing recruitment was going better in Scotland – and it was. Players and supporters of seventy-five Scottish teams had already enlisted. As the furore continued to gather momentum, the Unionist MP William Joynson-Hicks invited all eleven London teams to a meeting to discuss the formation of a Football Battalion.

The formation of the battalion, to be known as the Die Hards, was to be a turning point for football. But, in deciding to get fully involved in the war effort, football repeated the same fateful recruitment approach that had proven so painful for so many others on the Somme.

At 7.30 on the morning of 1 July 1916, after the most kinetic shelling in the history of warfare, the Battle of the Somme began. Amid the fear and pre-attack nerves, one man wrote two messages, neither of them for home. The Company Commander in the 8th Royal East Surrey Regiment, Captain Wilfred 'Billie' Nevill, had two footballs. He wanted his men to dribble them across the cratered no man's land. He had written on each. The first read 'The Great European Cup Tie Final – East Surreys v Bavarians, Kick-off at Zero'. Eccentrically, but accurately, the second announced simply 'No Referee'.

Nevill's wasn't a Football Battalion, but as the infantry entered into their final countdown he gave one ball to each of his platoons. He offered a prize for the first ball to be kicked into the German trenches. A private in the 8th Royal Sussex Regiment was looking up to the low sky, discoloured grey by the 1.5 million shells being lobbed over towards the dug-in Germans. As the barrage ceased, he described what he saw when the first soldier emerged from the trenches: 'As he did, he kicked off a football; a good kick, the ball rose and travelled well towards the German line. That seemed to be the signal to advance.'

Captain Nevill's award was never presented. The opening day of that bloody battle took the lives of 19,239 Allied troops. The precise spot where either ball stopped on that first charge was probably never officially recorded. Even if it was, the result is buried in a military grave in France, because the organiser of this peculiar football attack, Captain 'Billie' Nevill, was among the dead.

Like Rifleman Frank Edwards at Loos, there is much more to this than Nevill kicking a ball from the trenches as a morale-boosting distraction. Their actions, and the soldiers' responses, symbolised the centrality of football in British life at the time. For many, football was the conversation, debate and constant companion in the trenches. By the time of the Great War, the sport had completed its journey out of the nation's public schools and into the wider public's soul. It was the game of the Tommy and his officers. Both spoke football fluently. In a war that didn't discriminate about whose life it stole, football was one of only two things that most men in a class-conscious army had in common. The other was their godforsaken predicament.

Some regiments carried a football with them wherever they travelled. Fifteen-year-old Cyril Josie wrote home to his mum just before the Somme, asking her to send him a ball and a Bible. Football was a regular pastime behind their own lines – and, occasionally, as they charged towards the enemy's lines. But, for thousands of troops on the Western Front, football wasn't their escape from the war. It had been their trap door into it. Thousands had been recruited through football. For many, the journey to Loos, Flanders and the Somme had begun with a routine visit to cheer on their local football team. Their sport had transported them from a home football field to their foreign killing fields.

Many of the players, officials and fans served together in the 17th (Service) Battalion (1st Football) The Middlesex Regiment. It's well known that war makes comrades out of strangers. But for the first years of the conflict, it wasn't unusual in the British trenches for the man huddling next to you to be a friend from home, serving in a 'Pals Battalion'. The idea of these battalions seemed sound: friends, neighbours, relatives, school- and workmates joined up together and fought together. They were a recruitment phenomenon. Liverpool led the way in recruiting four battalions. It took just ten days to recruit the Accrington Pals Battalion. The Sheffield Pals came together in just forty-eight hours. The Glasgow Tramway had its own battalion of a thousand employee volunteers, and the Old 7th Fusiliers were recruited from London's Stock Exchange, banks and financial companies. And as more and more footballers answered the call, the 23rd and 27th Middlesex joined the 17th as Football Battalions.

But what was a celebrated recruitment success also turned into a terrible human disaster. The problem was that too many who signed up together then died together, and they did so at a rate that just couldn't be tolerated. A single shell crater in France could wipe out all the young men of what had up until then been an unheard-of British street. Of the 720 Accrington Pals, 548 were either killed or injured within just twenty minutes on the Somme. If anything, the Leeds Pals fared even worse: they lost 750 of their 900 City volunteers. By the end of the first hour in the Battle of the Somme, 1,700 men from Bradford lay dead or injured. Some workplaces, streets and villages lost most of their young men. The majority of the Chorley men who went over the top at the same time died. The Football Battalions lost more than 500 men in just eighteen days on the Somme.

The Pals Battalions were wound down, as too often a single battle would engulf so many towns in collective grief. All except what the journalist Arthur Mee described as the 'Thankful Villages' – those very few places that avoided loss. Sixteen thousand cities, towns and villages were haunted by loss of some scale during the conflict; only fifty-two villages were thankful. At the time of writing, there have been no places in Scotland or Ireland that have as yet been identified as having the good fortune to be 'thankful'.

At one level, it's perhaps understandable that some professional footballers had planned to leave the fighting to someone else. For pros, the act of simply volunteering came with the unique danger; even the slightest injury would prove fatal to their careers. Slow to start, but once it got going football was a real source of strength to the recruitment effort. Some clubs stood out from the crowd; near the top of that patriotic league were Clapton. The first prominent player to enlist in the Football Battalion was Fred 'Spider' Parker, the Clapton Orient captain. He was joined by nine of his teammates. Just behind 'The Spider' in the queue was Bradford City's centre-back Frank Buckley. Brighton's Archie Needham mobilised most of his team to sign up. It helped that military training rules were relaxed, allowing some players in the army to take part in team training and to play on Saturdays. Many footballers huffed and puffed their way through the army training sessions, claiming they found it tougher than any sports training they had ever been put through.

But the team that led the way was the team who in 1914 were at the head of the Scottish league, Heart of Midlothian. The entire first team enlisted; they were followed by 500 of their fans in time to fight on the Somme. The players who were then pulled together into a makeshift replacement Hearts team lost the league title. Seven of the Hearts first team lost their lives. To this day, Hearts supporters are rightly proud that their club, more than any other, properly and permanently commemorates their greatest ever heroes. Every year, fans and the successors to those who died, the first-team players, take part in an Edinburgh service of remembrance.

As football's war momentum spread, players and local personalities would often come onto the pitch to urge fans to join up. William Joynson-Hicks MP declared at a recruitment rally, 'I am inviting you to no picnic.' In what sounded like a manager's pre-match team talk, he told a crowd of potential recruits, 'It is no easy game against a second-rate team. It is a game of games...' and in a rhetorical flourish that unintentionally hinted at the truth of German military superiority, he added, '... against one of the finest teams in the world. It is a team worthy of Great Britain to fight.'

Fortunately for the Germans in a sporting sense, most of the footballers hadn't arrived on the Front in time to take part in the Christmas truce. But once the footballing fighters crossed the Channel they got involved in plenty of football, usually against other Allied units. On the first anniversary of the truce, on Christmas Day 1915, they played the Royal Engineers and scraped home 19-1. It was decided to strike a special commemorative medal after they defeated the 34th Brigade Royal Field Artillery 11-0 in June 1916. Some of the medals were never presented. By the time they were delivered to the Front, four of the Football Battalion had lost an infinitely more important contest against German field artillery.

While football as the national game attracted the nation's attention, it wasn't the only sport with a designated recruitment drive. Many sports did their own thing in their own way. But the formal involvement of other sports was in large part down to the efforts of the remarkable Mrs Cunliffe Owen, the only woman to ever raise a British Army battalion. She was a distant relative of the King, and enticed volunteers from all sports into what became known as the Sportsman's Battalions. In keeping with her standing as a high-society socialite, her recruitment centre was Europe's biggest hotel, the plush Hotel Cecil in London's Strand. This unlikely piece of military history, which was flooded with 1,500 applications in just the one month of September 1914, was demolished in the 1930s. It was turned into the HQ of oil giants Shell and BP. When not in The Strand, Mrs Owen could be found in her other five-star recruitment centres, Edinburgh's Royal Hotel and Glasgow's Central Hotel.

Men from every sport and from all over Britain responded to her call. This wasn't a cosy or cosseted public relations-driven deployment. They fought as fiercely as any other army recruits. So fiercely did they engage in their battle endeavours that they earned the battalion the nickname 'Hard as Nails'. Perhaps a ferocity of fighting spirit was to be expected from a group that included the middleweight boxing champion Private Harrison and the big-game hunter Corporal Canton. They served alongside recruits from more genteel sports, including the Yorkshire county cricketer Private Yates, and Sergeant Major Cumming, Britain's champion walker. But, despite all their fame, the bravery of the Sportsman's Battalions was probably only exceeded by their loss. Of the 4,762 who served in the Sportsman's Battalions, almost three-quarters, or 3,112, were either killed, wounded or missing by the conflict's close.

But despite the loss of so many other sportsmen, football contributed much more than any other sport and far more than just the Football Battalions. Within nine months of the war, 1,600 men had joined the Football Battalion. It was an act of sacrifice to be repeated just over two decades later in the Second World War, as was another generation of footballers. Perhaps the best known of these was the Bolton club captain Harry Goslin, who made an emotional war appeal in front of a 23,000-strong crowd at Burnden Park. He told them, 'This is something you can't leave to the other fellow; everybody has a share to do.' He led the entire team down to the local recruitment hall to join the 53rd (Bolton) Field Regiment. For six years they fought in France and north Africa. On one occasion, they were taken from the line to play King Farouk's side in Cairo. All except one made it home. The man who was by then known as Lieutenant Goslin was killed in Italy in 1943 when shrapnel ripped through his back.

It's impossible to place a precise figure on how many professional footballers volunteered in the 1914–18 war. The three designated Middlesex Battalions are only part of the story. Many players served in other units. England international Lieutenant Evelyn Lintott, the first professional footballer to receive a commission, was killed on the first day of the Somme, while serving with the Leeds Pals. Also killed in that harrowing battle was Private William Jonas, a prolific Clapton Orient goal scorer. As he lay dying, he told his friend who was comforting him, 'Best of luck, special love to my old sweetheart Mary Jane and best regards to the lads at Orient.' His football team's name was the last word to pass his lips.

Football felt the painful loss of men like Private Jonas. Of the 4,500 who served in the Middlesex 17th, 900 were lost forever. Most of the rest who returned were too injured or too old to resume their professional playing careers. The national sport, like the nation itself, wept over the destruction of so many of its best. So widespread was the death and injury toll among fighting footballers that in the last year of the war the National Football War Fund was created. Its only purpose was to support injured players who had fought and the families of the footballers who never returned.

So what did soldiers playing football on Christmas 1914 really achieve? A spontaneous soldiers' truce was a profound event. Symbolically, it was astonishingly powerful. The football played that day is the most famous match in history. No game more epitomises the poignancy of any sport; for a few hours, it helped turn enemies into simple opponents. But did it cause lasting change? Probably not. For those who were temporarily spared the horror of fighting, it was undoubtedly liberating. For those at home reading the belated reports, it was almost beyond belief. For many of the generals, it struck a bolt of fear that their men might be about to find more in common with those in front of them across the trenches than they had with those behind them directing the war.

But in any analysis of what changed the course of the war, the festive football is a high-profile fleeting footnote. It wasn't football but Christmas that provided the inspiration for the ceasefire between two predominantly Christian armies – and those few hours of peace changed almost nothing. Unquestionably, if the conflict had ended on Boxing Day 1914, the truce would be the most important moment of the twentieth century. But it didn't, and it isn't. What's more, the facts don't lie. Between the end of the temporary football truce and the beginning of the permanent ceasefire, millions more fighting men lost their lives. Rather than slowing down, the bloody conflict gathered pace and ferocity into 1915 and beyond. By the time all sides signed the Armistice on the eleventh hour of the eleventh day, the Great War had taken the lives of sixteen million men and women. A war that was supposed to be over in months ravaged the world for four long years.

But, by the time the few hours of peace ended, a war that was to be over by Christmas had simply paused for a single Christmas Day. The football achieved little other than to temporarily alter perceptions. Some still argue, with genuine commitment, that football helped accomplish what the combined efforts of the Pope and the US senate couldn't, which was a temporary halt in the slaughter.

But it wasn't what soldiers did as one-day footballers that changed the world. Rather, it was the bravery of thousands of professional and amateur footballers and hundreds of thousands of their fans as full-time warriors that altered history. In so doing, they helped save their country and undoubtedly rescued their sport. Footballing heroism took the sport from the verge of scapegoat status and placed it firmly at the heart of the public's affections. Gone were the assaults by the likes of Field Marshal Roberts and the animated 'something must be done' type of parliamentary hysterics directed at the Prime Minister. In their place was a newfound respect for the sport that had given the country thousands of individual but painful reasons to learn to love it afresh.

As the war ended, the English FA wasted no time. They met on the day immediately after the Armistice to discuss how to get things going again. Football's second chance can be best summarised by the non-footballing Colonel Henry Fenwick, who commanded the Football Battalion. As his men fought in the eye of the Battle of the Somme, he was quoted in the *Sporting Chronicle* paying an emotional tribute to them:

> I knew nothing of professional footballers when I took over this battalion. But I have learned to value them. I would go anywhere with such men. Their esprit de corps was amazing. This feeling was mainly due to football – the link of fellowship which bound them together. Football has a wonderful grip on these men and on the army generally.

In closing this chapter, and book, I can't help but feeling that perhaps now is the time for modern-day football to properly honour the heroism of those who were lost.

The nature of war and culture of football has changed in the century since that fleeting armistice. Mercifully, it is now unimaginable that almost 20,000 men could be killed in a single day's fighting. Football has also been transformed in a way that those brave men would never have believed possible.

At no time has it been more popular nor more prosperous. Even allowing for inflation, today's highest-paid footballer earns as much as the total combined income of a fifth of the entire British Army that fought from those rat-infested trenches back in 1914.

Modern football with its regular bling and occasional bluster can infuriate the purist in us all. The sport is now undoubtedly vogue in polite company. But it has never been a mere fashion; for real supporters it's part of who we are and how we live our lives. Clubs shouldn't treat their followers as spectators, as if they are passive ninety-minute observers, instead of head-and-heart fans.

But, for all its faults, the sport of Walter Tull, Ferenc Puskas and Alfredo Di Stéfano still has a magical allure to motivate in a way that no other game has ever been able to. Whether it is Ukrainian troops reaching not for a rifle but a football when confronted by Russian aggression; or the Palestinian teenagers I met whose suspicion immediately gave way to enormous smiles when I joined in their dusty kickabout with an air-free ball in a refugee camp in Jordan; or the Afghan trainee soldiers I watched taking a break from taking on the Taliban to play football against one another, while all the time heavily armed British troops prowled the sidelines to keep them safe from insurgents' attacks. Three situations, each of enormous complexity, all with different causes and with little in common but a love of football. No sport, no language and no government has that reach or influence.

I have written about events in history through the experiences of just eleven matches. But football's story isn't yet complete – far from it. This is the first generation where football is global and digital. Every minute of every day, somewhere in the world a child is kicking a ball or being introduced to the beautiful game for the very first time. For many, as they travel through life, football will become a constant companion. It will delight, disappoint and inspire. And in turn they will sustain a sport that can help to change the world all over again.

Acknowledgements

I would like to thank the following for all their advice and support: Claire Pryor, Mike Molloy, Jordan Galbraith, Pete Starkings, Andy Coyle, as well as Peter McDade and Rachel Parker for help with Spanish translations.

This book wouldn't have been possible without all of those who gave their time so generously to be interviewed for each of the chapters. I'd also like to thank the team at Biteback Publishing, as well as the *Daily Record* and *Daily Mirror* for access to their photography archives.

Bibliography

Banks, Simon, *Going Down – Football in Crisis. How the Game went from Boom to Bust*, Mainstream, 2002

Beevor, Antony, *The Battle for Spain: The Spanish Civil War 1936–1939*, Orbis Publishing, 2002

Best, Nicholas, *How The Great War Really Ended*, Weidenfeld and Nicolson, 2008

Bucks, Simon and Hanna, Ronnie, *20 Years of Breaking News*, Harper Collins, 2009

Burns, Jimmy, *Barca: A People's Passion*, Bloomsbury Publishing PLC, 1998

Burrowes, John, *Irish – The Remarkable Saga of a Nation and a City*, Mainstream Publishing, 2003

Canoville, Paul, *Black and Blue: How Racism, Drugs and Cancer Almost Destroyed Me*, Headline Publishing Group, 2008

Chippindale, Peter and Horrie, Chris, *Stick It Up Your Punter: The Rise and Fall of* The Sun, William Heinemann Ltd, 1990

Conn, David, *The Football Business. Fair Game in the '90s?*, Mainstream, 1997

Foley, Michael, *Hard as Nails: The Sportsman's Battalion of World War One*, Spellmount, 2007

Harris, Ed, *The Footballer of Loos: A Story of the First Battalion London Irish Rifles in the First World War*, The History Press, 2009

Heinrich, Arthur, 'The 1954 Soccer World Cup and the Federal Republic of Germany's Self-Discovery', *American Behavioural Scientist*, Volume 46, Part 11, 2003

Kapuscinski, Ryszard, *The Soccer War* (translated from Polish by William Brand), Granta Publications, 2007

Korr, Chuck and Close, Marvin, *More Than Just a Game, Football v Apartheid*, Harper Collins Publications, 2008

Mair, John and Keeble, Richard Lance, *Mirage in the Desert? Reporting the 'Arab Spring'*, Abramis Academic Publishing, 2011

Mandela, Nelson, *Long Walk to Freedom*, Little, Brown and Company, 1994

Merkl, Peter H., *The Federal Republic of Germany at Fifty: The End of a Century of Turmoil*, Macmillan Press Ltd, 1999

Mitchell, Andy, *Arthur Kinnaird: First Lord of Football*, CreateSpace Independent Publishing Platform, 2011

Nason, Anne, *For Love and Courage: Letters Home from the Western Front 1914–1917*, Preface Publishing, 2008

Peacock, L., *A History of Modern Europe*, Educational Books, 1987

Index